56:2 · October 2018

ENGLISH LANGUAGE NOTES

Latinx Lives in Hemispheric Context

MARIA A. WINDELL AND JESSE ALEMÁN, Special Issue Editors

T0341777

Latinx Lives

Latinx Lives
Aquí, Allá, y Ahora

MARIA A. WINDELL AND JESSE ALEMÁN

> These are facts.
> Let me show you my wounds: my stumbling mind, my
> "excuse me" tongue, and this
> nagging preoccupation
> with the feeling of not being good enough.
> . . . .
> Outside my door
> there is a real enemy
> who hates me.
> —Lorna Dee Cervantes, "Poem for the Young White Man"

Our current political climate calls for the affirmation of Latinx lives and the insistence on Latinx peoplehood, regardless of point of origin. It demands the rejection of the abject racism emanating from the US presidency, its pundits, media outlets, and congressional allies. It also demands a confrontation with electoral and population bases that benefit from, if not outright believe in, the race-baiting, fear-mongering discourses surrounding immigration, citizenship, job security, personal safety, and the ostensible sanctity of America's gone greatness. We make no pretense that such sentiments are new to the United States or unique to the present administration's *pendejadas*. Latinx peoples and their aspirations, ideas, stories, loves, labors, books, and bodies have for quite some time been on the run in the United States, with one foot in the grave from political, economic, social, cultural, and linguistic warfare. That Cervantes's 1981 poem continues to resonate with us is proof positive that Latinx lives, in any context, are already marked targets.

After all, "Let's make America great again" was Ronald Reagan's 1980 campaign slogan too, and there are "sharp-shooting goose-steppers round every corner" these days as well.[1] They showed up in Charlottesville wearing khakis and bearing tiki torches. It may seem we are enduring a moment of unprecedented white nationalism, but the lives, literatures, and letters of Latinx peoples remind

ENGLISH LANGUAGE NOTES

56:2, October 2018 DOI 10.1215/00138282-6960658
© 2018 Regents of the University of Colorado

us that living in the United States at any period has always been a struggle, survival, migration, and returns. It's been one of anonymity and targeted identification, crossings and dislocations, affirmations and negations, translations and transnationalisms—all under the weight of the X, which also marked the spot over the heart of subjects facing the firing squad. ("They're not aiming at you.")[2]

"Latinx Lives in Hemispheric Context" pushes against the violence of our current anti-immigrant moment by presenting the lives of Latinx people, communities, and bodies of writing across the hemisphere as resilient forms of expressive culture that speak to the here and now. We thereby heed María DeGuzmán's argument on the "here-ness" of Latinx studies: "Although the 'x' of Latinx is anonymous and reminds us of what has not yet been determined, the 'x' functions as a marker of presence. . . . The 'x' does not orient, but it does locate. It signifies, in shorthand, 'Here! ¡Aquí!' And this 'aquí' demarcates presence in a given space without that presence defaulting into assimilation as neutralizing or conforming absorption."[3] Beyond the possibility of reading Latinx as an inclusive, gender-fluid term that discards the binary Latina/o, framing X as *aquí* stakes a claim to Latinx presence ever more vital in our political climate. By exploring questions of migration, community, and archive, the issue interrogates how Latinx literary, cultural, and scholarly productions from the nineteenth century through today circulate throughout the Americas in much the same way as the lives and bodies of Latinx people migrate and mobilize. The following essays and position papers confront the historical and ongoing archival fragmentation of Latinx lives and narratives while assuming the "here-ness" and wholeness of our lives, literatures, and stories.

Migrant Bodies

Juan Poblete opens the collection with a position paper arguing that although coloniality remains a powerful force, we must imagine the possibility of a transamerican future free of fear. Claudia Milian's essay follows suit by demonstrating the need for such a future as it argues for the humanity of the Central American child over and against the survey used to process unaccompanied child minors who arrive in the United States without documentation. David Sartorius delineates how "papers" obtained at great cost and meant to signal belonging can also fail to do so, while Rachel Conrad Bracken examines how the United States regulates the bodies, rather than the papers, of Mexicans and Mexican-Americans in the US-Mexico borderlands. Anna Brickhouse's reflection on how Junot Díaz's *Brief Wondrous Life of Oscar Wao* can reframe events at the August 2017 rally in Charlottesville, Virginia, closes the first section. Combined, the pieces foreground the very processes of abjectification that Latinx bodies endure under the signs of citizenship, legality, and naturalization. Migrant bodies are marked bodies, X's already X'd out—often through the power of surveys and papers—before they ever arrive to become Latinx in the first place.

Equis/Excess

The second section makes a double movement. It marks the incomplete, fragmentary, and even forged nature of historically obscured Latinx archives; simultaneously, it excavates the excesses of *latinidad* that shape Latinx archives. Here the linguistic, racial, and national multiplicities that emerge through historical migration and colonization leave traces of *latinidad* for scholars to recover. Rodrigo Lazo opens the section by interrogating a literary-historical circulation of X that challenges the ostensible inclusivity of Latinx, and Ralph Bauer reminds us how a "hermeneutics of discovery" vexes the very hemispheric context we invoke as he calls for continued critique of the idea of discovery as both history and a paradigm of the Americas. With a critical turn to the archive, Anita Huizar-Hernández's essay discovers the forgery of *latinidad* at the heart of the 1895 Peralta land grant trial, in which Latinx race, gender, and sexuality become entwined in fictions of racial formation, while Alberto Varon's position paper about the fragmentary, migrant, multilingual, and multigeneric excesses of the Latinx archive insists on engaging the United States as a national framework for Latinx studies. John Alba Cutler's and Kelley Kreitz's essays take on such a challenge by working through both Latinx and Latin American frameworks. Cutler tracks printings of Rubén Darío's poetry to argue for a heterogenous genealogy of *modernismo* across Latinx print and reading cultures; Kreitz, alternatively, traces *modernismo's* emergence at the moment when the advent of electricity, the telephone, and the telegraph pressured notions of time and space in print. Even though the Latinx archive remains largely hidden to scholars outside Latino/a, Latin American, and hemispheric studies, its archival excess embodies the history of Latinx lives in hemispheric context: showing up again and again, in different iterations, across different times, and within different communities, known and familiar but also unrecognizable or a little bit changed—hidden and in excess, *aquí y de allá*.

Latinx Lives

The final section resists presumptions of fragmentation, tracking how geographic, (trans)national, linguistic, and ideological Chicanx and Latinx communities continually (re)shape themselves within and against forces of racism, xenophobia, nationalism, capitalism, and history. Marissa López argues for Chicanx studies and against pressure to adopt a broader Latinx framework. Exemplifying such an emphasis, Yolanda Padilla discusses how marginalized borderland print communities—particularly that of Laredo's *La crónica*—engage both Mexican and US traditions. Elise Bartosik-Vélez's position paper questions how translation, publication, and anthologization define national literary traditions, while Kenya C. Dworkin y Méndez argues for the importance of performance and "curriculum culture" in cohering Cuban émigré communities in the United States. Joshua Javier Guzmán closes the collection by reading the X of Latinx as a sign not of inclusivity but rather of the continued failure of language to represent *latinidad*. As Latinx, Chicanx, or Latina/o studies, our essays and position papers are also declarations: of story, knowledge, history, presence, community, and difference. They sound Spanish notes in an English-language journal to reassert, "Every day I am deluged with reminders / that this is not / my land / and this is my land."[4]

MARIA A. WINDELL is assistant professor of English at the University of Colorado Boulder. She is completing her first book project, tentatively titled *Transamerican Sentimentalism and Nineteenth-Century US Literary History*. Her work has appeared in *American Literary Realism*, *J19*, and *Nineteenth-Century Literature*.

JESSE ALEMÁN is professor of English and Presidential Teaching Fellow at the University of New Mexico. He is author of two dozen articles and essays on nineteenth-century American and US Latina/o literary histories and is editor (with Rodrigo Lazo) of *The Latino Nineteenth Century* (2016).

Acknowledgments

We wish to thank our authors for their excellent contributions, and we gratefully acknowledge the army of anonymous readers who generously reviewed essays. We thank Erica Sabelawski, *ELN*'s managing editor, for her editorial assistance. Laura Winkiel, *ELN*'s senior editor, has enthusiastically supported this issue from the start.

Notes

1   Cervantes, "Poem for the Young White Man," 35.
2   Cervantes, "Poem for the Young White Man," 35.
3   DeGuzmán, "Latinx," 220.
4   Cervantes, "Poem for the Young White Man," 36–37.

Works Cited

Cervantes, Lorna Dee. "Poem for the Young White Man Who Asked Me How I, an Intelligent, Well-Read Person Could Believe in the War between Races." In *Emplumada*, 35–37. Pittsburgh, PA: University of Pittsburgh Press, 1981.
DeGuzmán, María. "Latinx: ¡Estamos aquí!, or being 'Latinx' at UNC-Chapel Hill." *Cultural Dynamics* 29, no. 3 (2017): 214–30.

Dreaming Transnationally in America

JUAN POBLETE

Abstract Transnational circuits, as social practices, are not immaterial or virtual, but they do not depend on traditional understandings of one territorial location. Rather than fully and singularly determining the lives of its inhabitants, these local spaces belong now to a transterritory established by the physical, cultural, and imaginative labor of migrants connecting two such spaces, beyond the boundaries of one nation-state. Transnationalism, as a field of studies, has focused on these dynamics. Here they are used to address the question of a possible transnational politics *inside* the United States, connecting the lives of those who have the most and those who have the least, whether they are US nationals or foreign immigrants.

Keywords postsocial, transnationalism, Americanism/o

When the study of transnationalism began—in works such as Roger Rouse's "Mexican Migration and the Social Space of Postmodernism" (1991); Linda Basch, Nina Glick-Schiller, and Cristina Szanton Blanc's *Nations Unbound: Transnational Projects, Postcolonial Predicaments, and Deterritorialized Nation-States* (1994); and Peggy Levitt's *Transnational Villagers* (2001)—what was perceived as new in the lives of what were sometimes called transmigrants was their establishing transnational circuits. Transnational circuits were not immaterial or virtual, but they did not depend on traditional understandings of one territorial location. Rather than fully and singularly determining the lives of its inhabitants, these local spaces now belonged to a transterritory established by the physical, cultural, and imaginative labor of migrants connecting two such spaces, beyond the boundaries of one nation-state. As Rouse made clear, the labor performed by people in one of these places (Silicon Valley) as a proletarian force in the service sector of the knowledge economy allowed them to dream and plan for futures as small entrepreneurs and upwardly mobile Mexicans in another, their hometown of Aguililla, a southwestern Michoacán Mexican town.[1] As such, transnationalism seemed to offer a significant and perhaps unprecedented degree of political, economic, and cultural agency to people of relatively modest means, who could thus escape some of the limitations two nation-states had separately placed on their lives.

ENGLISH LANGUAGE NOTES

56:2, October 2018 DOI 10.1215/00138282-6960669
© 2018 Regents of the University of Colorado

As it turned out, these new ways of thinking the lives of migrants (transnationalism from below) coincided with the launch of the North American Free Trade Agreement (transnationalism from above), which—in a couple of decades, and with the help of subsidized US agricultural products—expelled millions of rural Mexicans from their lands by making their previous way of life, based on subsistence agriculture, impossible. Of course, the massive forced exodus to the North that followed did nothing but multiply the scale, the power, and the determination of migrants' transnationalism. In the meantime, while the neoliberal globalization of the Mexican countryside was taking place, millions of white blue-collar workers in the United States kept losing their jobs to outsourcing by the same forces, those leading the transformation from an industrial and relatively stable society to a postindustrial and much more unstable one. We now know that this was the way in which extraordinary wealth accumulation in a knowledge and immaterial service-based economy replaced the industrial and social compact of the welfare-state era. We know too that, in addition to considerable riches around the world, globalization produced extraordinary economic inequality, labor precarity, and social insecurity.

In the United States this resulted in the copresence, codependence, and mutual fear of those who have the most and those who have the least, manifesting as well in a generalized climate of insecurity for all those in between, often living paycheck to paycheck and always in danger of falling down socially. Those who have the least are composed of migrants, with few rights because of their frequent indocumentation, and downwardly mobile former industrial workers, desperately trying to find a place in the new economic and labor configurations. Those who have the most—whose gardens, houses, restrooms, health needs, restaurant meals, and so on are often serviced or supplied by immigrants of all kinds—fear those same immigrants who make their quality of life possible. White working-class citizens, experiencing their newly life-defining precarity, fear the migrants, criminalized minorities, and the lucky elites, and their resentment frequently surfaces as racism and neonationalism. Paradoxically, this postsocial condition, as I have called it elsewhere,[2] presents all the elements of a potential transnational politics *within* the United States, one that dares imagining trans-American futures that connect in a key different from fear, those bonds of copresence and codependence.

Such politics is powerfully proposed and explored in films such as Sergio Arau's *Day without a Mexican* and Alex Rivera's *Sleep Dealer*, in books such as Ruben Martinez's *Crossing Over: A Mexican Family on the Migrant Trail* and Sam Quinones's *Antonio's Gun and Delfino's Dream: True Tales of Mexican Migration*, and in novels such as Hector Tobar's *Barbarian Nurseries* and Cristina Henriquez's *Book of Unknown Americans*. In these cultural texts and in many others written and produced elsewhere, actually existing transnationalisms in America, or what I have elsewhere called true Americanism/o, begin to emerge.

....

JUAN POBLETE is professor of Latin American literature and cultural studies at the University of California, Santa Cruz. He is author of *Literatura chilena del siglo XIX: Entre públicos lectores y figuras autoriales* (2003); editor of *Critical Latin American and Latino*

Studies (2003) and *New Approaches to Latin American Studies: Culture and Power* (2017); and coeditor of *Andrés Bello* (2009), *Redrawing the Nation: National Identities in Latin/o American Comics* (2009), *Desdén al infortunio: Sujeto, comunicación y público en la narrativa de Pedro Lemebel* (2010), *Sports and Nationalism in Latin America* (2015), and *Humor in Latin American Cinema* (2015). His new books on the Chilean *crónica* writer Pedro Lemebel and the history of reading in Latin America are forthcoming.

Notes

1   Poblete, "Transnational Turn."
2   Poblete, "Americanism/o."

Works Cited

Poblete, Juan. "Americanism/o: Intercultural Border Zones in Post-social Times." In *Critical Terms in Caribbean and Latin American Thought: Historical and Institutional Trajectories*, edited by Ben Sifuentes Jáuregui, Yolanda Martínez–San Miguel, and Marisa Belausteguigoitia, 45–59. New York: Palgrave, 2015.

Poblete, Juan. "The Transnational Turn." In *New Approaches to Latin American Studies: Culture and Power*, edited by Juan Poblete, 32–49. London: Routledge, 2017.

Crisis Management and the LatinX Child

CLAUDIA MILIAN

Abstract   This article takes into consideration Valeria Luiselli's *Tell Me How It Ends: An Essay in Forty Questions*, a nonfictional work about unaccompanied Central American minors coming to the United States and the immigration questionnaire they must navigate to determine their US admissibility. The essay explores how the Northern Triangle's minor—the outré LatinX child—is made into the word on bureaucratic paper. It probes a genealogy of temporary American beginnings and delves into the expulsed Central American child as a newcomer, a migrant, and the beginning of something else: a LatinX phenomenon of—and in—crisis.

Keywords   Central American child migrant crisis, unaccompanied minors, questionnaire, LatinX

Tell Me How It Ends: An Essay in Forty Questions, a creative nonfiction undertaking by widely acclaimed Mexican novelist Valeria Luiselli, is "a deceptively slim volume," to give a précis of National Public Radio's view.[1] The account moves with an eye toward what became known, as a Wikipedia entry enumerates it, as the "2014 American immigration crisis."[2] This uncertain moment in American life refers to the influx into the United States of unaccompanied minors from Central America's Northern Triangle—El Salvador, Guatemala, and Honduras—or "the most murderous corner of the world," as renowned Salvadoran journalist Óscar Martínez construes it.[3] Their reasons for fleeing cannot be easily sloughed off: the children are escaping "extreme violence, persecution and coercion by gangs, mental and physical abuse, forced labor, neglect, abandonment."[4] The unauthorized entries were expected to reach seventy thousand in 2014 alone, an outpouring that led President Barack Obama to declare it a "humanitarian crisis."[5]

Luiselli enters this course of events as a volunteer interpreter for a New York City federal immigration court. "My task there is a simple one," she explains. "I interview children in court, following the intake questionnaire, and then translate their stories from Spanish to English."[6] Her main subject, Central American child migrants striving to exist, to say nothing of their presupposed questionable

ENGLISH LANGUAGE NOTES

56:2, October 2018   DOI 10.1215/00138282-6960680

motivations for defying their national origins—for not sticking to their *moira*—and illegally coming to the United States, deepens the urgency of Luiselli's work. Their stories are activated by a standardized American questionnaire—a mechanical list of unyielding items following a template, moving from one child to the ostensible monotonous sameness of the next one's responses. The sum of the questionnaire's forty parts presumably tells us all we need to know.[7] But a different history is burgeoning through the all-too-familiar Central American children, their life-and-death circumstances, and the way things work in the courtroom. Luiselli's approach revitalizes the immigration questionnaire's purpose by attenuating its routineness with a focus on the uniqueness of the responses.

Luiselli and the child migrant navigate a document in the service of national security, the rule of law, and public welfare. The questionnaire—a preliminary standardized American test—is a tool that measures, that now and then lets in, but that ultimately deports, time and again, the unauthorized migrant. The book's forty questions invite an analysis of the function of its very framework—the questions—as the Central American child is actualized in the public sphere through this test. How, we must ask, is the Central American children's humanity attended to via contemporary bureaucratic US documentation? Readers are forced to engage with the document to see a certain kind of Central American abject humanity, which is part of the problem. The questionnaire is a catalyst—a portal to enter the discussion of the US Central American presence through the minor. It is foundational to our understanding of the becoming of the Central American "thing," the unaccompanied minor, in the United States. But what is the questionnaire actually doing? How are Central American children made into the word on bureaucratic paper? My efforts attempt to create a language beyond the paper, so that the emergence of the problem child is understood.

The questionnaire—a file of information and personal experience—demonstrates a genealogy of temporary American beginnings. *Tell Me How It Ends* is a bid to "tell me how *you* begin"—how the outré LatinX child is configured within juridical archival projects, within American rhetoric and practice, and the historical space that does not admit Latino and Latina bodies. It is the US questionnaire—not the passport—that operates as a nexus of organizational attention, indicating the Central American child's unauthorized entry and providing a nebulous "history of the documentation of individual identity."[8] This form—as sociologist John Torpey speculates in connection to "the invention of the passport"—makes "their relevant differences knowable and thus enforceable," maintaining "documentary control" on their movement.[9] The questionnaire grants an identity that confers restricted access to American spaces, but through a matter where the why of this minor arises. Luiselli gives insight into how the child migrant interacts with perhaps one of the most contentious and tangled questions of our contemporary moment: "Why did you come to the United States?"[10] The why—*their* why—is beyond yes or no. It discloses a Central American sociopolitical reality that does not placate the public and limits the minor's being in the American world.

If, as philosopher Thomas Nail advances, the twenty-first century is "the century of the migrant," our epoch, too, is globally marked, in large scale, by the *child* migrant.[11] "Migration to developed states" by children and young people under twenty, affirms public policy scholar Jacqueline Bhabha, "has more than doubled in the last thirty-five years."[12] In cases when migrant children "did not have families to care for them," they "became the responsibility of diasporic community organizations from their countries of origin—Ethiopia, Iran, Vietnam, Somalia, Sri Lanka, El Salvador, Guatemala. Formal legal decisions were not taken on their behalf, and state entities did not take responsibility for their well-being."[13] Recall 2016 headlines that stressed the absence of protective attention for unaccompanied minors migrating to Europe. Thousands of moving children from Syria, Afghanistan, or Eritrea are missing or have been "accommodated" to the needs of the dark and intricate infrastructures of Greece and Italy's informal marketplaces. A BBC headline inquired, "Why are 10,000 migrant children missing in Europe?" The answer is disturbing: smugglers may be "turning the children they bring into Europe into the hands of traffickers to make more money. Those children might then be pushed into prostitution or slavery."[14] These migration patterns, routes of power, and forces of exploitation moving along with unaccompanied minors warrant studies from various researchers and experts in numerous fields and across geographies.

This juncture also merits new questions on mobility, the presence of children, and their restrictive US contexts alongside the everyday spaces of their lives. Transnational migrations, generally an adult-centered topic, are understood through assimilation, hyphenation, remittances, or full subjectivities. The "unaccompanied alien child," as the legal term describes them, navigates a number of worlds with—as the Mesoamerican corridor evinces—underworlds invariably lurking nearby. Central American minors—their agency, discoveries, and evolving stories—are fertilizing the field as well as the intellectual reach of Latino/a studies and its unlikely spaces in the Global South. But there is no final intellectual destination. How do the courses of these minors' mobility—their livelihood, the tensions, their different embodiments, the imprints they leave behind in movement, in detention, in US life, and in deportation processes—readjust the discursive edifice not so much of Latino/a ontological being but of deracinated emergence? By deracination I mean more than location or national uprootedness. It is a possibility to think about fragmentation, dissemination, and reconfiguration—an ungroundedness that decouples geographic fundamentality, specificity, and essentialism from the meaning of Latino and Latina in the United States, too. Latino/a is never fully situated in the world. The LatinX child's trajectory lends a hand in how these concerns with unpredictable starting points are disentangled.

Zigzagging our way through these conceptual thickets requires a brief explanation about the titular adjective moving this critical itinerary forward: LatinX. This gender-neutral denomination is deemed the current alternative to US Latino and Latina ethnoracial labels. LatinX—predominantly employed by scholars, activists, artists, and journalists—substitutes the terminological ilk of Latina/o, Latino/a, and Latin@. Online news outlets such as ColorLines, Fusion, *Huffington Post*, *Latina*, and Latino USA have been among the first to elucidate LatinX's meaning.[15] LatinX "first began to emerge within queer communities on the Internet in

2004."[16] It makes room "for people who are trans, queer, agender, non-binary, gender non-conforming or gender fluid," as the X rejects "the gendering of words especially since Spanish is such a gendered language."[17]

I do not quarrel about, or submit, "correct" definitions. I reflected elsewhere on LatinX's categorical uses and how it coevally bands together with a mélange of discourses and signifiers.[18] What attracts me about LatinX is its range of possibilities, its myriad pathways, and its wilting of conformity. The LatinX rhetorical gesture, as a matter of orientation in thought, is a ponderable one for our intellectual generation.[19] LatinX is more than just about Spanish as a gendered Romance language. The X is unknowable—or beyond knowing. The classification itself, LatinX, remains unknown, which is to say that we have rendered ourselves to the unknown—or the unknowns of unpredictable worlds. In this regard, LatinX can critically and imaginatively operate as "a guide to getting lost," to extract from essayist Rebecca Solnit, wherein we—quite riveted and wide awake—"leave the door open for the unknown, the door into the dark. That's where the most important things come from, where you yourself came from, and where you will go."[20] The Latin and the X are marked by, and prolong in, indeterminacy. Latin and X are capitalized to put their discursive functioning and communicative tensions in analytic play and to highlight how these dual-directional signifiers elicit continuous discernment. I steer toward LatinX in the context of unaccompanied Central American minors thrown into urgency, migration, detention, crises, questionnaires: the X of our actual moment in history. The X of the LatinX child subsumes many X's: lest we forget, there is more than one LatinX child. The scattered LatinX child lives at the margins of the unknown, of the double uncertainty of the X's of the Latino/a world and the American one. Its centrality of being is its abject, threatening knownness. The LatinX child has been depersonalized and dehumanized, far removed from the here and now.

This scrutiny delves into the broader concept of the expulsed Central American child as a newcomer, a migrant, and the beginning of something else: a LatinX phenomenon of, and in, crisis. By beginning I mean all that starts afresh: the LatinX child's inception is characteristic of how it came into being, as literary theorist and public intellectual Edward Said put forward.[21] His preoccupations come within range of the LatinX child, for "the notion of a beginning itself is practically tied up in a whole complex of relations. Between the word beginning and the word origin lies a constantly changing system of meanings."[22] Beginnings "inaugurate a deliberately *other* production of meaning": they are "a problem to be studied," "preparatory to something else."[23] Origins, by contrast, are passive, tied to "precedence and unchanging being," where "everything can be referred for an explanation."[24] While Central America is an origin—as in a "source," the first stage of existence, or, as Nail conjectures, the "socially fixed point *from which*" the LatinX child "departs"—I benefit from Said's cogitation on beginnings, as they do not subscribe to purity.[25] Beginnings are an ongoing process challenging the simplification of a subject to an origin or a point in time. Beginnings are vectors emphasizing direction.

This LatinX beginning—beginning of something else—requires that we wrestle, on and on, with "the tumbling disorder that will not settle down" for Latins looming under that capacious and changeable X.[26] The LatinX child advancing these pages begins through the Mesoamerican journey, at odds with the American child's safe domestic movements. Reflecting on childhood wanderings, getting lost, and its activation of the creative imagination, Solnit writes: "Children seldom roam, even in the safest places. Because of their parents' fear of the monstrous things that might happen (and do happen, but rarely), the wonderful things that happen as a matter of course are stripped away from them. For me, childhood roaming was what developed self-reliance, a sense of direction and adventure, imagination, a will to explore, to be able to get a little lost and then figure out the way back."[27] What does the LatinX child imaginatively conjure up during movement or "adventure"? Unaccompanied minors turn themselves over to the Border Patrol, to American bureaucracy, upon making it to the other side. There is a certain innocence in Solnit's passage. But the questionnaire's LatinX child is already inscribed into a transcriptive practice. Which is to say that we need another beginning to Luiselli's end. For the LatinX child, "roaming" is at odds with their journey. The LatinX child locomotes with particular motivation and will. The LatinX traveler is still a child, and still unable to move through the bureaucracy of their final destination.

Anthropologist Susan J. Terrio sets forth that "when the number of unaccompanied children crossing the US–Mexico border from October 2013 to June 2014 surged to 57,525, moral panic centered on the threat of criminality and disease they posed."[28] The reader thrust into Luiselli's text vis-à-vis an exigent crisis learns how movement and detention inaugurate—indeed, usher along—the LatinX child, or the ex-child who does not quite fall back to childhood. Let us consider, too, that there is another X child in Luiselli's enterprise: her unnamed five-year-old daughter, a key questioner who often asks her, "So, how does the story of those children end?"[29] Through her child's eye—another witness account—we see an unbreakable feedback between mother and daughter. Luiselli's titular intent could just as readily be amended to *(You) Tell Me How It Ends (Mamá)*, or even *(You) Tell Me How It Ends (Mamá, Because It's Different from How Your Story Ended)*. The Central American minor is perhaps the most X of the children that are "out there." What is LatinX in relation to child migrants? What is a LatinX life, given its dissonances, incoherence, and fluctuating borders? How are their LatinXness *and* AmericanXness put into words? I pursue these concerns through an unfolding LatinXness underpinned by notions of nascency, one that, like the Central American child, is intangible, deracinated, aspirational, far from unified, transcends "the nation," and struggles to "make sense."

Tell Me How It Ends obliges readers to sift through historical antecedents of the questionnaire and its circulations and to try to find a working order of the racialized Central American child in it. I start by drawing on a brief overview of surveys and the narratives they have proffered to the nation as well as its citizens— illustrating, during these beginning moments of Central American inscription, that "the future is only the stuff of some kids," as performance studies theorist José Esteban Muñoz made known.[30] From there, I interrogate the meanings of US crisis in Central American life.

The Central American Minor/The Minor Central American

Migration from Central America to the United States is not a recent occurrence. Sociologist Norma Stoltz Chinchilla and political scientist Nora Hamilton note that the isthmus's civil wars during the 1980s—coupled with "the effects of Hurricane Mitch and other natural disasters in the 1990s, and deteriorating economic conditions, as well as a demand for immigrant labor in certain U.S. labor markets"— set in motion their steady migratory flows.[31] Since "a substantial number of Central American immigrants are undocumented," they add, this "constitutes an important obstacle to their economic success, limiting the kinds of jobs available to them and resulting in frequent exploitation of their labor. In contrast to Cubans and Vietnamese, Salvadorans, Guatemalans, and Nicaraguans were not accepted as refugees during the 1980s, and very few were able to obtain asylum."[32]

Sociologist Pierrette Hondagneu-Sotelo underscores that "Salvadoran and Guatemalan women and men left their countries in haste, often leaving their children behind, as they fled the civil wars, political violence, and upheaval."[33] Journalistic endeavors such as Sonia Nazario's *Enrique's Journey*—originally a six-part *Los Angeles Times* series from 2002, which earned the Pulitzer Prize for Feature Writing—looked into the psychological impact of gendered migrations on Central American families.[34] Nazario chronicled how Enrique, a teenager, traveled alone from Honduras to search for his mother in the United States, feeling, as some Central American children frequently do, abandoned. Central American children are not, clearly, the first or the last to take a questionnaire. Yet the survey—how it ideologically strengthens itself and keeps tabs on the unwanted migrant child—gives "birth" to expellable intruders who are seen precisely because of their "illegality" and Central Americanness. The questionnaire is a legitimate form that makes these undocumented subjects speak and legible to a social order. Central American children are foregrounded as nomadic and oral—at odds with the written records structuring the nation and its families.

Historian Sarah Igo imparts that "the promise of empirical surveys," with its prying inquisitiveness, is "to disclose the society to itself."[35] Mass surveys entered the public domain after World War I, "telling Americans 'who we are,' 'what we want,' and 'what we believe.'"[36] Doubtlessly, there are "many other ways to envision America, beginning with works of literature, photography, and history."[37] "Americans today," Igo proceeds, "are accustomed to a seemingly endless stream of questions from survey researchers, political pollsters, marketers, and census takers. Being studied, and being privy to the results, is an understood and unexceptional feature of modern life. It is perhaps the principal way that we know ourselves to be a part of the national community."[38] Contemporary US life is inundated with countless types of questionnaires shared on social media. Personality tests, dating profiles, and "our obsession with online quizzes" manifest "a nonstop, exhausting performance" of selfhood.[39] MIT psychologist and cultural analyst Sherry Turkle emphasizes that the quizzes' function "is to share it, to feel 'who you are' by how you share who you are."[40]

This globally networked relationality—or untiring "linking" of the technological self that is always *on*—involves an active makeover that recurrently performs and reveals a new kind of temporal life. But this reworking of the self cannot be neatly connected to unsummoned, unaccompanied Central American children and the "confessional" responses required in off-line questionnaires for US courtrooms. "As you make your way down its forty questions," Luiselli avers, "it's impossible not to feel that the world has become a much more fucked-up place than anyone could have ever imagined."[41] These children's stigmatized bodies are a mismatch. They cannot, on the face of it, afford quality things and habitually tinker with the self through smart technological gadgets. Unable to readily catch up to the ongoing, updated reinvention encountered online, they come across as distant from the American everyday. And the questionnaire, as applied to administered Central Americans in US courtrooms, upholds the value of American organizational life, of an efficient American bureaucracy that competently deports them. The disruption is not the procedural paper logic that writes them off, or the history of American intervention that has produced these displacements. The Central American minor is disruption embodied.

But I want to follow, for a bit, the historical thread of the questionnaire and its associations to notions of geography, pedigree, racial hierarchies, and moral characteristics. Evan Kindley's *Questionnaire* keeps a finger on the pulse of nineteenth-century efforts to draft surveys envisioning "a world remade by asking the right questions."[42] Another way to put it may be that the "right" questions asked by the "right" kind of people led to a "righted" world, as English explorer and anthropologist Francis Galton intended. A cousin of Charles Darwin, Galton coined the scientific and social movement known as eugenics in 1883 and is recognized for this form's early and meticulous uses. He designed questionnaires promoting the development of the sciences of anthropometrics, statistics, and evolutionary biology. Galton's surveys—"scientific investigations"—were fortuitous. Parents became "family historians," preserving a "trustworthy record" of their "biological experience" through their children.[43] These family catalogs gave rise to "the baby book, a popular genre that continues to flourish today."[44]

Galton's investment in purity, development, and fitness from infancy onward coincided with the extreme representation, during England's Victorian age (1837–1901), of Máximo and Bartola, two "diminutive, primary microcephalic" Central American siblings.[45] Known for their "'dwarfish and idiotic' appearance," they toured both sides of the Atlantic.[46] A Spanish trader approached Máximo and Bartola's parents to take them from El Salvador to the United States and cure them of their "imbecility."[47] Arguably, Máximo and Bartola are the genesis of Central American "unaccompanied minors." Later sold to an American, the brother and sister were refashioned as "Aztec children" by their owner-manager, who metamorphosed them into objects of "vivid interest" at a time when Americans "thirsted for more information about the natural history of their own continent."[48] The "Aztec Lilliputians" were guests of President Millard Fillmore at the White House and created "quite a stir" in England.[49] They were exhibited at P. T. Barnum's American Museum in New York and before the Ethnological Society of London. Máximo and Bartola also met the royal family at Buckingham Palace. They progressed from "sensation to specimen"—having been declared "a new type of humanity, only three feet high"—as literary scholar Robert D. Aguirre reveals.[50] Máximo and Bartola had been rendered, in a word, inanimate objects. They performed for their own moment in time, foreshadowing the grotesqueries of the Central American future.

This snapshot casts light on the rhetorical and processual building up of the questionnaire, especially during industrialization and during a time of change. In the 1880s the number of excluded classes in the US immigration system grew, as historian Mae Ngai has discussed, "to comprise the mentally retarded, contract laborers, persons with 'dangerous and loathsome contagious disease,' paupers, polygamists, and the 'feebleminded' and 'insane,' as well as Chinese laborers."[51] Victorian scholar Sally Mitchell writes that across the Atlantic the textures of every-day life, "the physical and technological surroundings in which people lived, the patterns of their education and work and recreation and belief, were [all] utterly transformed."[52] This transition period parallels our contemporary time, with the digitization of life. Yet the more connected we are digitally, the more disconnected we become. Sentimentality and the representation of emotions are attributed to inanimate children like Máximo and Bartola—not unlike the projected dark brown-ness and stillness of minors in a questionnaire. Obsessive scientific approaches and racialized lenses are applied to "things," to "monstrous" differences that help hege-monic subjects understand their normality and superiority. But it is a "monstrosity" that must be kept afar. Terrio expounds that "terms such as *racial purity* have largely disappeared from public usage, but racial thinking is expressed in coded language about work, education, immigration, and entitlements."[53] Organizational and man-agerial control does not trail too far behind. Anthropologist David Graeber reminds us of this when he observes that bureaucratic procedure "invariably means ignoring all the subtleties of real human existence and reducing everything to simple pre-established mechanical or statistical formulae. Whether it's a matter of forms, rules, statistics, or questionnaires, bureaucracy is always about simplification."[54]

Luiselli attempts to limn, sardonically, America's normative fears when it comes to the child migrant from Central America—a region that, in foreign affairs journalist Tim Marshall's rendering, "has little going for it by way of geography but for one thing. It is thin."[55] Marshall posits a different relation to the area and its human subjects, a new sense of getting caught up in "that" Central American "thin(g)": that trivial thin thing. Luiselli writes:

> In varying degrees, some papers and webpages announce the arrival of undocumented children like a biblical plague. Beware the locusts! They will cover the face of the ground so that it cannot be seen—these menacing, coffee-colored boys and girls, with their obsidian hair and slant eyes. They will fall from the skies, on our cars, on our green lawns, on our heads, on our schools, on our Sundays. They will make a racket, they will bring their chaos, their sickness, their dirt, their brownness. They will cloud the pretty views, they will fill the future with bad omens, they will fill our tongues with barbarisms. And if they are allowed to stay here they will—eventually—reproduce.[56]

To be clear: I admire Luiselli's oeuvre, her thoughtfulness, and, as she demonstrates, her readiness and skill to witness, translate, and discharge the concrete problem back to her American addressees. *Tell Me How It Ends* is a testament that the Central American minor has not been kicked out of the American world so silently. Luiselli raises awareness—"a transformation of consciousness," as author Nathaniel Popkin rightly gauged in *Lit Hub*—and appeals to a US goodness that will engender reason and dignity to Central American children.[57] It is almost as though the reader is privy to Luiselli's Latina becoming. She is an alien—a "nonresident alien" wanting to become a "resident alien"—wrestling with the green card questionnaire and the unresolvable question "Why did you come to the United States?"[58] I understand her intended irony in the aforementioned excerpt, a tricky thing to capture. Yet the ease of the prose—the circulation of this cultural representation—does not read as ironic. The passage sounds eerily like eugenics. To whom are these words of "disfigurement" directed? These signifiers conceivably legitimate these minors' geopolitical and racial differences—marking them as "real." Central American differences are unchangeable. Most ironically, isn't that why they are policed, detained, and deported in the first place?

Ultimately, what does such a passage contribute? Can we grasp "their" difference only through this repetition of saturated difference? *What* is *this* LatinX child's difference? The LatinX child may not be called a rapist or a predator in the US lingua franca, as undocumented adults are usually dubbed. But perhaps Luiselli's double-edged comments about this political problem are unerring to the extent that the semiotics applied to the unlawful child migrant's racialized meanings are not so color-blind. This racialization is at odds with how, as constitutional scholar Patricia Williams has pointed out, US children in predominantly white schools are told by "well-meaning teachers" such hackneyed expressions as "Color makes no difference" and "It doesn't matter whether you're black or white or red or green or blue."[59] Seemingly, the LatinX child—none or all of the above—is muffled in the classroom and remains outside the colorings of this colorless palette, of this discursive elision of race. The Central American child becomes what "we" already "know" "it" is, or, as Luiselli synthesizes it, "barbarians who deserve subhuman treatment."[60]

Binding the minor to the precision of the survey's questions, we only "know" Central American children as juridical subjects, as an impure matter on which American power will be exercised. Not an American child, but more like a contemptible child without discipline and with a slew of undesirable attributes, this minor treads a path far from straight and narrow. Who are they, what are their origins, and where are their parents? Luiselli explains that "the process by which a child is asked questions during the intake interview is called screening."[61] She continues:

> Right before the first formal interview question, a line floats across the page
> like an uncomfortable silence:
>   Where is the child's mother?___father?___

There are no family trees to reconstruct this "floating" population: only blank lines resting, "floating" on genealogical "imperfection." They surface as empty, anonymous X's "filled" by a blank univocality unified by abandonment and unknowability. The Central American child transfigures into the LatinX child, coming to us from a different "Latin" world. And yet its adjacent AmericanXness is never far behind: LatinXness and AmericanXness have been birthed in crisis. This child's relatives are nonrelatives. The LatinX child's "authenticity" is the X that looks odd, that duplicates, that is both paper and paperwork. The X of blank-headedness and bureaucratic runaround. The X of heightened exclusion. The X that requires the LatinX child to be "realistic." The X of not knowing where or how it will end up. The X that drops by. The X of stigma and confinement. The X that cannot cross out the (Northern Triangle) error. The LatinX child is resistant to closure.

"Too often, the spaces remain blank," Luiselli divulges; "all the children come without their fathers and their mothers. And many of them do not even know where their parents are."[62] These are families in crisis. Buried in a particular "grammar book," as literary theorist Hortense J. Spillers might put it, this Central American "baby"—a "notorious bastard" that is always Mama's, Papa's, and the nation's "maybe"—grows into "a resource for metaphor."[63] The absence of the mother and father for the Central American child evolves into a "territory of cultural and political maneuver."[64] Central American minors become illegitimate children with illegitimate claims. Spillers's methodological conception of US historical order as it relates to black womanhood, enslavement, and African American family structures is, needless to add, distinct from migrant children who "try to turn themselves in to the migra, or Border Patrol, as soon as possible."[65] Yet I return to Spillers's work to deliberate on this migrant "anomaly"—on Central American "faults" and "failures" from early childhood—and the new kind of "grammar," the "altered human factor" produced in transit.[66] "The migration of children," Luiselli regards with keen attention, "is reorganizing and redefining the traditional family structure."[67]

The Central American child is "unthinkable."[68] To trouble this pronouncement further: it is not the minor per se who is unthinkable. Central American children and their ballooning numbers are simply unthinkable *in* the United States—and extraordinarily unthinkable in the American long run. Seen as such, these minors "deserve," as Bhabha has it, punitive treatment, punitive intervention, and punitive measures that return them "to the places they fear."[69] Their predicament—and the ugliness that surrounds their plight, to say nothing of their unhealthy nations—exhibits an unfitness registering the isthmus's dangers and pathologies. LatinX children can never really speak of a *new* life, only attest to their ever-present abjection. Their "floating" explanations steadily go south—taking these minors, literally, back to Central America.

Luiselli swiftly resurrects a passage from a Reuters story in which the news agency reported that "looking happy the deported children exited the airport on an overcast and sweltering afternoon. One by one, they filed into a bus, playing with the balloons they had been given." Calling this far-from-festive sight an "uncanny image," Luiselli "cannot stop reproducing" it "somewhere in the dark back of our minds."[70] Reuters's characterization of deportation as "fun and games" is, shall we say, haunting, almost suggesting that expelled children must play—or, rather, that adult readers must be comforted by—the positive role of happiness under these circumstances. The balloon is like a goody of care, a party favor, a temporary consolation prize. The balloon and the minor are easy to puncture and deflate: deflatable goods for deflatable children. Children and balloons, both familiar in daily life, become strange and unfamiliar. They are the contents of an awkward and outrageous performance that "fits" in the culture of a detention and deportation system through a different form of "crisis management." There is no management model to improve the practice of admitting Central American children into the United States, just the coordination of mass expulsions.

The LatinX child is pliable. Childhood and adulthood are on the same hostile footing. The Central American minor (as in: under the legal age of full responsibility) interchangeably becomes a minor Central American (meaning: someone who has a low rank, status, or position)—enacting an ideological Lilliputianness at the juridical level. The diminutiveness of the LatinX child—a descendant of Máximo and Bartola's, so to speak—evokes magnification: the magnification of smallness through time. Lilliputianness is a metaphor for Central America and the Central American. The questionnaire mirrors this shortness by condensing and minimizing its subject. The fantastical smallness of Máximo and Bartola makes a return as the little LatinX child is shortened through his or her questionnaire responses in our modern day. After all, immigration judge Jack H. Weil has argued that "three- and four-year-olds can learn immigration law well enough to represent themselves in court. I've taught immigration law literally to three-year-olds and four-year-olds. It takes a lot of time. It takes a lot of patience. They get it. It's not the most efficient, but it can be done."[71]

The LatinX child is expected to possess the brainpower to figure out US immigration law and to competently serve as its own legal counsel. This child acts out a legally sanctioned bizarre irrationalism. The LatinX child stages the juridical mode of recognition by which it is identified: its abject problems. But there is no sense of American ethics and obligation to the Central American child who appears to arrive ex nihilo. Three additional judges publicly challenged Weil: "A typical three-year-old cannot tie her shoes, count to 100, peel a banana, or be trusted not to swallow marbles."[72] Luiselli mentions the cognitive stumbling blocks presented by the form's last ten questions. They "are the most difficult because they refer directly to the gangs. Smaller children look back at you with a mixture of bewilderment and amusement if you say 'bands of organized criminals,' maybe because they associate the word 'bands' with musical groups."[73] The LatinX child, "targeted on the basis of racialized national identities," is framed to articulate its own grounds of expulsion.[74] Ngai's words ring true: if "the illegal immigrant cannot be constituted without deportation—the possibility or threat of deportation, if not the fact"— neither can the LatinX child.[75] Illegality, detention, and deportation are its iconic status.

One is not a detached observer. Luiselli speaks of two Guatemalan sisters, five and seven years old, whose mother saved enough money to bring them up north through a coyote or, as one of the girls says, "a man."[76] They prepared for their journey in this way:

> The day before they left, their grandmother sewed a ten-digit number on the collars of the dress each girl would wear through the entire trip. It was a ten-digit number the girls had not been able to memorize, as hard as she tried to get them to, so she had decided to embroider it on their dresses and repeat over, and over, a single instruction: they should never take this dress off, not even to sleep, and as soon as they reached America, as soon as they met the first American policeman, they were to show the inside of the dress's collar to him. He would then dial the number and let them speak to their mother. The rest would follow.[77]

Luiselli calls attention to the "ten-digit number." This incomprehensible phone number—as unknowable as XXX-XXX-XXXX—cannot be repeated memoriter. It cannot come any farther than Luiselli's qualifier: the ten-digit number. At times US businesses make phone numbers catchier by using letters or phrases in place of digits. But this ingenious grandmother clears this obstacle by fashioning her own system of communication. By the same token, there is no punctual sense of clock and calendar time—no one knows the length of this arduous and risky journey, just the descriptor "through the entire trip." The girls are "timed" by the number of borders they continue to cross in their coded, unchangeable dresses, a sort of borderlands uniform in this Mesoamerican space of "standard stranded time," as it were. They are "timed," as well, by their bodies—children's bodies keeping up with adult paces, a coyote's speed, moving forward—which assume, one can only speculate, a physical and psychological toll. Their grandmother tells their story of crossing boundaries through her needlework—stitching a US recognizable, registered, and working number, a "good" number, on a collar to be shown, like official documentation, to American government agents on arrival. But this dress is a different activation of caller ID, let's say, for one cannot predict who will access and dial the ten digits: a US police officer or a member of a gang or an organized crime group. The dress and its discreet phone number presage life and death, good and bad news, farness and nearness, childhood home and detention center, crossing with fear and living with fear.

"The children that arrived here, one must remember, are also the children that made it. The children that made it through Mexico, which is really like hell for Central American migrants," Luiselli told *Democracy Now!* Central American vulnerability along the hazardous Mesoamerican route has been widely explored in academic studies, journalistic feature and news writings, films, and documentaries.[78] Anyone who crosses over has more than made it. Their perseverance across borders is "life beyond life": "Survival is not simply that which remains but the most intense life possible."[79]

Problem Children

Communication scholars Timothy L. Sellnow and Matthew W. Seeger outline that crises connote unpredictable, threatening, and high-uncertainty occurrences bringing about a sense of collapse, disruption, and harm.[80] These exigencies can include the humanities crisis; an existential breakdown or midlife crisis; a social crisis; a health crisis or pandemic; natural disasters like earthquakes, tsunamis, tornadoes, and hurricanes; environmental catastrophes like lead seeping into drinking water, global warming, drought, nuclear disaster, and an oil spill; financial disasters; an energy crisis; terrorist attacks; or a "specific, unexpected, non-routine event or series of events that create high levels of uncertainty and a significant or perceived threat to high priority goals."[81] "The dizzying array of crisis narratives," as anthropologist Janet Roitman alludes to them, determines "the post hoc judgment of deviation, of failure."[82] The LatinX child migrant is a visually excessive sign of repetitive crisis and failure. The LatinX minor's forecast is gloomy: it is a futurity that cannot be. LatinX kids are a liability and tend to meet with the same kind of ending. Can one imagine what a Central American child in crisis can become? Can a LatinX child move beyond alienness? Perhaps 2014 indicates a bigger extremity: that of Central American negation, the disavowal of their humanness.

How did this grave US emergency resonate in Central America? Public discourse of a state of crisis propelled Óscar Martínez to report on the phenomenon. The investigative journalist's account—"Los niños no se van: Se los llevan" ("The Children Don't Leave: They Take Them")—questions the perceived homogeneous entity of the "unaccompanied child migrant."[83] Martínez pushes for greater interpretive complexity vis-à-vis the decisions Central Americans make to move and engage in what still amounts to an open future. His article tracks down the nuances within contexts of violence, family separation, and the business of human smuggling. Martínez avoids the term crisis: it dehumanizes the Central American minor's perils and trauma. Children are not a crisis. "What has changed in the last few months," he asks, writing in July 2014, "so that tens of thousands of Central American children flee from violence?" Martínez infers that "if El Salvador's children would leave because of the violence alone, thousands and thousands would've left. We've been violent for a long time before fifty-two thousand children left." He consults with the pseudonymous "Señor Coyote," who has been in the human smuggling business since 1979. Mr. Coyote "boasts being one of El Salvador's first coyotes. When he began to *coyotear*," or smuggle, "he even ran ads for 'safe travel to the United States' on newspaper pages, listing his office number." Mr. Coyote's métier entails making headway through Mexico, getting the children to the other side, and training them "to forget they went with a coyote."

More remarkable is a point made almost en passant, proffering insights about a LatinXness in transit and its temporary identifications. Mr. Coyote mentions that "many children passed through with the papers of Puerto Ricans or Dominicans." Martínez does not untangle the degrees of otherness that Central American children undertake at geographic and cultural crossroads and in an active process of "Latinization." Their modifications touch on a LatinXness of being: minors must "forget" about the adults guiding them from point X to point X and assume an accompanying "citizenship" from another country. Puerto Rican or Dominican papers facilitate the Central American child's mobility farther north, uprooting the child from his or her "origins," but beginning again as something else. These documents assign another layer of meaning to the LatinX minor.

Can we even quantify the dizzying array of Latin copiousness in these "Puerto Rican" and "Dominican" border crossings? What do we make of this deracinated but dispersed, "underage" but legal, and hidden but well-paced "Latinidad"—or, rather, these legal iterations of Dominicanness and Puerto Ricanness in Mesoamerica? Puerto Rican US citizenships circulating through Mesoamerican undocumented migrations intimate broad "alien" movements. Puerto Ricans are US citizens, of course, and the domain of a flexible Puerto Ricanness in this Central American moment punctuates a paradoxical "foreignness." An often-unrecognized US citizenship is activated through the transitory "Americanness" of Central Americans. The LatinX migrant, hailing from elsewhere, is "naturalized" to other homelands. Martínez imparts another kind of resistance to restrictions that carve out family spaces. "If parents don't have a real choice to take their children in a legal way," he concludes, "if parents don't see that violence shows signs of declining significantly in Honduras, Guatemala, or El Salvador, if many of those parents no longer wash dishes but have established, after years of sacrifice, their own business, then what? If the United States, Guatemala, El Salvador, or Honduras does not give them an option, a coyote will give it to them. Parents will always want to have their children by their side."

Central American movements continue. They are about far more than immigration forms. *Tell Me How It Ends* is, sure, about the comprehensive American questionnaire and its cultivation of alien personae. Luiselli tells us, in this sense, how the LatinX child begins: in movement, in deportation, in questions, and in new affiliations. The LatinX child is starting another production of meaning. The LatinX child is beginning here and there.

CLAUDIA MILIAN is associate professor of Romance studies and director of the Program in Latino/a Studies in the Global South at Duke University. She is author of *Latining America: Black-Brown Passages and the Coloring of Latino/a Studies* (2013) and editor of a special issue of *Cultural Dynamics*, "Theorizing LatinX" (2017). Milian is also coeditor of two special issues: "Interoceanic Diasporas and the Panama Canal's Centennial" in *The Global South* (2012) and "U.S. Central Americans: Representations, Agency, and Communities" in *Latino Studies* (2013). She is at work on her second book, tentatively titled *LatinX: Present Tense and Tensions.*

Acknowledgments

I gratefully acknowledge the participants of the 2017 Duke University–Durham University faculty workshop "Borders: Regimes, Disposability: A Symposium on Migration and State Violence" for their optimism, encouragement, and comments, from which this essay has benefited: Francisco-J. Hernández Adrián, Peter Baker, Marc Botha, Russell Contreras, Michaeline Crichlow, John Morán González, Kirsten Silva Gruesz, Noam Leshem, Kerstin Oloff, and Janet Stewart. I want to give a big shout-out to the students in my spring 2017 autobiography and memoir seminar, particularly Elizabeth Barahona, Betty Chen, Kathleen Marsh, Leslie Turner, and Alexandra Wisner. Special thanks to and admiration for my fabulous community of first readers and my BFFs, Eduardo Contreras, R. Galvan, and Miguel Segovia, for always going above and beyond with their feedback, word-by-word generosity, and unparalleled thoroughness and thoughtfulness.

Notes

1   Powers, "'Tell Me How It Ends.'"
2   Wikipedia, "2014 American Immigration Crisis."
3   Martínez, *History of Violence*, xviii.
4   Luiselli, *Tell Me How It Ends*, 12.
5   Gordon, "70,000 Kids Will Show Up Alone."
6   Luiselli, *Tell Me How It Ends*, 7.
7   Luiselli, *Tell Me How It Ends*, 40.
8   Robertson, *Passport in America*, 3.
9   Torpey, *Invention of the Passport*, 2–3.
10   Luiselli, *Tell Me How It Ends*, 7.
11   Nail, *Figure of the Migrant*, 1.
12   Bhabha, *Child Migration*, 2.
13   Bhabha, *Child Migration*, 2.
14   Merriman, "Why Are 10,000 Migrant Children Missing in Europe?"
15   See Logue, "Latina/o/x"; Funes, "Ever Wondered What 'Latinx' Means?"; Latino USA, "Latinx"; Reichard, "Why We Say Latinx"; and Rivas, "What We Mean When We Say Latinx."
16   Ramirez and Blay, "Why People Are Using the Term 'Latinx.'"
17   Ramirez and Blay, "Why People Are Using the Term 'Latinx.'"
18   Milian, "Extremely Latin, XOXO."
19   See Chandler, *X*.
20   Solnit, *Field Guide*, 4.
21   Said, *Beginnings*, 174–75.
22   Said, *Beginnings*, 5–6.
23   Said, *Beginnings*, 13–14.
24   Said, *Beginnings*, 174.
25   Nail, *Figure of the Migrant*, 14.
26   Said, *Beginnings*, 50.
27   Solnit, *Field Guide*, 7.
28   Terrio, *Whose Child Am I?*, 10.
29   Luiselli, *Tell Me How It Ends*, 55.
30   Muñoz, *Cruising Utopia*, 95.
31   Chinchilla and Hamilton, "Central America," 328.
32   Chinchilla and Hamilton, "Central America," 333.
33   Hondagneu-Sotelo, *Doméstica*, 53.
34   Nazario, "Enrique's Journey." See also Nazario, *Enrique's Journey*.
35   Igo, *Averaged American*, 2.
36   Igo, *Averaged American*, 3.
37   Igo, *Averaged American*, 4.
38   Igo, *Averaged American*, 2–3.
39   Maloney, "Our Obsession with Online Quizzes."
40   Maloney, "Our Obsession with Online Quizzes."
41   Luiselli, *Tell Me How It Ends*, 10.
42   Kindley, *Questionnaire*, 11.
43   Galton, *Record of Family Faculties*. See also Galton, *Life History Album*.
44   Kindley, *Questionnaire*, 14.
45   Bogdan, *Freak Show*, 127–28.
46   Bogdan, *Freak Show*, 127–28.
47   Bogdan, *Freak Show*, 127–28.
48   Bogdan, *Freak Show*, 128–30.
49   Bogdan, *Freak Show*, 130.
50   Aguirre, *Informal Empire*, 105.
51   Ngai, *Impossible Subjects*, 59.
52   Mitchell, *Daily Life in Victorian England*, xiv.
53   Terrio, *Whose Child Am I?*, 9.
54   Graeber, *Revolutions in Reverse*, 51.
55   Marshall, *Prisoners of Geography*, 226.
56   Luiselli, *Tell Me How It Ends*, 15.
57   Popkin, "Translating This Broken World."
58   Luiselli, *Tell Me How It Ends*, 8–10.
59   Williams, *Seeing a Color-Blind Future*, 3.
60   Luiselli, *Tell Me How It Ends*, 84.
61   Luiselli, *Tell Me How It Ends*, 11.
62   Luiselli, *Tell Me How It Ends*, 11.
63   Spillers, "Mama's Baby, Papa's Maybe," 66.
64   Spillers, "Mama's Baby, Papa's Maybe," 67.
65   Luiselli, *Tell Me How It Ends*, 20.
66   Spillers, "Mama's Baby, Papa's Maybe," 70.
67   Luiselli, *Tell Me How It Ends*, 48.
68   Luiselli, *Tell Me How It Ends*, 12.
69   Bhabha, *Child Migration*, 207.
70   Luiselli, *Tell Me How It Ends*, 16.
71   Markon, "Can a 3-Year Old Represent Herself in Immigration Court?"
72   Markon, "Former Judges Challenge Official."
73   Luiselli, *Tell Me How It Ends*, 73.
74   Terrio, *Whose Child Am I?*, 15.
75   Ngai, *Impossible Subjects*, 58.
76   Luiselli, *Tell Me How It Ends*, 56.
77   Luiselli, *Tell Me How It Ends*, 57.
78   Goodman, "Mexican Writer Valeria Luiselli." See, e.g., Sandoval-García, *Exclusion and Forced Migration*; Sassen, "Massive Loss of Habitat"; Basok et al., *Rethinking Transit Migration*; Martínez, *Beast*; *La jaula de oro* (*The Golden Dream*), dir. Diego Quemada-Diez (2013); and *Which Way Home*, dir. Rebecca Cammisa (2009).
79   Derrida, *Learning to Live Finally*, 52.
80   Sellnow and Seeger, *Theorizing Crisis Communication*, 2–4.
81   Sellnow and Seeger, *Theorizing Crisis Communication*, 6–7.
82   Roitman, *Anti-crisis*, 41–42.
83   Martínez, "Los niños no se van." All the passages quoted in this section are from this news article. All translations are mine.

Works Cited

Aguirre, Robert D. *Informal Empire: Mexico and Central America in Victorian Culture.* Minneapolis: University of Minnesota Press, 2005.

Basok, Tanya, Danièle Bélanger, Martha Luz Rojas Wiesner, and Guillermo Candiz. *Rethinking Transit Migration: Precarity, Mobility, and Self-Making in Mexico.* New York: Palgrave Macmillan, 2015.

Bhabha, Jacqueline. *Child Migration and Human Rights in a Global Age*. Princeton, NJ: Princeton University Press, 2016.

Bogdan, Robert. *Freak Show: Presenting Human Oddities for Amusement and Profit*. Chicago: University of Chicago Press, 1988.

Chandler, Nahum Dimitri. *X: The Problem of the Negro as a Problem for Thought*. New York: Fordham University Press, 2014.

Chinchilla, Norma Stoltz, and Nora Hamilton. "Central America: Guatemala, Honduras, Nicaragua." In *The New Americans: A Guide to Immigration since 1965*, edited by Mary C. Waters, Reed Ueda, and Helen B. Marrow, 328–39. Cambridge, MA: Harvard University Press, 2007.

Derrida, Jacques. *Learning to Live Finally: The Last Interview*, translated by Pascale-Anne Brault and Michael Naas. Hoboken, NJ: Melville House, 2007.

Funes, Yessenia. "Ever Wondered What 'Latinx' Means? This Video Will Explain." *ColorLines*, April 3, 2017. www.colorlines.com/articles /watch-ever-wondered-what-latinx-means -video-will-explain.

Galton, Francis. *Record of Family Faculties*. London: Macmillan, 1884.

Goodman, Amy. "Mexican Writer Valeria Luiselli on Child Refugees and Rethinking the Language around Immigration." *Democracy Now*, April 18, 2017. www.democracynow.org/2017/4/18 /mexican_writer_valeria_luiselli_on_child.

Gordon, Ian. "70,000 Kids Will Show Up Alone at Our Border This Year: What Happens to Them?" *Mother Jones*, July–August 2014. www .motherjones.com/politics/2014/06/child -migrants-surge-unaccompanied-central -america.

Graeber, David. *Revolutions in Reverse: Essays on Politics, Violence, Art, and Imagination*. London: Minor Compositions, 2011.

Hondagneu-Sotelo, Pierrette. *Doméstica: Immigrant Workers Cleaning and Caring in the Shadows of Affluence*. Berkeley: University of California Press, 2007.

Igo, Sarah Elizabeth. *The Averaged American: Surveys, Citizens, and the Making of a Mass Public*. Cambridge, MA: Harvard University Press, 2007.

Kindley, Evan. *Questionnaire*. New York: Bloomsbury, 2016.

Latino USA. "Latinx: The Ungendering of the Spanish Language." Podcast. National Public Radio, January 29, 2016. www.npr.org/2016 /01/29/464886588/latinx-the-ungendering-of -the-spanish-language.

Logue, Josh. "Latina/o/x." *Inside Higher Ed*, December 8, 2015. www.insidehighered.com /news/2015/12/08/students-adopt-gender -nonspecific-term-Latinx-be-more-inclusive.

Luiselli, Valeria. *Tell Me How It Ends: An Essay in Forty Questions*. Minneapolis: Coffee House, 2017.

Maloney, Devon. "Our Obsession with Online Quizzes Comes from Fear, Not Narcissism." *Wired*, March 6, 2014. www.wired.com/2014 /03/buzzfeed-quizzes.

Markham, Lauren. *The Far Away Brothers: Two Young Migrants and the Making of an American Life*. New York: Crown, 2017.

Markon, Jerry. "Can a 3-Year Old Represent Herself in Immigration Court? This Judge Thinks So." *Washington Post*, March 5, 2016. www .washingtonpost.com/world/national-security /can-a-3-year-old-represent-herself-in -immigration-court-this-judge-thinks-so/2016 /03/03/5be59a32-db25-11e5-925f -1d10062cc82d_story.html?utm_term= .6bd406e35804.

Markon, Jerry. "Former Judges Challenge Official Who Said 3-Year-Olds Can Represent Selves in Immigration Court." *Washington Post*, March 15, 2016. www.washingtonpost.com/world /national-security/former-judges-challenge -official-who-said-three-year-olds-can-represent -themselves-in-immigration-court/2016/03/15 /d9cb0538-eaaf-11e5-b0fd-073d5930a7b7_ story.html?utm_term=.ac101c88e78e.

Marshall, Tim. *Prisoners of Geography: Ten Maps That Explain Everything about the World*. New York: Scribner, 2015.

Martínez, Óscar. *The Beast: Riding the Rails and Dodging Narcos on the Migrant Trail*, translated by Daniela Maria Ugaz and John Washington. London: Verso, 2013.

Martínez, Óscar. *A History of Violence: Living and Dying in Central America*. New York: Verso, 2016.

Martínez, Óscar. "Los niños no se van: Se los llevan." *ElFaro.net*, July 13, 2014. elfaro.net/es/201407 /noticias/15683/Los-ni%C3%B1os-no-se-van- se-los-llevan.htm.

Merriman, Helena. "Why Are 10,000 Migrant Children Missing in Europe?" BBC, October 12, 2016. www.bbc.com/news/world-europe -37617234.

Milian, Claudia. "Extremely Latin, XOXO: Notes on LatinX." *Cultural Dynamics* 29, no. 3 (2017): 121–40.

Mitchell, Sally. *Daily Life in Victorian England*. Westport, CT: Greenwood, 1996.

Muñoz, José Esteban. *Cruising Utopia: The Then and There of Queer Futurity*. New York: New York University Press, 2009.

Nail, Thomas. *The Figure of the Migrant*. Stanford, CA: Stanford University Press, 2015.

Nazario, Sonia. "Enrique's Journey: A Six-Part Times Series." *Los Angeles Times*, September 29, 2002. www.latimes.com/nation /immigration/la-fg-enriques-journey-sg -storygallery.html.

Nazario, Sonia. *Enrique's Journey: The Story of a Boy's Dangerous Odyssey to Reunite with His Mother.* New York: Random House, 2007.

Ngai, Mae M. *Impossible Subjects: Illegal Aliens and the Making of Modern America.* Princeton, NJ: Princeton University Press, 2004.

Popkin, Nathaniel. "Translating This Broken World: How to Tell a Refugee's Story." *LitHub*, April 26, 2017. lithub.com/translating-this-broken-world-how-to-tell-a-refugees-story.

Powers, John. "'Tell Me How It Ends' Offers a Moving, Humane Portrait of Child Migrants." National Public Radio, April 6, 2017. www.npr .org/2017/04/06/521791352/tell-me-how-it -ends-offers-a-moving-humane-portrait-of -child-migrants.

Ramirez, Tanisha Love, and Zeba Blay. "Why People Are Using the Term 'Latinx.'" *Huffington Post*, July 5, 2016. www.huffingtonpost.com/entry /why-people-are-using-the-term-latinx_us_ 57753328e4b0cc0fa136a159.

Reichard, Raquel. "Why We Say Latinx: Trans and Gender Non-conforming People Explain." *Latina*, August 29, 2015. www.latina.com /lifestyle/our-issues/why-we-say-LatinX-trans -gender-non-conforming-people-explain.

Rivas, Jorge. "What We Mean When We Say Latinx." *Fusion*, April 13, 2017. fusion.net/what-we -mean-when-we-say-latinx-1794092929.

Robertson, Craig. *The Passport in America: The History of a Document.* Oxford: Oxford University Press, 2010.

Roitman, Janet. *Anti-crisis.* Durham, NC: Duke University Press, 2014.

Said, Edward W. *Beginnings: Intention and Method.* New York: Basic, 1975.

Sandoval-García, Carlos. *Exclusion and Forced Migration in Central America: No More Walls*, translated by Kari Meyers. New York: Palgrave Macmillan, 2017.

Sassen, Saskia. "A Massive Loss of Habitat: New Drivers for Migration." *Sociology of Development* 2, no. 2 (2016): 204–33.

Sellnow, Timothy L., and Matthew W. Seeger. *Theorizing Crisis Communication.* Malden, MA: Wiley-Blackwell, 2013.

Solnit, Rebecca. *A Field Guide to Getting Lost.* New York: Viking, 2005.

Spillers, Hortense J. "Mama's Baby, Papa's Maybe: An American Grammar Book." *diacritics* 17, no. 2 (1987): 65–81.

Terrio, Susan J. *Whose Child Am I? Unaccompanied, Undocumented Children in U.S. Immigration Custody.* Berkeley: University of California Press, 2015.

Torpey, John. *The Invention of the Passport: Surveillance, Citizenship, and the State.* Cambridge: Cambridge University Press, 2000.

Wikipedia. "2014 American Immigration Crisis." n.d. en.wikipedia.org/wiki/ 2014_American_immigration_crisis.

Williams, Patricia. *Seeing a Color-Blind Future: The Paradox of Race.* New York: Noonday, 1997.

Paper Trails

DAVID SARTORIUS

Abstract   This essay reflects on the materiality of migration with a focus on passports and other kinds of documentary permissions for travel. It argues that throughout the history of the Americas passports have acquired meanings exceeding contemporary associations with national citizenship that are discernible in literary works and in the archival record. It looks to documentary practices in Latin America and the Caribbean to decenter the United States from studies of border crossing and Latinx subjectivities, suggesting intersecting hemispheric practices that delineate the relative importance of being documented or undocumented.

Keywords   passports, migration, documentation, undocumented

Early in "Caroline's Wedding," a short story in Edwidge Danticat's *Krik? Krak!* (1995), the Haitian-American narrator admits that "in my family, we have always been very anxious about our papers."[1] When she received her US naturalization certificate, she wanted to run through Brooklyn "waving the paper like the head of an enemy rightfully conquered in battle"; when she surrendered that document to submit a passport application—because her mother believes that "a passport is truly what's American"—she "suddenly felt like unclaimed property."[2] I have recalled these lines frequently since I began reading news reports in 2013 about decisions in the Dominican Republic to revoke the citizenship and initiate the deportation of thousands of Haitian immigrants and Dominicans of Haitian descent. Images of protesters in Santo Domingo and near the border with Haiti showed people holding their Dominican passports in the air—or, in the absence of a passport, some other state document that proved (now if only to themselves) that they belonged in the country. It does not require a radical act of historical imagination to connect these stories: to wonder what has informed Haitians' choices to migrate to the United States or the Dominican Republic, to think about the sliding-door consequences of opting for one over the other, and to notice how meaningful state-issued identity documents became in both cases.

The politics of papers encompass everything from state border policing and the surveillance of individuals to migrant subjectivities and survival strategies to thorny questions of language and terminology. Fourteen years before Race

ENGLISH LANGUAGE NOTES

56:2, October 2018 DOI 10.1215/00138282-6960691

Forward's "Drop the I-Word" campaign began in 2010 to discourage referring to immigrants as "illegal," a group of three hundred Africans in France occupied the Saint-Bernard Church in Paris and began a hunger strike for legal residency. In French public discourse, references to their "paperless" legal status became a shorthand for their precarity, and the *sans-papiers* movement thus made the lack of identity papers a defining attribute of France's immigrants. Even as the term *undocumented migrant* has become the preferred substitute for *illegal alien* in US parlance, it bears noting that both terms produce an exclusionary status that denies rights to many. (Indeed, the *New York Times* style guide cautions that "undocumented," a term "preferred by many immigrants and their advocates . . . has a flavor of euphemism.")[3] But the proliferation of references to the undocumented, no matter their valence, invites an opportunity to ask new questions about migration, status, and identity. What does it mean, as a normative condition, to be "documented"? What have identity papers meant to migrants? What does attending to the paper technologies of migration render visible?

It is a success of the hemispheric turn in Latinx studies that the answers to these questions no longer necessarily begin and end in the contemporary United States. Looking across the Americas and to the past for answers helps denaturalize the fictions of legality that make associations between citizenship and documentation so prominent today. Quotidian practices of documenting identity and belonging are an integral feature of Latin America's past, from notary-transcribed copies of parish baptismal records to freedom papers carried by the formerly enslaved. The documentary requirements that migrants face have often begun in their points of departure—locales that, in turn, developed paper regimes to regulate the arrival of those coming from the United States, as nineteenth-century travel writing makes abundantly clear. Throughout the hemisphere, passes for transit within territorial boundaries and passports to travel beyond them did not always correspond to clearly defined borders, national identities, or even state sanction. The ubiquity of these practices exposes the myopia of focusing only on the United States as the preeminent border-policing and document-issuing polity in the hemisphere.

For migrants themselves, the significance of identity papers in this transnational context thus far exceeds what being documented or not signifies in the United States, and it demands our greater consideration. As we continue to explore the meanings of migration, we can find insights in the pocket-sized protections and permissions that have written people into a certain kind of existence, authorized their mobility and residence, and shaped a sense of themselves. At the end of "Caroline's Wedding" we learn of the sacrifices made for the narrator to obtain her passport: "We had all paid dearly for this piece of paper, this final assurance that I belonged in the club. It had cost my parent's marriage, my mother's spirit, my sister's arm."[4] But what about those Dominican passports that have failed to protect other Haitian migrants in recent years? Attending to migration's paper trails should also acknowledge the relative *un*importance of being documented: when other objects mean much more to someone than a visa, a passport, or a green card; when the procedures for identity papers have been less standardized and consequential; and when a lack of state legibility may represent a deliberate exclusion or a strategic evasion.

DAVID SARTORIUS is associate professor of history at the University of Maryland and author of *Ever Faithful: Race, Loyalty, and the Ends of Empire in Spanish Cuba* (2013). He is at work on a history of passports, race, and the materiality of migration in Cuba and the Caribbean. He is coeditor of *Social Text* and a member of the organizing collective of the Tepoztlán Institute for the Transnational History of the Americas.

Notes

1   Danticat, *Krik? Krak!*, 158.
2   Danticat, *Krik? Krak!*, 158.
3   Siegal and Connolly, *New York Times Manual*, 156.
4   Danticat, *Krik? Krak!*, 214.

Works Cited

Danticat, Edwidge. *Krik? Krak!* New York: Vintage, 1996.
Siegal, Allan M., and William G. Connolly. *The New York Times Manual of Style and Usage*. 5th ed. New York: Three Rivers, 2015.

Borderland Biopolitics

Public Health and Border Enforcement in Early Twentieth-Century Latinx Fiction

RACHEL CONRAD BRACKEN

Abstract This article situates early twentieth-century Latinx fiction within the inter-twined histories of public health and border surveillance along the Rio Grande to reveal a "borderland biopolitics" unique to the US-Mexico border region. Drawing on three early twentieth-century novels—Daniel Venegas's *Adventures of Don Chipote*, Américo Paredes's *George Washington Gómez*, and Jovita González and Eve Raleigh's *Caballero*—it adds another layer of historical nuance to studies of Latinx literature by demonstrating the profound, pervasive influence that epidemiological science and public health policy have had in shaping national identity politics in the borderlands. Because militarized border control evolves from public health efforts, reframing analyses of Latinx fiction to read for public health provides fresh insight into institutionalized forms of discrimination and social injustice that continue to condition Latinx lives in the US-Mexico borderlands.
Keywords   citizenship, medicalized nativism, biopolitics, public health, border control

The US-Mexico borderlands are a hybrid space, home to the descendants of native peoples and Spanish colonists, Anglo-Americans and African slaves. Unsurprisingly, these borderlands have long been fraught multiethnic and multi-lingual territory, bearing the scars of recurrent violence and exploitation. "It's not a comfortable territory to live in, this place of contradictions," Gloria Anzaldúa writes in the preface to her landmark treatise *Borderlands/La Frontera: The New Mestiza*. "Hatred, anger, and exploitation are the prominent features of this landscape," she continues, reflecting on the traumatic legacies of settler colonialism, Manifest Destiny, border patrol, and predatory labor practices.[1] Born of this landscape, early twentieth-century Latinx fiction similarly bears the traces of US territorial expansion and border enforcement protocols—rooted in quarantine and immigrant medical inspection—which structure the violent, contradictory borderland culture Anzaldúa recounts. As Marcos Cueto and Steven Palmer note, the "social and political consequences of disease and health have been at the center of hemispheric history," although, they lament, the histories of medicine and public health have received relatively sparse scholarly attention.[2] Answering Cueto and Palmer's call

ENGLISH LANGUAGE NOTES

56:2, October 2018 DOI 10.1215/00138282-6960702
© 2018 Regents of the University of Colorado

for increased scrutiny of health care in hemispheric history and tracing the evolution of what Alison Bashford names "medico-legal border control," this article situates early twentieth-century Latinx fiction within the intertwined histories of public health and border surveillance along the Rio Grande to reveal what I name a "borderland biopolitics" unique to the US-Mexico border region.[3]

I begin by excavating the history of quarantine and immigrant medical inspection as a precursor to formalized border surveillance along the Rio Grande, looking to the ways in which the geopolitics of immigration, public health history, and border enforcement resonate within Daniel Venegas's 1928 picaresque *Las adventuras de Don Chipote o cuando los pericos mamen* (*The Adventures of Don Chipote; or, When Parrots Breast-Feed*, hereafter referred to as *Don Chipote*). Attending to the novel's candid descriptions of border quarantine measures and immigrant medical inspections in the article's first section, "Exclusion," I trace how public health protocols give rise to policies meant to limit transnational movement and exclude "undesirable" populations. In the following section, "Surveillance," I survey how the exclusionary borderland biopolitics uncovered in *Don Chipote* condition the accounts of Latinx life in the US-Mexico borderlands narrated in Américo Paredes's *George Washington Gómez: A Mexicotexan Novel* and Jovita González and Eve Raleigh's *Caballero: A Historical Novel*—both drafted in the 1930s but unpublished until the 1990s. The medicalization of Mexican immigrants and migrant workers at the border reemerges in these novels as a need to surveil a racial other. Thus, by uncovering the legacy of border quarantine and immigrant medical inspection in *Caballero* and *George Washington Gómez*, I add another layer of historical nuance to studies of Latinx literature by demonstrating the profound, pervasive influence that epidemiological science and public health policy have had in shaping national identity politics in the borderlands.

Exclusion: Border Patrol and/as Public Health

In this section I draw on social histories of medicine at the border to attend to the confluence of immigrant medical inspection, public health policy, and border patrol illustrated by *Don Chipote*'s cynically frank accounts of border crossing. In the Chipotes' failed attempts to legally immigrate, I contend, Venegas demonstrates the biopolitical impulses of twentieth-century US border control policies—policies that have evolved from nineteenth-century quarantine protocols and the racist conviction that "dirty" Mexicans played host to communicable diseases. Seeking the life of wealth and ease promised to him by the lying loafer Pitacio—who returns to Mexico with enchanting tales of his successes in "the land of Uncle Sam"[4]—Don Chipote must first make it past the US Public Health Service (USPHS) officers stationed in El Paso/Ciudad Juárez. For Don Chipote, who doesn't "speak any *toq inglis*" (*DC*, 27), what the novel's narrator snidely describes as "the procedure that the American government had created expressly for all Mexicans crossing into their land" is disorienting, though not entirely unpleasant (35). Led to the showers with brusque efficiency and ordered to strip, Don Chipote is teased by "his fellow countrymen" (35), who unceremoniously undress in preparation for the showers, delousings, disinfections, medical inspections, and interviews required of each immigrant and migrant worker who routinely passes through "the *gringo* border station" (35) in El Paso. Naive and oblivious to the nationalist power play unfolding via immigrant medical inspection at the border, Don Chipote eagerly complies:

> He thought that if this was the only thing he had to do, it was not worth fussing over. After taking off his clothes, he was naked as a jaybird, putting his grubby little paws in a box of powdered disinfectant, then hitting the showers. . . .
>
>   It was no small task for Don Chipote to scrub off all the grime that covered his body. An advocate of the saying that "the bark protects the tree," the washings that he had given himself were few and far between, and even those only came when a storm had fallen upon the fields. Be that as it may, however, he enjoyed having stripped off the husk he wore, and even more so when he figured that this was all he needed to do to cross into American territory. (35–36)

Characterized by "grubby little paws" and a rugged bark of dirt and grime, Don Chipote seems hardly human as he enters the border station and steps into a shower. Assuming that a thorough scrubbing will enable him "to cross into American territory," he inadvertently aligns "America" with cleanliness and Mexico with both filth and antiquated folk wisdom: "The bark protects the tree." Indeed, the description of Don Chipote's ritual cleansing does little to contest stereotypical portrayals of the "dirty" Mexican or to oppose eugenic notions of racial inferiority. Rather, by likening "our hero" to plants and trees and animals—Don Chipote and his dog, Skinenbones, share the same "delight of a warm shower" (36)—the narrator's account of this scene identifies the hapless Don Chipote as "natural." It is not a compliment. Uncivilized and undomesticated, bathing only when caught in the rain, Don Chipote is not merely provincial but primitive. His unwashed body defies the sterile rationality of American sanitary science.

  Dirty Don Chipote is a caricature of the Mexican immigrant as imagined by paranoid border patrol officers—filthy and simple, he is capable of bringing disease across the border. Having lived all of his life in a small village one month's walk south of the border, however, Don Chipote knows nothing of immigration politics, racial discrimination, or the English language used by border patrol officers. He "could not understand why they treated him that way," with an overt mix of impatience and disgust, but he does not discern the dehumanizing border inspection as anything other than a minor inconvenience far outweighed by the promise of admission to the United States (*DC*, 35). He is oblivious to the complex "technologies of statecraft" that, drawing on the nascent fields of eugenics, criminology, anthropology, sociology, and bacteriology, rely on immigrant medical inspection to pathologize Latinx bodies in the borderlands and thus, as Celeste Menchaca explains, to "simultaneously create, mark, and read the (in)admissible migrant body."[5] Medical inspection, Menchaca insists, emerges in the early twentieth century as a technology of surveillance that, by visualizing Latinx bodies as "vectors of disease," both imaginatively produces the US-Mexico border and prefaces the strategies employed by today's Customs and Border Protection officers.[6] The "presumed scientific objectivity" of US health officials at the border "gave wide circulation to constructed categories of Mexicans as unclean, ignorant of basic hygiene practices, and unwitting hosts for communicable disease," Natalia Molina likewise notes.[7] It is just such a "scientifically" informed fear of the Mexican as disease vector that justifies the invasive medical inspection Don Chipote endures in El Paso. Ultimately, and unsurprisingly, Don Chipote is denied entry because he does not speak English; fails to provide the proper documentation, such as a birth certificate, a passport, and a certificate of medical examination; and cannot pay the eight-dollar "head tax" required of immigrants.[8] Yet, despite his "grubby little paws" and "the grime that covered his body," our hapless hero is disease free. This truth is of little consequence in the transnational borderland communities forged along the Rio Grande, however, wherein Mexican and Mexican-American border crossers— often migrant workers like Don Chipote and the novel's narrator—were presumed filthy, lousy, diseased, and/or degenerate and so were disproportionately subjected to the degrading manifestations of biomedical exclusions and surveillance executed by the USPHS.[9]

Through the novel's narrator, a character equally more sophisticated and more cynical than the provincial Don Chipote, Venegas exposes the ideological pretexts—often openly racist, nationalist, and even eugenic—that underlie border "protection." Himself a migrant worker, the narrator has been subjected to his fair share of public baths, delousings, and interrogations; he pities Don Chipote's parochial naïveté and, as Paul Fallon observes, "draws readers in to sympathize with the protagonists as he alludes to the common experiences of exploitation."[10] Reflecting on Don Chipote's unduly optimistic trust in border inspection, he observes, with affected disbelief, "There thou hast it. Don Chipote [is] actually taking pleasure in the first humiliation that the *gringo* forces on Mexican immigrants!" (*DC*, 35). And there are many more humiliations to come. Indeed, forced vaccinations, clothing shrunk or ruined by steam cleaning, and exposure to dangerous fumigants—the pesticide Zyklon B was later used in Nazi gas chambers[11]—were the norm for "Mexican laborers[, who] were required to carry bath certificates and undergo disinfection once a week."[12] Moreover, the intrusive, degrading protocols for medical inspection opened the door to further indignities; the El Paso bath riots of 1917 erupted, in part, because health officers were rumored to have taken and shared nude photographs of working women forced to disrobe and comply with disinfection procedures.[13] With the juxtaposition of Don Chipote's guileless faith in the mechanisms of border control and the narrator's impatient incredulity, Venegas thereby draws attention to the process of border medical inspection, exposing it as demeaning, exploitative, perhaps even unnecessary.

In the decades following the Treaty of Guadalupe Hidalgo, US quarantine laws evolved into a federally regulated immigration policy relying heavily on medical inspection. These laws and policies were outgrowths of the Chinese Exclusion Act of 1882, which established a legal precedent for restricting immigration based on race or ethnicity, as well as of advances in bacteriology and epidemiology, which lent scientific authority to "the fear and stigma associated with filth, labor mobility, and outsider status" and thus justified policies designed to "exclude, disinfect, or expel ethnic migrants or minorities as part of nation-building efforts."[14] In 1891 the US federal government assumed authority over immigration, which, according to Amy Fairchild, "created the machinery for federal officers to inspect and exclude immigrants" by permitting "medical officers of the [USPHS] to inspect and issue a medical certificate to all immigrants suffering from a 'loathsome or dangerous contagious disease.'"[15] Then, in late 1916, the medicalization of immigration policy—and of Latinx border crossers—intensified in response to an outbreak of typhus in El Paso. It was during the USPHS's "iron-clad" quarantine in early 1917 that the stringent bathing, disinfection, and delousing protocols Venegas recounts with Don Chipote's border crossing were instated; although the epidemic abated within the year, these quarantine procedures remained in effect until the early 1940s.[16]

The coincidence of international market forces, burgeoning nativist sentiment, and the racist medicalization of immigrant bodies—what Alan Kraut terms "medicalized nativism"[17]—culminated in the National Origins Act of 1924, which established a rigid quota system, and the creation of the US Border Patrol to enforce the federal government's new immigration protocols. These quotas severely restricted immigration from Asian and eastern European nations, essentially imposing a "whites-only" immigration system, and required immigrants to secure visas—contingent on medical inspection—from US consular agents abroad before immigrating. Notably, these restrictions did not apply to nations in the Western Hemisphere, so that southwestern growers and railroad companies would still have access to cheap Mexican migrant labor. American agribusiness relied on migrant labor and therefore benefited from a relatively permeable national border.[18] Nativist sentiment persisted in effectively transnational communities, however, and border crossers—whether pursuing permanent relocation in the United States or simply commuting from Juárez to the wealthy neighborhoods of El Paso for work—were subject to the baths, delousings, and medical inspections mandated by federal immigration policy. These procedures were not only dehumanizing but expensive; many, like Don Chipote, crossed the border illegally—that is, without passing through an official port of entry as mandated by the 1907 Immigration Act and without undergoing medical inspection—to avoid dangerous fumigation, forced baths and vaccinations, and prohibitive head taxes. To reduce the incidence of unregulated border crossing, the Immigration Act of 1929 criminalized illegal immigration; subsequently, unlawful border crossers were subject to fines, imprisonment, and deportation while southwestern growers secured greater control over an already exploited labor source.[19] A federal system of immigrant restrictions and requirements in the US-Mexico borderlands, as well as a militarized border patrol, thereby emerged out of the infrastructure built by public health agencies.

With Doña Chipote's later border crossing, in pursuit of her husband, Venegas demonstrates how eugenics complements epidemiology in shaping early twentieth-century borderland biopolitics; anti-Mexican sentiment, fueled by quarantine and border enforcement, cast the "Mexican race" as dirty, lousy, and lazy. In the early twentieth century a eugenic assessment of Mexican racial inferiority justified restrictive immigration legislation, including the aforementioned National Origins Act, by inciting fear that Mexican immigration would precipitate "a severe drain on the state's charity and welfare institutions."[20] This fear was magnified, Alexandra Minna Stern explains, by the stereotypical portrayal of Mexican women "as hyper-breeders whose sprawling broods of deprived children threatened to drain public resources."[21] "Rudely" turned away by an overworked *gringo* border agent and taken, "with great care and shoves, to the middle of the bridge with their noses pointed towards their homeland," Doña Chipote and her children are denied legal entry to the United States and must resort to illegally crossing the Rio Grande (*DC*, 136, 140–42). A dangerous "hyperbreeder," Doña Chipote, with her innumerable clutch of "Chipotitos," is turned away because she and her children are likely to become public charges, sapping state resources rather than invigorating the national economy. Thus Venegas's account of Doña Chipote's border crossing, as well as the novel's previous description of Don Chipote's disinfection, underscores the intimate entanglements of restrictive immigration policies, infectious disease control, and border security that constitute the intricate borderland biopolitics evolving in the United States at the turn of the twentieth century—a vast governmental infrastructure designed to manage an increasing, and increasingly diverse, national population.

The borderland biopolitics revealed in these episodes—rigorous disinfection procedures and a eugenic evaluation of "fitness"—demonstrate governmental strategies for regulating the health and character of the US population by designating potential border crossers as either risks or assets. But Doña Chipote's crossing showcases, as well, the dangerous permeability of national borders and the limits of border regulation, and, in this way, Venegas's novel resists the authority of the US government's early twentieth-century border enforcement efforts. Both Don and Doña Chipote are denied legal entry to the United States, but both make their way across the border with relative ease once they have paid a coyote to lead them. They simply remove their shoes, roll up their pants, and wade through the Rio Grande (*DC*, 42–43, 141). "They didn't need any papers, nor to pay anyone to cross a river," Doña Chipote realizes. "And so, in this way, and shivering from the cold, they crossed the border and found themselves in the infamous United States," Venegas unceremoniously reports (141). Collapsing the distinction between the river, a geographic feature, and the border, a geopolitical entity, Doña Chipote undermines the state's authority to curtail the movement of populations within and across territorial borders. Venegas's matter-of-fact narration normalizes this defiance, as does the remarkably sparse attention he devotes to his protagonists' border crossings—especially in view of the thoroughness with which he narrates their every bowel movement throughout the novel. "Nothing worth recounting happened to our pilgrims during their journey," Venegas writes of Doña Chipote's trip to El Paso, for example. She "had planned for her journey with a handful of diapers. Her littlest Chipotito soon went through them all. And, one by one, throughout the journey, they were seen flapping out the train window, fully loaded with digested food" (135). This detail is seemingly unnecessary, even unnecessarily vulgar, but I would like to consider the possibility that the abundance of scatological references operates as yet another attempt to thwart US border control. The borderlands are mutable, visceral spaces populated by living—eating, breathing, and, yes, defecating—people, Venegas bawdily insists. For this reason, an imaginary, geopolitical border line cannot contain the messy chaos of life in borderlands communities, which are shaped by the fluid interchange of bodies, labor, goods, and germs among a transnational population.

Restrictive immigration policies ostensibly designed to preserve "America's" health and prosperity by stemming the spread of contagion rely on an artificially rigid perception of the border distinguishing one nation from another, one population from another. Yet, as the Chipotes' illegal border crossings attest, there is nothing natural about national borders; they are perpetually redrawn by war and conquest, theft, colonization, and revolution—a reality I explore in more depth in the following section. Nevertheless, law and policy make the arbitrary meaningful, as the histories of border health and immigration I have recounted here reveal. Designating Mexican immigrants and migrant workers a threat to the health and safety of US citizens, the practice of quarantine, medical inspections, and mandatory sterilization procedures—shower baths, head shaving, delousing, and disinfection with harmful chemicals—imagined the Mexican "race" as other: other than white, other than American. Race was thus inextricably linked to citizenship and national belonging via medicalized nativism and, as Stern demonstrates, an overtly eugenic motivation to preserve the hereditary fitness of the (white) "American race" by excluding those deemed racially other. In the US-Mexico borderlands, US quarantine law and immigrant medical inspection simultaneously create and "defend" the nation's borders from unwanted immigrants and infectious disease, thereby imagining the nation into being, both geographically and ideologically, via the regulatory mechanisms of a biopolitical state.

Surveillance: Borders, Citizenship, and Belonging

Don Chipote's depictions of early twentieth-century border enforcement protocols faithfully recount the restrictive, exclusionary biopolitics of border control, but the legacy of quarantine and border enforcement likewise persists in Latinx novels that do not directly thematize either border crossing or immigrant medical inspection. These novels register a culture of biopolitical surveillance that exceeds border checkpoints, where taxes, literacy tests, and medical inspections exclude "undesirable" immigrants but also, as Fairchild contends, assimilate foreign-born laborers. Only a relatively small percentage of immigrants were denied entry because they failed a medical inspection, Fairchild explains, especially in the southwestern United States, where there was a need for cheap labor to build railroads and to fuel expanding agribusiness.[22] Border enforcement by way of medical surveillance served primarily a disciplinary, rather than an exclusionary, function, she argues: to acculturate immigrant and migrant laboring forces to US industrial expectations.[23] It is this push for assimilation within early twentieth-century borderland biopolitics—one that requires ongoing surveillance to mitigate the threat posed by the pathologized Mexican body—that I explore further in this section.

Here I uncover the large-scale, lasting effect that the degrading treatment of Mexican immigrants and migrant workers at border inspection stations has had on Latinx identity in the borderlands, evident in the ways by which borderland biopolitics permeate two fictional accounts of Mexican-American subjectivity: Paredes's *George Washington Gómez* and González and Raleigh's *Caballero*.[24] While neither novel addresses quarantine or immigrant medical inspection directly, both negotiate cultural identity, national belonging, and life in the borderlands according to the racialized medicalization of Latinx bodies and Anglo-American nationalism cultivated through medico-legal border control. That is, although these novels question the authority of border control by foregrounding the temporal contingency of national borders and resisting negative stereotypes of the Mexican immigrant— and the figure Paredes names the "Mexicotexan," a native or naturalized US citizen with Mexican heritage—as dirty and thereby dangerous, they nevertheless internalize the medicalization of the Latinx body as one that requires biopolitical surveillance. The protagonists of *Caballero* and *George Washington Gómez* are or will soon become legally American citizens, but they remain unassimilable, other, pathologized by border patrol protocols rooted in quarantine and immigrant medical inspection. Both novels were drafted in the 1930s, during the Great Depression and, consequently, amid the first large-scale deportation of Mexican and/or Mexican-American laborers from the United States,[25] yet both recall earlier eras of border turmoil; *Caballero* recounts the Mexican-American War and the Treaty of Guadalupe Hidalgo, while *George Washington Gómez* opens with racial tensions and retributive violence catalyzed by the transnational politics of the Mexican Revolution (1910–20) and concludes with the onset of World War II. Both texts therefore situate the fraught border politics of the 1930s within a much longer history of bloodshed and exploitation in contested border territories, "remember[ing] the past," as J. Javier Rodríguez observes, "to comment on [their] own present."[26]

Recalling the history of Anglo-American settlement in Mexican territory ceded to the United States with the Treaty of Guadalupe Hidalgo and the often violent land disputes that followed, *Caballero* and *George Washington Gómez* interrogate the sociopolitical construction and thus the temporal contingency of national borders. These novels remind us that the United States' claim to land south of the Nueces River is relatively recent, thereby unsettling established, Anglocentric perceptions of the nation, citizenship, and national belonging in the borderlands. "We do not choose to be dirty *Americanos*," Don Santiago's sister, Doña Dolores, indignantly insists. "We are Mexicans, our mother land was Spain. Not all of their laws can change us, for we are not them. *Americanos*, indeed!"[27] Here Doña Dolores's reliance on the dismissive moniker "dirty *Americanos*" effectively subverts and redirects the pathologization of Mexican bodies at the US-Mexico border. In this moment González and Raleigh write early twentieth-century medicalized nativism back onto nineteenth-century US territorial expansion and, in so doing, pathologize Anglo-American bodies, instead. Demonstrating the versatility of this rhetorical maneuver—the pathologization of the other—Doña Dolores's impassioned outburst undermines early twentieth-century border security protocols and immigrant medical inspections rooted in a fear of the alleged "dirty Mexican." Likewise, although the history of US expansion that Paredes recounts in *George Washington Gómez* is grittier than the romanticized history González and Raleigh imagine in *Caballero*, it mirrors the same narrative patterns: the "dirty *Americanos*" invaded

Mexican territory and "made it Gringo land by force. But no force of theirs can make us, the land's rightful people, Gringo people," George's uncle Feliciano defiantly avers.[28]

Though they live on land governed by the United States and must therefore submit to the laws of this land, neither Feliciano nor Doña Dolores identifies as an American. Pride in their heritage leads them to eschew "American" cultural identity, yet their heritage continues to be both socioculturally and politically weaponized by Anglo-Americans who, like the bedraggled "pioneers" wishing to settle on Don Santiago's rancho, "considered themselves justified in stealing the lands of the Mexicans" (*C*, 195). "Even if it's theirs they're only Mexicans," the settlers rationalize. "We be white folks and this is the United States, ain't it?" (194–95). The impoverished trespassers conflate race and the rights of citizenship, falling back on falsehoods of racial superiority to insist that the United States is—or ought to be—a nation of "white folks," even in formerly Mexican territory. This protoeugenic racial awareness is anachronistic—borderlands historians trace the evolution of race as a social construct, the racialization of Mexicans, and eugenic perceptions of white supremacy back to the institution of border protection protocols following the end of the Mexican-American War[29]—yet foreshadows how race will be deployed as a rationale for segregation, for violence, and for limiting Mexican-American citizenship rights, and those of other racial minorities, in the early twentieth century. Like their hidalgo neighbors and unlike the novel's white pioneers, the Mendoza y Soría family is well educated, wealthy, and cultured and owns land, yet neither land rights nor legal citizenship can ensure social capital or grant them access to the privileged because hegemonic echelons of society—particularly when land grants and federal law preference white Americans. It is not the Mexican immigrant who poses a threat to the Anglo-American body politic, *Caballero*'s and *George Washington Gómez*'s histories thereby set out to prove, but rather the *Americano* expansionist who should be both feared and reviled. Whether they characterize Anglo-Americans as filthy trespassers, ruthless Gringo thieves, or foolish children playing at nation building, these novels insist that national belonging is determined not through landowning or legal citizenship but through the exclusion and surveillance of nonwhite bodies instead.

Foregrounding the fluidity of national borders, the histories of US expansion presented in *Caballero* and *George Washington Gómez* not only unsettle Anglo-American territorial sovereignty north of the Rio Grande but also expose the culture of biopolitical surveillance, cultivated through quarantine protocols and immigrant medical inspection, that molds the complexities of Mexican-American identity, subjectivity, and citizenship in the borderlands. Both "part of the land" (*GWG*, 148) and "the land's rightful people" (103), Mexicotexans are distinct from "Gringo people," whose authority is backed by racially discriminatory laws, corrupt politicians, and violence. "The Mexicotexan has a conveniently dual personality," Paredes sardonically observes. "When he is called upon to do his duty for his country he is an American. When benefits are passed around he is a Mexican and always last in line" (195). Although legally American citizens, the Mexicotexan inhabitants of former Mexican territory are not culturally "American," nor are they granted equal protection under laws that strip them of power and property. Thus the Mexicotexan is a paradox and a hybrid, at once citizen and alien.[30] The struggle to comprehend this discriminatory duality prescribes the Mexicotexan's coming of age in historically fraught borderland territories, as it does for Paredes's young protagonist, who "develop[s] simultaneously in two widely divergent paths. In the schoolroom he was an American; at home and on the playground he was a Mexican. . . . The eternal conflict between two clashing forces within him produced a divided personality" (147). This "eternal conflict" is insurmountable in part, I argue, because it is rooted in border surveillance technologies that irrevocably pathologize the Latinx body in order to protect the Anglo-American body politic.

The persistent pathologization of Latinx bodies is evident in the opening pages of *George Washington Gómez*, wherein the local physician, Doc Berry, exercises the authority to police the movement of Mexicotexan bodies in the borderlands because he alone can alleviate the Texas Rangers' anxieties concerning Latinx ethnic identity. In this scene George's father, Gumersindo, is stopped by a group of Rangers who struggle to identify—and thus to evaluate the threat posed by—the "stocky, red-haired man of about thirty" traveling alongside the doctor (*GWG*, 11). "The two sour-faced Rangers were staring at the red-haired man," Paredes writes,

> as though trying to place him. The man fidgeted in his seat and avoided their eyes. Finally, one of the Rangers spoke, "What's your name, feller?"
>
> "He doesn't speak much English," Doc Berry said.
>
> "Mexican, eh?" said MacDougal. "For a minute there I thought he was a white man." He looked steadily at the man, who began to show signs of nervousness.
>
> "He's a good Mexican," Doc said. "I can vouch for him."
>
> "He's okay if you say so, Doc," MacDougal answered. "But it's getting kinda hard these days to tell the good ones from the bad ones. Can't take any chances these days. But he's all right if you say so." (12)

This scene is notable for the way in which it dehumanizes Gumersindo, who is referred to throughout simply as "the man." Not only does he remain unnamed in Paredes's narration of this scene, but he is also denied the opportunity to introduce himself by Doc Berry's explanation, "He doesn't speak much English." Though nearly able to pass as white, Gumersindo is ultimately reduced to his ethnicity: "Mexican." Furthermore, it takes the doctor's perspicuity to correctly diagnose George's father, and it is only on the doctor's insistence that he is "a good Mexican" that the Rangers allow him to pass unmolested. The Ranger MacDougal cannot trust his own instincts, admitting that he cannot "tell the good ones from the bad ones," which is a frightening admission from a law enforcement agent. It is the doctor, then, who acts as a gatekeeper—who must be responsible for accurately categorizing and assessing the threat posed by Latinx bodies in the borderlands. This scene mirrors the border checkpoint Don Chipote passes through in El Paso, and Doc Berry's evaluation of Gumersindo's character is akin to immigrant medical inspection. Here, however, the pathologization of the Mexican body is oblique—operating below the surface of the novel's plot—but the physician's authority to restrict or permit the movement of Latinx bodies within the borderlands echoes a long history of medico-legal border control and borderland biopolitics.

When looking to the similar pathologization of Latinx bodies in *Caballero*, we must acknowledge that the novel recalls a much earlier moment in US history—a time prior to the founding of the American Medical Association and the professionalization of American medicine, as well as a time before germ theories of contagion had replaced miasmatic models of infection[31]—when physicians did not yet wield Doc Berry's cultural authority. Rather than the physician, then, it is the priest who offers counsel to the Mexicotexans of Matamoros in *Caballero*, although Padre Pierre's advice for the Mendoza y Soría children troublingly resembles Doc Berry's dismissive paternalism—the doctor's wheedling assurance that Gumersindo is "a good Mexican"—and the eugenic rationale espoused by the Anglo-American settlers who trespass on Don Santiago's ranchero. Padre Pierre encourages Don Santiago's son, Luis Gonzaga, to follow Captain Devlin to Baltimore for a formal art education and advocates for the Mendoza y Soría daughters' marriages to Anglo-American men because, he explains, Lieutenant Warrener and Red McClane represent "the more virile race now," and "Texas will never again be ruled by the Mexicans" (*C*, 158). "Should Susanita or Angela marry one of the boys in their circle," he speculates, "their children will be ordinary in looks and intelligence, their tastes and tendencies downward" (158). Pseudoscientifically concluding that the Mexican "race" is both in decline and inferior to an Anglo-American population, Padre Pierre offers a eugenic speculation that internalizes the racist undertones of an exclusionary borderland biopolitics, both excavating the mid-nineteenth-century roots of the late-century conflation of Mexican as disease vector and anachronistically inserting early twentieth-century medicalized nativism into the border politics of the Mexican-American War. That is, although *Caballero*'s plot precedes germ theories of disease, immigrant medical inspection, and even federal regulation of immigration in the United States, early twentieth-century borderland biopolitics shaped by these forces nonetheless color *Caballero*'s fictional history and Padre Pierre's suggestion that degenerate Mexicans are in need of Anglo-American surveillance.

When read as a "national allegory," as José Limón insists we ought to interpret *Caballero*'s marriage plots, Susanita's, Angela's, and Luis Gonzaga's "marriages" model how, to survive in the borderlands, the Mexicotexan must yield to Anglo-American superiority and surrender to governmental surveillance.[32] Alternatively, Pablo Ramirez suggests that the novel, and Padre Pierre in particular, deliberately draws on scientific theories of race, inheritance, and degeneracy to counter twentieth-century eugenic thought. The novel critiques twentieth-century eugenicists' obsession with racial purity, Ramirez contends, and instead celebrates hybridity "as a way of creating a more vigorous and healthy citizenry."[33] Repudiating stereotypes of Mexicans as filthy, lousy carriers of "loathsome and contagious diseases,"[34] stereotypes that reduce Mexican people to the germs of contagion, *Caballero* celebrates the fine qualities—Susanita's natural beauty, Angela's humble grace, Luis Gonzaga's artistic talent, and Alvaro's commanding leadership—that the children of Don Santiago promise to pass on to their offspring. Pairing the novel with González's ethnographic work, Ramirez argues that *Caballero*'s intercultural marriage plots—the love shared by Susanita and Lieutenant Warrener, the practical union of Angela and Red McClane, and Luis Gonzaga's homoerotic partnership with fellow artist Captain Devlin—"integrate Mexicans into the nation by . . . expanding the category of whiteness to ensure their full political participation."[35] It is a compelling conclusion because it promises peace, an end to outmoded patriarchal power structures, and the demise of an economic system reliant on peonage, yet recasting the Mexicotexan as a genealogical asset is, at best, saccharinely idealistic and, at its worst, incredibly reductive.[36] Although "expanding the category of whiteness" to include the Mexicotexan resists the pathologization of Latinx bodies in the borderlands—if Mexicotexans have always already been white, then they cannot pose a racial threat to the Anglo-American body politic—it leaves the basic tenets of eugenics intact. Moreover, to make the Mexicotexan white is to erase the multiethnic, multicultural roots of Latinx identity, to ignore the complexity of life in the borderlands, and to concede Anglo-American superiority. The intercultural marriage plot has often symbolized reconciliation and peaceful cohabitation,[37] but the Mendoza y Soría children's partnerships with US military men, I argue, register instead the far-reaching legacy of militarized, governmental surveillance essential to borderland biopolitics. These marriages do, as Ramirez claims, "integrate Mexicans into the nation," but only insofar as they permit the US government to regulate the lives of both legally and socioculturally subordinate Mexicotexans in the borderlands, thereby ameliorating this population's dangerous otherness and destroying the patriarchal Mexican aristocracy that Don Santiago represents.

This culture of surveillance—the close scrutiny of dangerous, diseased, or degenerate Latinx bodies, as well as the biopolitical management of Mexicotexan sociopolitical and genealogical assets—is magnified in *George Washington Gómez*. At the novel's close, its protagonist, who has changed his name to George G. Gómez and who, like the Mendoza y Soría children of *Caballero*, has chosen an Anglo-American spouse, returns to his uncle's farm in Jonesville-on-the-Grande.[38] George appears to have rejected his Latinx heritage and adopted Anglo-American cultural values, but his *gringo* persona does not fit him well—"you look uncomfortable in that suit," Feliciano notices (*GWG*, 299). Feliciano is uncannily perceptive, isolating in George's uncomfortable clothes a deeper discomfort with the identity that his nephew has assumed as an adult; for George Washington Gómez, as Leif Sorensen notes, "assimilation into the US is not a seamless fit."[39] Caught between his desire to resist and to assimilate, the adult George G. Gómez remains plagued by the "eternal conflict" of dual subjectivity that plagued his childhood self.[40] Rather than a celebrated "leader of his people," as his parents had once hoped, George Washington Gómez has become a spy—"a first lieutenant in counter-intelligence" whose "job is border security" (300, 299). Working to secure the border against Mexican militants, he perpetuates a dehumanizing system of border patrol built on the pathologization of Mexicans and Mexicotexans.

That Paredes's novel closes with this startling scene, in which the object of surveillance has become the surveilling agent, demonstrates how completely his protagonist has internalized the borderland biopolitics of medico-legal border control.[41] As a spy, George "undertake[s] the representational work of identification through a process of recognition and naming of the singularities of race and ethnicity," Crystal Parikh explains, effectively assuming responsibility for border "quarantine" and immigrant inspection, although without any medical affiliation.[42] He inhabits the role, previously filled by Doc Berry, of evaluating who along the border is a "good Mexican" and who, alternatively, poses a threat to national security. Taken together, *George Washington Gómez's* opening and closing scenes mirror the evolution of medico-legal border control from primarily a public health effort—by way of quarantine orders and immigrant medical inspection in the latter half of the nineteenth century—to militarized border enforcement via armed patrols and federally operated border security stations in the 1930s. "I am doing what I do in the service of my country," George explains in the face of his uncle's palpable disappointment, although also, he concedes, in service to his career. Feliciano's reply to George's unsatisfying excuse is bitterly dismissive: "Does 'your country' include the Mexicans living in it?" George says only, "I'd rather not go into that again," but the answer, of course, is no (*GWG*, 302). The Mexican—not the "Mexican-American" or "Mexicotexan"—is unassimilable because pathologized, only ever a threat to the American body politic despite his or her citizenship status. Because "Mexicans will always be Mexicans," George concludes, they will always need surveillance (300).

Conclusion

Amid territorial disputes and the revision of citizenship laws, epidemiological science and eugenic anxieties shaped evolving conceptions of race and national identity that have influenced generations of thought about borders and populations.[43] Part of the transnational history of medico-legal border control, early twentieth-century Latinx fiction—including *Don Chipote, Caballero*, and *George Washington Gómez*—exists within a vast network of legislation, policy, institutional protocols, nativist rhetoric, and sociocultural norms that collectively constitute what I have named "borderland biopolitics." Attending to the legacy of public health policy and practice in Latinx texts that do not directly thematize illness, contagion, or immigrant medical inspection reveals the lasting influence of epidemiological thinking on evolving perceptions of social obligation, state power, and national belonging. Public health policies at the border—in the form, especially, of immigrant medical inspections, forced baths, and delousings—must therefore be recognized among the "ideological state apparatuses" that, as Héctor Pérez contends, shape Latinx subjectivity by culturally and politically subordinating Texas Mexicans in the borderlands.[44] Like schools and "state authorized historical accounts" of US expansionism,[45] the imbricated public health policies and immigration control protocols that together manifest borderland biopolitics mold the systems and structures of US national culture and racial politics. Reframing our analysis of Latinx fiction to foreground the structural determinants of Mexicotexan subjectivity— reframing to read for public health—provides fresh insight into institutionalized forms of discrimination and social injustice that continue to condition Latinx lives in the US-Mexico borderlands.

RACHEL CONRAD BRACKEN is assistant professor of family and community medicine at Northeast Ohio Medical University. Her work, which explores the intersections of American literature and public health history, also appears in *Hektoen International: A Journal of Medical Humanities, Big Data and Society*, and the collection *Transforming Contagion: Risky Contacts among Bodies, Disciplines, and Nations* (2018).

Acknowledgments

My sincerest gratitude to all who read and offered feedback on early drafts of this piece: Kirsten Ostherr, Joe T. Carson, my anonymous reviewers, and especially Maria A. Windell and Jesse Alemán, who provided thorough and generous guidance.

Notes

1   Anzaldúa, *Borderlands/La Frontera*, 19.

2   Cueto and Palmer, *Medicine and Public Health*, 1. Within the past fifteen years, a growing number of scholars have interrogated the imbricated histories of medicine, public health, nationalism, and the construction of racial difference. See also Stern, "Buildings, Boundaries, and Blood"; Fairchild, *Science at the Borders*; Mckiernan-González, *Fevered Measures*; Molina, "Borders, Laborers, and Racialized Medicalization"; and Menchaca, "Crossing the Line."

3   Bashford, "At the Border," 344. My conception of a borderland biopolitics builds on a Foucauldian framework and follows the work of Bashford, who insists that "public health must be understood as bio-political, as an important modern 'rationality' of government" (348). Where recent studies of biopolitics and immigration interrogate the contemporary utility of Foucault's work on biopolitics, I trace the emergence of a biopolitical apparatus in the US-Mexico borderlands that, in trying to protect the nation from foreign contagion, has routinely pathologized Latinx bodies. See Nail, "Crossroads of Power"; and Bird and Short, "Cultural and Biological Immunization."

4   Venegas, *Adventures of Don Chipote*, 30 (hereafter cited as *DC*).

5   Menchaca, "Crossing the Line," pars. 3 and 2.

6   Menchaca, "Crossing the Line," pars. 1 and 15; see also Fairchild, *Science at the Borders*, 39–47.

7   Molina, "Borders, Laborers, and Racialized Medicine," 171.

8   Menchaca, "Crossing the Line," par. 14.

9   "Mexicans were commonly associated with typhus, plague, and smallpox in the 1920s," Stern argues in *Eugenic Nation*, 21.

10   Fallon, "Staging a Protest," 118.

11   Romo, *Ringside Seat to a Revolution*, 240–43.

12   Fairchild, *Science at the Borders*, 155.

13   Mckiernan-González, *Fevered Measures*, 182–90.

14   Mckiernan-González, *Fevered Measures*, 170–71.

15   Fairchild, *Science at the Borders*, 14.

16   For a detailed account of the 1916–17 typhus outbreak and subsequent quarantine, as well as resistance to invasive, dehumanizing quarantine protocols, see Stern, *Eugenic Nation*, 60–67; and Mckiernan-González, *Fevered Measures*, 164–97.

17   Kraut, *Silent Travelers*, 3.

18   For more on the passage of the National Origins Act and the establishment of the US Border Patrol, as well as the nativist sentiment, eugenic impulses, industrial interests, and lobbying power of southwestern agribusiness underlying this legislation, see Hernández, *Migra!*, 27–34; Fairchild, *Science at the Borders*, 215–18; and Stern, *Eugenic Nation*, 16, 24, 67–68, 73–79.

19   Championed by South Carolina senator Coleman Livingston Blease, the Immigration Act of 1929—known colloquially as "Blease's bill"—authorized more stringent monitoring and regulation of immigration along the US-Mexico border, setting the tone for contemporary debates regarding undocumented immigration. See Hernández, "How Crossing the US-Mexico Border Became a Crime."

20   Stern, *Eugenic Nation*, 57.

21   Stern, *Eugenic Nation*, 21.

22   Fairchild, *Science at the Borders*, 4–5.

23   Fairchild, *Science at the Borders*, 16.

24   To the issue of coauthorship, see Limón, "Mexicans, Foundational Fictions, and the United States," 348; and Limón, "Introduction," xviii–xxii.

25   Molina recounts the change in popular opinion concerning immigration policy in the US Southwest with the Great Depression in *How Race Is Made in America*, explaining how "as jobs disappeared, so did the justification for allowing an open immigration policy with Mexico" (60). For more on US deportation and repatriation efforts, see also 34–38.

26   Rodríguez, "*Cabellero's* Global Continuum," 132. Similarly, Limón orients the novels' plots relative to armed conflict in the borderlands ("Introduction," xv–xvii).

27   González and Raleigh, *Caballero*, 9 (hereafter cited as *C*).

28   Paredes, *George Washington Gomez*, 102–3 (hereafter cited as *GWG*).

29   For more on the conceptual evolution of race at the border, see Stern, *Eugenic Nation*; Molina, "Borders, Laborers, and Racialized Medicine"; Molina, *How Race Is Made in America*; Menchaca, "Crossing the Line"; and Mckiernan-González, *Fevered Measures*.

30   Pablo Ramirez notes that a crucial distinction between legal citizenship and cultural identity took shape in the early twentieth century as immigration from South and Central America, Asia, and eastern Europe accelerated and both scientific and sociocultural concepts of race

evolved. *Citizen* did not necessarily connote "American," Ramirez clarifies in "Resignifying Preservation," 24.

31   Lester S. King provides a comprehensive overview of germ theory, which attributed disease to discrete microbes rather than filth and foul odors, in chapter 7 of *Transformations in American Medicine*, esp. p. 142. For an account of medical practice's regulation—from education to licensure—and professionalization in the United States, see Starr, *Social Transformation of American Medicine*.

32   See Limón, "Mexicans, Foundational Fiction, and the United States"; and Limón, "Nations, Regions, and Mid-Nineteenth-Century Texas," esp. 105–8.

33   Ramirez, "Resignifying Preservation," 22.

34   US Public Health Service, *Regulations*, 5.

35   Ramirez, "Resignifying Preservation," 36.

36   Limón likewise concedes that *Caballero* entertains an overly romanticized and likely unrealistic series of marriages ("Mexicans, Foundational Fictions, and the United States," 346, 349).

37   Limón observes, for example, that "in *Caballero*, as in all such romances, the marriage of initially star-crossed lovers projects the wished-for consolidation of the groups they semiallegorically represent" ("Mexicans, Foundational Fictions, and the United States," 350). He acknowledges both the idealism and the flaws inherent in *Caballero's* marriages. Similarly, Monika Kaup contends that the novel's marriage plots "allegorize the post-1848 political accommodation between the Anglo and the Mexican social order in South Texas" and forge "interethnic political alliances through kinship bonds" ("Unsustainable *Hacienda*," 565; see also 573).

38   A number of critics have offered brilliant commentary on the significance of George Washington Gómez's name as a symbol of his—and, by extension, all Mexicotexans'—fraught national and racial identity, notably Saldaña-Portillo, "'Wavering on the Horizon of Social Being,'" esp. 151–55; and Saldívar, "Borderlands of Culture," esp. 277–79, 284–85. Leif Sorensen likewise notes the symbolic significance of "the Americanization encoded in [George's] given name and the counterdiscourse of indigenism that coalesces around his nickname, Guálinto" ("Anti-*corrido* of George Washington Gómez," 117).

39   Sorensen, "Anti-*corrido* of George Washington Gómez," 111.

40   A self-proclaimed "borderland bildungsroman," *George Washington Gómez* both interrogates and complicates its protagonist's divided

subjectivity; for more on these themes, see Sorensen, "Anti-*corrido* of George Washington Gómez"; and Parikh, "Ethnic America Undercover," esp. 265–69.

41   The trope of the "traitorous informant" frequently appears in minority literature, Crystal Parikh contends, and "allegorizes the crises of the 'ethnic intellectual' as a self-representing agent within minority discourse" ("Ethnic America Undercover," 251).

42   Parikh, "Ethnic America Undercover," 263.

43   Mckiernan-González, *Fevered Measures*, esp. 5–6.

44   Pérez, "Voicing Resistance on the Border," 30.

45   Pérez, "Voicing Resistance on the Border," 30.

Works Cited

Anzaldúa, Gloria. *Borderlands/La Frontera: The New Mestiza*. 3rd ed. San Francisco: Aunt Lute, 2007.

Bashford, Alison. "At the Border: Contagion, Immigration, Nation." *Australian Historical Studies*, no. 120 (2002): 344–58.

Bird, Greg, and Jon Short. "Cultural and Biological Immunization: A Biopolitical Analysis of Immigration Apparatuses." *Configurations* 25, no. 3 (2017): 301–26.

Cueto, Marcos, and Steven Palmer. *Medicine and Public Health in Latin America: A History*. New York: Cambridge University Press, 2015.

Fairchild, Amy L. *Science at the Borders: Immigrant Medical Inspection and the Shaping of the Modern Industrial Labor Force*. Baltimore, MD: Johns Hopkins University Press, 2003.

Fallon, Paul. "Staging a Protest: Fiction, Experience, and the Narrator's Shifting Position in 'Las Aventuras De Don Chipote o Cuando Los Pericos Mamen.'" *Confluencia: Revista hispanica de cultura y literatura* 23, no. 1 (2007): 115–27.

González, Jovita, and Eve Raleigh. *Caballero: A Historical Novel*, edited by José Limón and María Cotera. College Station: Texas A&M University Press, 1996.

Hernández, Kelly Lytle. "How Crossing the US-Mexico Border Became a Crime." *Conversation*, April 30, 2017. theconversation.com/how-crossing-the-us-mexico-border-became-a-crime-74604.

Hernández, Kelly Lytle. *Migra! A History of U.S. Border Patrol*. Berkeley: University of California Press, 2010.

Kaup, Monika. "The Unsustainable *Hacienda*: The Rhetoric of Progress in Jovita González and Eve Raleigh's *Caballero*." *Modern Fiction Studies* 51, no. 3 (2005): 561–91.

King, Lester S. *Transformations in American Medicine: From Benjamin Rush to William Osler*.

Baltimore, MD: Johns Hopkins University Press, 1991.

Kraut, Alan M. *Silent Travelers: Germs, Genes, and the Immigrant Menace*. Baltimore, MD: Johns Hopkins University Press, 1994.

Limón, José. "Introduction." In *Caballero: A Historical Novel*, edited by José Limón and María Cotera, vii–xxviii. College Station: Texas A&M University Press, 1996.

Limón, José. "Mexicans, Foundational Fictions, and the United States: *Caballero*, a Late Border Romance." *MLQ* 57, no. 2 (1996): 341–53.

Limón, José. "Nations, Regions, and Mid-Nineteenth-Century Texas: History in *On the Long Tide* and *Caballero*." *Amerikastudien/American Studies* 53, no. 1 (2008): 97–111.

Mckiernan-González, John Raymond. *Fevered Measures: Public Health and Race at the Texas-Mexico Border, 1848–1942*. Durham, NC: Duke University Press, 2012.

Menchaca, Celeste. "Crossing the Line: A History of Medical Inspection at the Border." *KCET*, June 24, 2014. www.kcet.org/shows/artbound /crossing-the-line-a-history-of-medical -inspection-at-the-border.

Molina, Natalia. "Borders, Laborers, and Racialized Medicalization: Mexican Immigration and US Public Health Practices in the Twentieth Century." In *Precarious Prescriptions: Contested Histories of Race and Health in North America*, edited by Laurie B. Green, John Mckiernan-González, and Martin Summers, 167–83. Minneapolis: University of Minnesota Press, 2014.

Molina, Natalia. *How Race Is Made in America: Immigration, Citizenship, and the Historical Power of Racial Scripts*. Berkeley: University of California Press, 2013.

Nail, Thomas. "The Crossroads of Power: Michel Foucault and the US/Mexico Border Wall." *Foucault Studies*, no. 15 (2013): 110–28.

Paredes, Américo. *George Washington Gomez: A Mexicotexan Novel*. Houston: Arte Público, 1990.

Parikh, Crystal. "Ethnic America Undercover: The Intellectual and Minority Discourse." *Contemporary Literature* 43, no. 2 (2002): 249–84.

Pérez, Héctor. "Voicing Resistance on the Border: A Reading of Américo Paredes's George Washington Gómez." *MELUS* 23, no. 1 (1998): 27–48.

Ramirez, Pablo. "Resignifying Preservation: A Borderlands Response to American Eugenics in Jovita Gonzalez and Eve Raleigh's *Caballero*." *Canadian Review of American Studies* 39, no. 1 (2009): 21–39.

Rodríguez, J. Javier. "*Caballero's* Global Continuum: Time and Place in South Texas." *MELUS* 33, no. 1 (2008): 117–38.

Romo, David. *Ringside Seat to a Revolution: An Underground Cultural History of El Paso and Juárez, 1893–1923*. El Paso, TX: Cinco Puntos, 2005.

Saldaña-Portillo, María Josefina. "'Wavering on the Horizon of Social Being': The Treaty of Guadalupe-Hidalgo and the Legacy of Its Racial Character in Américo Paredes's *George Washington Gómez*." *Radical History Review*, no. 89 (2004): 135–64.

Saldívar, Ramón. "The Borderlands of Culture: Américo Paredes's *George Washington Gómez* and Chicano Literature at the End of the Twentieth Century." *American Literary History* 5, no. 2 (1993): 272–93.

Sorensen, Leif. "The Anti-*corrido* of George Washington Gómez: A Narrative of Emergent Subject Formation." *American Literature* 80, no. 1 (2008): 111–40.

Starr, Paul. *The Social Transformation of American Medicine: The Rise of a Sovereign Profession and the Making of a Vast Industry*. New York: Basic, 1982.

Stern, Alexandra Minna. "Buildings, Boundaries, and Blood: Medicalization and Nation-Building on the U.S.-Mexico Border, 1910–1930." *Hispanic American Historical Review* 79, no. 1 (1999): 41–81.

Stern, Alexandra Minna. *Eugenic Nation: Faults and Frontiers of Better Breeding in Modern America*. 2nd ed. Berkeley: University of California Press, 2016.

US Public Health Service. *Regulations Governing the Medical Inspection of Aliens: Miscellaneous Publication no. 5*. Washington, DC: US Government Printing Office, 1917. books .google.com/books?id=Y9wEAAAAYAAJ &oe=UTF-8.

Venegas, Daniel. *The Adventures of Don Chipote, or, When Parrots Breast-Feed*, edited by Nicolás Kanellos, translated by Ethriam Cash Brammer. Houston: Arte Público, 2000.

En Homenaje a Latinx Studies
From Charlottesville, August 2017

ANNA BRICKHOUSE

Abstract This short essay was written in the days after white supremacists and neo-Nazis invaded the campus of the University of Virginia and downtown Charlottesville, many of them heavily armed and dressed for combat. After offering a brief reflection on how Latino/a/x studies shaped her scholarly trajectory as someone not trained in this field as a graduate student, the author asks how the field can help reimagine this particular political moment. The essay reads Junot Díaz's *Brief Wondrous Life of Oscar Wao* forward in time—as an anticipatory history illuminating the last US presidential election.
Keywords Junot Díaz, anticipatory history, Rafael Trujillo, Black Lives Matter

Latino, Latina, Latinx: the field has ineluctably shaped my thinking since the earliest stages of my career. As a graduate student, I learned from José David Saldívar's *Dialectics of Our America* that I wanted not to "master" an American field—the ostensible goal of my PhD exams—but to help in *constructing* one: the project of discerning and writing an "oppositional American literary history," in his terms, still motivates me now.[1] While working on my first book, I drew lasting inspiration from Kirsten Silva Gruesz's *Ambassadors of Culture*. She urged Americanists to envision nothing less than "a new form of U.S. cultural history"—"one that would unseat the fiction of American literature's monolingual and Anglocentric roots" with a deeply historicized but nongenealogical history of Latino writing.[2] In those early days, though, I never thought of myself as working in Latino studies per se—in part because my first graduate training was in African American studies, and I had yet to recognize the vital links between the two fields. Still, I felt a nascent kinship with the Latino field, even if I embraced other terms that pronounced my affiliation: transamerican, hemispheric, multilingual. Later I recruited speculative figures and geographies that drew me closer: Hispanophone Squanto, Virginia as a part of greater Mexico, the "unsettlement" of America. I have never been fully at ease with an autobiographical idiom, and this account of my intellectual trajectory is perhaps unorthodox for the genre of the position paper. Somehow the only position I can naturally assume at this moment, however, is a personal one: I feel gratitude to Latina/o studies. I also feel, in the two years since the last US

ENGLISH LANGUAGE NOTES

56:2, October 2018 DOI 10.1215/00138282-6960713
© 2018 Regents of the University of Colorado

presidential election, a new responsibility, small but nevertheless important to me, to name my intellectual debts with greater precision. I do not have the training, or the research and teaching record, to claim a place in Latina/o studies. But I do wish for a stronger language of solidarity with the field in its current Latinx unfolding, and with those who have long made it flourish as a body of scholarship alongside their engagement and activism.

I could express this sense of gratitude by turning to any number of examples, but today my thoughts are on a novel that is also a work of research and scholarship: Junot Díaz's unforgettable *Brief Wondrous Life of Oscar Wao*. I have in fact thought often about this novel since the day after the election, when I woke up, like the rest of the world, in a daze. As I trudged to work and looked around to see if the land-scape was as different as I felt it to be, I found myself repeating, mantra-like, the words from the famous opening passage: "They say it came first from Africa, car-ried in the screams of the enslaved, that it was the death bane of the Tainos, uttered just as one world perished and another began; that it was a demon drawn into Creation through the nightmare door that was cracked open in the Antilles. Fukú americanus . . . fukú . . . a curse or a doom . . . the curse and the doom of the New World."[3] When I realized that I was murmuring these lines, stuck like a pop song in my head, I was caught up short. Why did I need them on this particular day? As readers of Díaz well know, *fukú* is untranslatable, voiced in screams and death banes, a word born centuries ago, in the Caribbean, of indigenous genocide and African slavery—the two founding human-made catastrophes of a New World now cursed by calamities outside its own making or control. By the twentieth cen-tury, as narrator Yunior tells it, fukú is a contagion, carried out of the West Indies in the "rucks and suitcases and shirt pockets" of US "soldiers, technicians, and spooks" who have carried out another illegal invasion of the Dominican Republic in 1965. And *fukú*—in Yunior's words, "just a little gift from my people to America: a small repayment for an unjust war"—now explains all inexplicable disaster in the United States.[4]

So on the day after the election, as I walked along in confused recollection of the TV spectacle from the night before, when commentators flailed around, strug-gling to understand why the supposed rationalism of political science had failed, why the numbers had failed to predict the outcome, I suddenly heard Yunior's voice whispering the answer: "It's fine if you don't believe, because no matter what *you* believe, fukú believes in you."[5] To say that the recognition brought comfort would be wrong, but the novel began to offer me an interpretive frame that was in itself empowering—almost as if I could hear Yunior talking to me directly: "Profe-sora, *please*. You *know* it's true. Putin himself said it a few days before the election during all the outrage over Russian tampering. He said it! 'What, is America now a Banana Republic?'"[6] The Putin speech was both a disavowal and a taunting half admission of cyberhacking along with a commentary on the contemporary social and economic stratification of the United States. But filtered through Díaz's novel, I heard Putin pronouncing a more deeply historical irony. He was pointing out that the United States might now be a country as easily installed with a dictator as it once snapped dictators into place like Legos in the original "banana republics"—indeed, as the United States once installed a dictator in the Dominican Republic.

The name of that dictator is central to Díaz's novel. On the day after the 2016 election, it came eerily back to me: *Trujillo*. In the 1990s Neil Larsen put it this way: "Few individuals, perhaps not even [Rafael] Trujillo himself, could foresee the pervasiveness and sheer capacity for entrenchment of a power viewed by most at the time as a temporary usurpation."[7] To me, this described the whole primary season, and every day leading up to Tuesday, November 8. Again I could imagine what Yunior might say: "You think the T to the R to the U in Trujillo and Tru** is a *coincidence*?" Trujillo ran his own brutal campaign to make the Dominican Republic great, a.k.a. white, again. Trujillo was a known narcissist. He opposed the free press. He preferred large crowds shouting their allegiance over any (unrigged) electoral process. He was famous for sexual coercion and rape and, in Yunior's words, for "fucking every hot girl in sight, even the wives of his subordinates, thousands upon thousands upon thousands of women."[8] He too operated on the premise that he could grab them all—as Yunior might say, by the *toto*—with the absolute impunity of power. Yunior, I think, would call this a fukú-driven recurrence. He would tell us that Trujillo is back, this time with a one-syllable but still recognizable Anglicized name that just happens to rhyme with his legendarily favorite rape-able part of the female body: the rump.

Yunior thus helped me understand *RUMP, in all his orange, spray-tanned, clownish horror, as a mere *yanqui* copy of an insidious Latin American original— one trained by US Marines, born of occupation, and now, perhaps, revisited on his former creators. This in turn has helped me see how Díaz's novel offers a particular kind of "anticipatory" political history, to borrow a concept from the environmental humanities. While an old pragmatist aphorism teaches that those who do not remember history's atrocities are condemned to repeat them, an anticipatory history proceeds in part by acknowledging that the narrative assumption of progress toward a better future will ultimately falsify the story told. Its premise is that future catastrophe is imminent and that the destruction of the past must be documented and parsed for resources with that very knowledge in mind. So while Díaz's fukú figures "the longue durée of the coloniality of power in the Americas," as Jennifer Harford Vargas has aptly noted, it may also offer a way of better understanding and intervening in the future that it anticipates.[9]

I felt the edge of the novel's anticipatory history again during the weekend of August 11–12, 2017, when white supremacists and neo-Nazis invaded the campus of the University of Virginia and downtown Charlottesville, many of them heavily armed and dressed for combat. Like Trujillo, who exchanged presents with Adolf Hitler, attesting to their shared belief in genocide—a copy of *Mein Kampf,* an ironwork of swastikas—the Charlottesville invaders made symbolic gestures invoking the German Nazi regime. Like Trujillo's troops, they both presented a spectacle meant to terrorize with an explicit message of anti-Semitism and racism and enacted physical violence and murder. Díaz's novel, in telling the story of Trujillo as fukú, draws vital anticipatory connections between these disparate temporal moments with its account of a Dominican regime that systematically sought the end of black life within its national borders. But it also sings, to a Latin beat, a virtual hymn of anticipatory history about a movement yet to be born, with its relentlessly moving attestation, even in the face of a death announced already in the novel's title, that Black Lives Matter: just as Oscar's life, made brief by institutionalized racial violence, is tendered forth by Díaz's narrative in all its exquisite wondrousness.

ANNA BRICKHOUSE is professor of English and American studies at the University of Virginia. Her first book, *Transamerican Literary Relations and the Nineteenth-Century Public Sphere* (2004), was awarded the Gustave O. Arlt Award from the Council of Graduate Schools as well as Honorable Mention for the American Studies Association's Laura Romero First Book Prize. Her second book, *The Unsettlement of America* (2014), was a cowinner of the *Early American Literature* Book Prize and winner of the Modern Language Association's James Russell Lowell Prize as well as Honorable Mention for the ASA's John Hope Franklin Prize. She is researching a project on translation and catastrophe.

Notes

1 Saldívar, *Dialectics of Our America*, 12.
2 Gruesz, *Ambassadors of Culture*, 4.
3 Díaz, *Brief Wondrous Life of Oscar Wao*, 1.
4 Díaz, *Brief Wondrous Life of Oscar Wao*, 4.
5 Díaz, *Brief Wondrous Life of Oscar Wao*, 5.
6 ZeroHedge.com, "Putin Asks."
7 Larsen, *Reading North by South*, 59.
8 Larsen, *Reading North by South*, 2.
9 Vargas, "Dictating a Zafa."

Works Cited

Díaz, Junot. *The Brief Wondrous Life of Oscar Wao.* New York: Riverhead, 2007.

Gruesz, Kirsten Silva. *Ambassadors of Culture: The Transamerican Origins of Latino Writing.* Princeton, NJ: Princeton University Press, 2002.

Larsen, Neil. *Reading North by South: On Latin American Literature, Culture, and Politics.* Minneapolis: University of Minnesota Press, 1995.

Saldívar, José David. *The Dialectics of Our America: Genealogy, Cultural Critique, and Literary History.* Durham, NC: Duke University Press, 1991.

Vargas, Jennifer Harford. "Dictating a Zafa: The Power of Narrative Form as Ruin-Reading." In *Junot Díaz and the Decolonial Imagination*, edited by Monica Hanna, Jennifer Harford Vargas, and José David Saldívar, 201–27. Durham, NC: Duke University Press, 2016.

ZeroHedge.com. "Putin Asks: 'Is America Now a Banana Republic.'" *Millennium Report*, October 27, 2016. themillenniumreport.com/2016/10/putin-asks-is-america-now-a-banana-republic.

Before Latinx
X and *Cartas de un Americano*

RODRIGO LAZO

Abstract   The article suggests that the fashionable use of the term *Latinx* overlooks the historical context of Spanish-language publications in which the gender distinction Latina/o is important. Focusing on the anonymously published *Cartas de un Americano* (London, 1826), a collection of letters written in New York and Philadelphia, the article notes the importance of male-centered homosocial relations and epistolary form for this transatlantic publication. When considering the history of textual production, should *Latinx* be viewed as a misnomer created by contemporary US politics? Does *Latinx* erase particularities of the Spanish language in a country that has never wanted to accept its Hispanophone historical dimensions?
Keywords   Latinx, Latino history, *Cartas de un Americano*, Spanish-language US publishing, nineteenth-century Latinos

In the 1980s Frank Del Olmo made a convincing case to readers in California that the term *Latino* was preferable to the bureaucratic and Anglo-sounding *Hispanic*. Del Olmo based his arguments predominantly on the derivation of *Latino* from *Latinoamericano/a*, which is common usage in Latin America. He also believed *Hispanic* homogenized a heterogeneous people. But tucked into Del Olmo's articles were references to *Latino* being preferred by young people. And he suggested that young people "are more in touch with what is happening in the Latino community than is the federal government."[1] Del Olmo's gesture toward youthful insight registers a historical situation, a moment when a significant number of people changed their preferred term of identification. In another historical turn, today many undergraduates prefer to call themselves Latinx so as to bypass the oppressive gender impositions of *Latino/a*. This Xist neologism, which sounds like either "Lateen-X" or "Latin-X," is attractive to a new generation. But for scholarly work that purports to be hemispheric or historical in that it deals with contexts from other centuries, *Latinx* is at best a misnomer, at worst a fad reminiscent of the passé *Latin@*. Considering that in the United States, official history disavows the Spanish language as a dimension of US culture, the term *Latinx* runs the danger of linguistically situating *latinidades*

ENGLISH LANGUAGE NOTES
56:2, October 2018   DOI 10.1215/00138282-6960724
© 2018 Regents of the University of Colorado

in the monolingual Anglophone wing. As such, it misses the point of historical scholarship that aims to be transamerican and sensitive to language difference.

Here is one example of how a historical situation can provide a different power of *X*. Almost two hundred years ago X was the signatory to a Spanish-language collection of letters written in New York and Philadelphia and published in London: *Cartas de un Americano sobre las ventajas de los gobiernos republicanos federativos* (*Letters of an American concerning the Advantages of Federal Republican Governments*). The occasion for the publication of these letters were debates about constitution formation raging in new Latin American countries in the wake of independence from Spain. The anonymously published *cartas* offered a debate over constitutions established in Mexico and other countries and also touted the success of the US Constitution in establishing a prosperous country. A product of transamerican movement and transatlantic print-culture processes, the letters were drafted at first by Vicente Rocafuerte, a roving intellectual who later became Ecuador's president. Rocafuerte took the letters to London and handed them to José Canga Argüelles, a Spanish economist and government minister who had gone into exile in London for his liberal views. Canga Argüelles arranged for the printing.[2] Rocafuerte initiated the project because he wished to see Gran Colombia (a large territory that included present-day Colombia, Ecuador, and Venezuela) with a federal government comparable to that of the United States instead of a centralized unitarian approach or a dispersal into a confederation. The federal-unitary tension would play an important part in the histories of several Latin American nations, including Argentina.

The anonymously published *Cartas* signed by an *X* was in keeping with the many epistolary exchanges penned by Latin American intellectuals in Philadelphia and the northeastern United States in the early nineteenth century. Addressed to an unknown reader (and thus implying general readership), the *cartas* open with salutations such as "Amigo mio" (My friend) or "Mi dulce y apreciado amigo" (My sweet and respected friend), emphasizing personal attachment as a condition of political conversation. The letters close complementarily with a variety of affectionate phrases, including "su afmo. amigo y servidor" (your most affectionate friend and servant) and "Q.S.M.B.," an abbreviation for "que su mano besa" (with a kiss to your hand). The affectionate epistolary elements are part of an artifice meant to persuade readers in what is a rhetoric of public political conversation. In the opening letter, X enters a print debate "con la franquesa de nuestra amistad, con la concisión propia del estilo epistolar, y con el ardiente deseo que me asiste de contribuír al bien de nuestra patria" (with the frankness of our friendship, with the succinctness of epistolary style, and with the ardent desire that you assist me in contributing to the good of our patria).[3] X concludes the first letter by assuring the recipient that "mi correspondencia no saldrá del estrecho recinto de nuestra amistad" (my correspondence will not go beyond the guarded confines of our friendship).[4] Rather than the crossing of genders implied by *Latinx*, this usage of *X* is an example of an elite brotherhood participating in a transamerican exchange of letters. In this case, men engaged in a homosocial exchange that included sweet salutations.

The *X* signature in *Cartas* presents a writer who could plug into numerous American sites where constitutions were being written and rewritten. As an unknown variable, *X* signals a deterritorialization of the writing subject into a general hemispheric American. This American(o) was not tethered to one location by nationality or social position. The choice of *X* in this book was a curious gesture in that it could have been the mark of an illiterate person and thus could imply inclusivity. But the more rarefied influence of Rocafuerte is clear in letters that display familiarity with *The Federalist* and other books on constitutional theory. As the signatory, X associated himself with hemispheric Americanism and positioned federalism in opposition to Europe. X is influenced by transamerican movement and can be an American(o) in any country in the Americas. As such, X is a product of a historical age of transamerican independence and is an example of a writer of Spanish-language books out of the United States with transatlantic connections. *Cartas de un Americano* reminds us of the historicity of *X*, which in this case should be read as "equis."

RODRIGO LAZO is professor at the University of California, Irvine, and director of the Humanities Core Program. His book *Letters from Filadelfia: Early Latino Literature and the Trans-American Elite* is forthcoming.

Notes

1   Olmo, "Latinos by Any Other Name Are Latinos."
2   Rocafuerte, *Vicente Rocafuerte*, 50.
3   *Cartas de un Americano*, 5–6.
4   *Cartas de un Americano*, 7.

Works Cited

Cartas de un Americano sobre las ventajas de los gobiernos republicanos federativos. In *Colección Rocafuerte*, edited by Neptalí Zúñiga. Quito: Gobierno del Ecuador, 1947.

Olmo, Frank del. "Latinos by Any Other Name Are Latinos." *Los Angeles Times*, May 1, 1981.

Rocafuerte, Vicente. *Vicente Rocafuerte, un Americano libre*, edited by José Antonio Fernández de Castro. Mexico City: Secretaría de Educación Pública, 1947.

The White Legend

Edmundo O'Gorman, Hemispheric Studies,
and the Paradigm of New World Exceptionalism

RALPH BAUER

Abstract   This position paper offers a reflection on Edmundo O'Gorman's seminal *La invención de América* as a critique of the New World exceptionalism underwriting much of twentieth-century hemispheric American studies. It suggests that the paradigm of New World exceptionalism emerges, as a state of exception, from the modern Western (Protestant) idea that America was discovered by Europeans in the fifteenth century, or that America was ever "discovered" by anyone at all. This exceptionalist paradigm of discovery can be understood in terms of a "White Legend" that structurally depends on the idea of the "Black Legend" of the Spanish conquest, for, contrary to conventional wisdom, it was the conquest of America (not its "discovery") that *legitimated* the modern idea of discovery in international law and science.
Keywords   Edmundo O'Gorman, invention of America, discovery in international law and science, hemispheric American studies, New World exceptionalism

There is a hardy Anglo-American tradition that conceives of the origins of America as the result not of a conquest but of a discovery. Thus, Anglophone historians of America since the seventeenth century have preferred words such as *plantation, settlement,* and *colonization* to describe the English presence in America following its "discovery." The phrase *the conquest of America* hereby inevitably refers to sixteenth-century Spanish America, which appears as a temporary relapse into medievalism that seventeenth-century English colonists had been called on to rectify.[1] The "Black Legend" and the "White Legend"—the story of the inordinate cruelty of the Spanish conquest of America and the story of the English "discovery" of a virginal America, respectively—thus became the two interdependent founding myths of Anglo-American settler colonialism. The founders of the United States are therein seen as the heirs not of Hernando Cortés the conqueror but of Christopher Columbus the discoverer.[2] Hence, in the United States, Columbus Day is celebrated but not Cortés Day, even though Columbus never came any closer than Cortés to a place that later became a part of the United States. By contrast, the sixteenth-century Spanish conquest has appeared in the modern Anglo-American

ENGLISH LANGUAGE NOTES

56:2, October 2018 DOI 10.1215/00138282-6960735
© 2018 Regents of the University of Colorado

historical imagination as a sort of historical parenthesis within the "Age of Discovery"—the roughly two hundred years between Columbus's landfall and the publication of Isaac Newton's *Principia*. According to the White Legend, it was an age when Western culture broke through the traditional confines of the book-bound circle of classical knowledge; liberated itself from the inherited religious superstitions of the medieval "Dark Ages"; and ushered forth the modern age of empiricism, progress, and even scientific "revolution." Columbus's first transatlantic journey is hereby seen as *the* watershed event that propelled Western culture on its distinctly modern path, a path that not only broke with its own medieval past but also set it apart from other non-Western cultures in the world. Why, asked the popular American historian Daniel Boorstin, did not the Chinese, the Arabs, or the Indians discover America? The reason, in his view, was an essential difference in the history of humanity between those "solar" cultures that, like the modern West, prize innovation over tradition and those "lunar" cultures, like those founded by Chinese, Arabs, or Indians, that prize tradition over innovation. "My hero is Man the Discoverer," he declared; "the world we now view from the literate West . . . had to be opened for us by countless Columbuses. . . . All the world is still an America."[3]

Today few historians specializing in the study of the early modern period, the early Americas, or the history of science still subscribe to Boorstin's heroic (and racist) account of "the discoverers" as the unequivocal heralds of universal human progress. Many historians have emphasized the disastrous demographic, ecological, and cultural consequences of Columbus's discovery for those who were discovered, even describing it as an "American Holocaust."[4] More broadly, the Columbian Exchange following Europe's discovery of America has been seen as the beginning of the Anthropocene, the epoch in global history in which "many geologically significant conditions and processes are profoundly altered by human activities."[5] Even the very idea of a European "discovery" of America in 1492 by Columbus has come under critical scrutiny. However, much of this debate has revolved around the question of who was "first" to discover America—the Norse, possibly even Phoenicians, Africans, and Chinese, not to mention Native Americans.[6] The question of discovery has become, in this school of thought, a mere question of perspective.[7] An understanding of discovery as a "matter of viewpoint" is fundamentally flawed, however, for it presupposes not only that the various accounts of discovery (Native American, Norse, African, Chinese, European, etc.) constitute a single tradition but also that all these groups conceived of their presence in the Americas as the consequence of a "discovery." Yet, if surviving oral and textual traditions are any indication, most (if not all) Native American cultures conceived of their presence in the Americas as the result not of a "discovery" but, similar to Old World peoples, of various acts of genesis after which they have always been there.[8] Thus the notion of a "prediscovery" of America—whether it was by Native Americans, Africans, Chinese, or Vikings—is based on a modern Western ideology that is hardly less Eurocentric than the claim that America was discovered by Columbus in 1492. The controversy about who was "first" has hereby merely reinforced a particularly hardy form of New World exceptionalism that underwrote much of hemispheric American studies in the twentieth century. It is an exceptionalism that is predicated on the notion that, while most of the world simply *was*, America was *discovered*.

It is this ontological notion of America as a "New World" that the Mexican philosopher of history Edmundo O'Gorman once called a "geographic hallucination" when asked to comment on Herbert Eugene Bolton's famous proposal that the Americas "have a common history."[9] In his own works in hemispheric American studies, *La idea del descubrimiento de América* (1951) and *La invención de América* (1958), O'Gorman had pursued a "hermeneutical" approach that built on the philosophical critiques of Martin Heidegger to argue that, before being able to discover something, one has first to hold or develop a *concept of its possibility*—a "fore-understanding" (*Vorverstehen*).[10] Hence O'Gorman argued that before Europeans could "discover" America, they had first to *invent* the idea of a world with a fourth part—an idea that was impossible to conceive within the epistemic structure of traditional Christian cosmology, which acted as a sort of "cosmic jail" that committed its mental prisoners to the tripartite composition of the world on the doctrinal grounds that the *imago mundi* and its populations must be accounted for by the descendants of the three sons of Noah.[11] O'Gorman therefore challenged us to inquire not into the history of the discovery of America but into the history of "the *idea that America was discovered*." Such a project would yield insights, he suggested, into "the historical nature of the New World and the meaning of its history" for modernity at large.[12]

More than half a century later O'Gorman's critique still stands as an important reminder that the problem of discovery can never be approached as a question of positivist historiography but only as a question of intellectual history, philosophical hermeneutics, and literary tradition. However, while O'Gorman's critique of modern positivist historiography has been seminal in subsequent postcolonial and poststructuralist criticism in early American studies, its effect has been that the historical problem of the modern "hermeneutics of discovery"—the history of the idea of what it means to discover something—has largely been ceded to an often Eurocentric historiography and philosophy of science and international law ("the rights of discovery"), while it has been all but ignored in (post)colonial and hemispheric American studies.[13] In light of the recent "hemispheric turn" in American studies, it may be an opportune time to revisit O'Gorman's critique and interrogate not only the history of the idea that America was discovered but also how the idea of the discovery of America became the *paradigm* of what Giorgio Agamben has called the "state of exception" in the history of science and of international law—of Boorstin's notion that, for the modern discoverer, "all the world is still an America."[14]

RALPH BAUER is associate professor of English and comparative literature at the University of Maryland. His publications include (coedited with Marcy Norton) "Entangled Trajectories," a special issue of *Colonial Latin American Review* (2017) and (coedited with Jaime Marroquín Arredondo) *Translating Nature: Cross-Cultural Histories of Early Modern Science* (forthcoming). His monograph *The Alchemy of Conquest: Science, Religion, and the Secrets of the New World* is forthcoming.

Notes

1   See Cañizares-Esguerra, *Puritan Conquistadors*;
    see also Jennings, *Invasion of America*.
2   See Bauer, "Colonial Discourse and Early
    American Literary History."
3   Boorstin, *Discoverers*, 8, xv–xvi.
4   Stannard, *American Holocaust*.
5   Gibbard and Walker, "The Term
    'Anthropocene.'"
6   See Kolodny, *In Search of First Contact*. For
    other accounts of "prediscovery," see Van
    Sertima, *They Came before Columbus*; Menzies,
    1421; and Forbes, *American Discovery of Europe*.
7   Selye, *From Dream to Discovery*, 88.
8   For the best account of Native American stories
    of origin with a hemispheric scope, see
    Brotherston, *Book of the Fourth World*.
9   O'Gorman, "Do the Americas Have a Common
    History?"
10 O'Gorman, *La idea del descubrimiento de
    América*; O'Gorman, *Invention*. See also Dussel,
    "Philosophy in Latin America in the Twentieth
    Century," esp. 16–19.
11 O'Gorman, *Invention*, 129.
12 O'Gorman, *Invention*, 41.
13 I adapt the phrase *hermeneutics of discovery* from
    Fleming, "Introduction," 7, 8. See also
    Fleming, *Milton's Secrecy*, 1–4.
14 Agamben, *State of Exception*, 41, 25.

Works Cited

Agamben, Giorgio. *State of Exception*, translated by
    Kevin Attell. Chicago: University of Chicago
    Press, 2005.
Bauer, Ralph. "Colonial Discourse and Early
    American Literary History: Ercilla, the Inca
    Garcilaso, and Joel Barlow's Conception of a
    New World Epic." *Early American Literature* 30,
    no. 3 (1995): 203–32.
Boorstin, Daniel J. *The Discoverers*. New York:
    Vintage, 1985.
Brotherston, Gordon. *Book of the Fourth World:
    Reading the Native Americas through Their
    Literature*. Cambridge: Cambridge University
    Press, 1992.
Cañizares-Esguerra, Jorge. *Puritan Conquistadors:
    Iberianizing the Atlantic, 1550–1700*. Stanford,
    CA: Stanford University Press, 2006.
Dussel, Enrique. "Philosophy in Latin America
    in the Twentieth Century: Problems and
    Currents." In *Latin American Philosophy:
    Currents, Issues, Debates*, edited by Eduardo
    Mendieta, 11–53. Bloomington: Indiana
    University Press, 2003.
Fleming, James Dougal. "Introduction." In *The
    Invention of Discovery: Humanism, Science,
    and Hermeneutics*, edited by James Dougal
    Fleming, 1–13. Aldershot: Ashgate, 2011.
Fleming, James Dougal. *Milton's Secrecy*. Aldershot:
    Ashgate, 2009.
Forbes, Jack. *The American Discovery of Europe*.
    Urbana: University of Illinois Press, 2007.
Gibbard, P. L., and M. J. C. Walker. "The Term
    'Anthropocene' in the Context of Formal
    Geological Classification." *Geological Society,
    London, Special Publications*, no. 395 (2014):
    29–37.
Jennings, Francis. *The Invasion of America: Indians,
    Colonialism, and the Cant of Conquest*. Chapel
    Hill: University of North Carolina Press, 1975.
Kolodny, Annette. *In Search of First Contact: The
    Vikings of Vinland, the Peoples of the Dawnland,
    and the Anglo-American Anxiety of Discovery*.
    Durham, NC: Duke University Press, 2012.
Menzies, Rowan Gavin Paton. *1421: The Year China
    Discovered the World*. New York: Bantam, 2004.
O'Gorman, Edmundo. "Do the Americas Have
    a Common History?" In *Do the Americas Have
    a Common History? A Critique of the Bolton
    Theory*, edited by Lewis Hanke, 103–11. New
    York: Knopf, 1964.
O'Gorman, Edmundo. *La idea del descubrimiento de
    América: Historia de esa interpretación y crítica
    de sus fundamentos*. Mexico City: Centro de
    Estudios Filosóficos, 1951.
O'Gorman, Edmundo. *The Invention of America*.
    Westport, CT: Greenwood, 1972.
Selye, Hans. *From Dream to Discovery*. New York:
    McGraw Hill, 1964.
Stannard, David E. *American Holocaust: Columbus
    and the Conquest of the New World*. New York:
    Oxford University Press, 1992.
Van Sertima, Ivan. *They Came before Columbus: The
    African Presence in Ancient America*. New York:
    Random House, 2003.

Forging a Borderlands Baroness

Latinx Identity and Racial Uncertainties in the 1895 Peralta Land Grant Trial

ANITA HUIZAR-HERNÁNDEZ

Abstract In 1895 a woman from California named Sofia Peralta-Reavis leaped into the national spotlight when her husband, James Reavis, sued the federal government for confirmation of her title to the Peralta Land Grant, an enormous Spanish land grant in the territories of Arizona and New Mexico. At the highly publicized trial that followed, it came to light that the evidence Reavis had presented to the court to prove the existence of the Peralta Land Grant and his wife's title to it was forged. This essay uses the trial transcript to recover the woman at the center of the scandal, arguing that Sofia Peralta-Reavis's fraudulent embodiment of a wealthy Spanish baroness unmasks the fluidity and fragility of racial categories, gender, and authenticity in the late nineteenth-century borderlands.
Keywords nineteenth-century United States, Southwest borderlands, land grants, Latinx racial identity

On June 17, 1895, a woman from California named Sofia Peralta-Reavis took the stand at the US Court of Land Claims in Santa Fe, New Mexico. Despite her humble beginnings as an orphaned child, Peralta-Reavis leaped into the national spotlight when she, together with her husband, James Reavis, presented a claim before the court that they held title to 12 million acres of land in central Arizona Territory. According to the claim, Peralta-Reavis was the descendant of Don Miguel Nemecio Silva de Peralta de la Córdoba y García de Carrillo de las Falces, otherwise known as the first baron of Arizona, who received the land from the king of Spain in thanks for his service to the Spanish crown. A century later Reavis traveled the globe to collect archival evidence that proved that his wife, Peralta-Reavis, was the only living descendant of the baron and the sole inheritor of his eponymous Peralta Land Grant. Armed with facsimiles of maps, wills, codicils, and baptismal records from Spain, Mexico, and southwestern United States, James and Sofia Reavis presented their claim to the US government for confirmation.

At the US Court of Land Claims, US attorney Matthew G. Reynolds and his special assistant, Severo Mallet-Prevost, the two government attorneys assigned to the Peralta Land Grant case, made a shocking accusation: the archival evidence

ENGLISH LANGUAGE NOTES

56:2, October 2018 DOI 10.1215/00138282-6960746
© 2018 Regents of the University of Colorado

Reavis had collected, which proved the existence of the grant and his wife's title to it, had been forged. There had never been a baron of Arizona or a Peralta Land Grant, and Peralta-Reavis was not the descendant of Spanish nobility. Instead, according to Reynolds, her real name was Sofia Treadway, and she was the illegitimate daughter "of one John A. Treadway by an Indian squaw commonly known and called Kate."[1] In court Reynolds alleged that Reavis was a con artist who had used his wife as a pawn in a land grab that he had spent the better part of two decades planning.

Thus the trial to determine the validity of the Peralta Land Grant became a trial to verify Peralta-Reavis's identity. In her study of another contentious Spanish land grant case, María Montoya argues, "The problem of land grants in the American Southwest is largely a problem of translation."[2] Reavis saw an opportunity to exploit this problem of translation by inventing and claiming a land grant that never existed, preying on the ignorance that allowed for mistranslations and, in this extreme case, counterfeits. However, because of the central role of Peralta-Reavis's identity in her husband's con, the trial to confirm the land claim transformed into a hotly contested debate over Peralta-Reavis's claim that she was the Spanish heiress to the vast and valuable grant. Precisely because her claim was eventually shown to be baseless, the arguments presented by both sides to prove or disprove her identity point to the fluidity and fragility of racial categories, gender, and authenticity in the nineteenth-century borderlands.

The nearly successful transformation of Peralta-Reavis from a poor, mixed-race, illegitimate child into a wealthy Spanish baroness is a testament to the unstable positionality of late nineteenth-century Latinx people in general, and women in particular, and the far-reaching consequences of that instability. Though the United States' victory against Mexico introduced a new racial hierarchy in the Southwest, its decisive political triumph did not similarly translate into a definitive cultural conquest. The binary racial hierarchy the United States introduced did not fully replace the tiered Spanish system, and the testimonies of the witnesses called by both Reavis and Reynolds affirm that, in this context, proving (or disproving) a person's Latinx identity was easier said than done. Though the government eventually proved that Peralta-Reavis was not in any sense who she claimed to be, the conversations surrounding her identity reveal lingering anxieties about how the US-Mexico War altered not only the physical but also the cultural borders of the United States, and what the lasting consequences of those shifted borders would be. Read in this way, the Peralta Land Grant trial transcript archives reveal not only a land fraud but also the fault lines of the late nineteenth-century US racial imaginary.

Although the transcript of a trial that took place in the US Court of Land Claims may seem like an odd place to find a Latinx life in hemispheric context, it is impossible to understand Peralta-Reavis and the Peralta Land Grant trial in any other way. Though she played a central role in the Peralta Land Grant saga, what studies do exist about the case fail to explore how the debates surrounding her identity reveal the complex interaction among authenticity, racial identity, and citizenship in the US Southwest.[3] A hemispherically situated Latinx studies approach, with its contestation of national, linguistic, and historical borders,[4] is uniquely capable of exploring how these complexities play out not only in the

Peralta Land Grant case but also, more important, in the broader context of the history of the US Southwest.

The robust recovery of the Peralta Land Grant case and Peralta-Reavis's role in it therefore challenges what Rodrigo Lazo describes as "a tendency in U.S. society to exclude or forget certain cultural and political resonances, particularly those that emerge from immigrant communities whose populations are not easily integrated into an Anglo or a black/white conception of the nation."[5] These forgotten cultural and political resonances include the hemispheric collisions brought about by the US-Mexico War, which unsettled the temporal and spatial borders of the US Southwest, and how that unsettlement impacted the people living there. The ambiguity the war created made the story of Peralta-Reavis as a Southwest Cinderella both possible and precarious. As coverage of the Peralta Land Grant trial gripped the nation, her disputed identity quickly became a shorthand for debates about belonging in the borderlands, highlighting the simultaneous centrality and instability of race and ethnicity to questions of citizenship and its accordant rights. Consequently, a close reading of the legal adjudication of Peralta-Reavis's forged Spanish identity allows for a recovery of the always already forged nature not only of Latinx identity but also of racial identity writ large.

Hemispheric Legacies, Latinx Mobilities: The Invention of Sofia Peralta-Reavis

When James Reavis took the stand in Santa Fe, Reynolds grilled him about one of the more unbelievable parts of his story: his chance meeting on a train in California with his future wife, Sofia Peralta-Reavis, the lone heiress for whom he had been searching. Though Reynolds's questions highlight the implausibility of such a serendipitous encounter, the terms both he and Reavis use to describe the meeting further underscore the fluidity of racial identity in general, and Latinx identity in particular, in the late nineteenth-century US Southwest. Reynolds begins:

> Q: Now, what name was she going by at the time you so met her on the train?
> A: The name she gave me as her adopted name was Treadwell.[6]
> Q: You suspected by reason of her appearance that she was of Spanish origin?
> A: Certainly. That was the only inducement for speaking to her.
> Q: You were then looking for a long lost heiress to the property?
> A: That idea had not occurred to me when I spoke to her. It was simply that she was a Spanish beauty and I a young man—quite natural, in my opinion.[7]

It is not surprising that Reavis would describe the first interaction he had with his wife in terms of "natural" attraction.[8] His comments, however, also strategically position Peralta-Reavis's identity, her "Spanish origin," as immediately and unequivocally obvious.[9] In his testimony, it is clear that Reavis intends to bolster his wife's claim to the Peralta Land Grant by affirming the irrefutability of her Spanish identity. Legally, to be a credible heiress for the Spanish land grant, Peralta-

Reavis needed to be able to claim Spanish ancestry. However, proving it was easier said than done. Reavis knew that the forged documents he presented to the court were meaningless without the identity he had forged for his wife, who brought those documents to life in a specific social reality that depended on the legibility of her identity to validate his claim. Reavis's careful construction of Peralta-Reavis as an "heiress" and a "Spanish beauty" are therefore more than just details; they affirm her racial identity through a mediated discourse about her sexuality designed to prove the validity of her inherited claim.

Of course, the irony of Reavis's plot was that it depended simultaneously on the belief that identity was indisputable and the reality that it was mutable. The tension these opposing forces created is precisely what precipitated Peralta-Reavis's passing. Elaine Ginsberg affirms that "passing is about identities: their creation or imposition, their adoption or rejection, their accompanying rewards or penalties."[10] The court's confirmation or rejection of Peralta-Reavis's claim to an authentic Latinx identity promised to bring her husband either a reward, the confirmation of his title to the Peralta Land Grant, or a penalty, the discovery of his deception. But more was at stake in Peralta-Reavis's passing than the title to a piece of land. Ginsberg continues, "Passing is also about the boundaries established between identity categories and . . . the individual and cultural anxieties induced by boundary crossing."[11] The construction of and responses to the counterfeit narrative that created Peralta-Reavis demonstrate the unsettling permeability of racial boundaries in the late nineteenth century. A wide cultural chasm separated Sofia Treadway from Sofia Peralta-Reavis, yet one woman was nearly able to bridge that divide by appearing and behaving convincingly as someone she was not.

In this way, the debates that consumed the trial regarding Peralta-Reavis's racial identity and that are foreshadowed in the exchange between Reavis and Reynolds underscore the falsity of the fixity of Latinx identity in particular, and racial categories in general. In his study of *The Woman in Battle*, an 1876 narrative that describes a cross-dressing Cuban woman named Loreta Janeta Velazquez who had fought as a Confederate soldier in the US Civil War, Jesse Alemán affirms that the debate surrounding the accuracy of Velazquez's story "speaks to the impossibility of authenticity altogether. Gender, race, and nation are sartorial performances that dislodge stable identity markers, wreaking havoc . . . on ideologies, national institutions, and literary histories that demand readable signs of subjectivity."[12] The Peralta Land Grant trial transcript similarly forecloses appeals to authenticity by recording the vigorous debates surrounding Peralta-Reavis's identity. That such debates could happen in the first place is proof that late nineteenth-century racial and national categories were fluid, subjective, and, ultimately, impossible to define.

The specifics of how this racial uncertainty operated and what its consequences were are clear in the contradictory testimony of two key witnesses, one called by Reavis and the other by Reynolds, who provided contrasting accounts of Peralta-Reavis's ancestry. Reavis's key witness, R. C. Hopkins, was a translator in the surveyor general's office who had traveled with Reavis to Guadalajara to verify the authenticity of the Peralta Land Grant papers.[13] There Reavis and Hopkins became such good friends that Peralta-Reavis later lived with Hopkins as a boarder in his home.[14] When Reavis called Hopkins to the stand, he questioned him about his impression of Peralta-Reavis:

> Q: During the time that Sofia was at your house, wasn't it distinctly understood that she was Spanish, and nothing else?
> A: That is my recollection. I do not now remember anything to the contrary.
> Q: If there had been an intimation that she was Indian, would you certainly remember it?
> A: I have no recollection of any suggestion that she was an Indian.[15]

In contrast to Reavis's earlier affirmation of his wife's Spanish identity as self-evident, here he prompts Hopkins to confirm her identity in relation to another racial category, that of Indian. Indeed, Hopkins does confirm that Peralta-Reavis was Spanish by *denying* that she was Indian. In the late nineteenth century such a claim had complex racial resonances and important consequences for US citizenship. Half a century before Hopkins took the stand, the Treaty of Guadalupe Hidalgo had promised the rights and privileges of citizenship, including the right to own property,[16] to Mexicans living in what had been northern Mexico and was now the southwestern United States, so long as they were not Indians.[17] This demand to distinguish a national identity (Mexican) from an imagined ethnic identity (not Indian) provoked confusion regarding which US racial categories Mexican people fell into and instigated a national conversation about the "Mexican Question,"[18] or how to categorize these new subjects within US racial hierarchies. Whereas Indians were wholly discounted as barbaric others,[19] Mexicans, whose heritage meant that they were part native and part European, occupied a more liminal position in this hierarchy, embodying an ambiguous "off-white" racial identity.[20]

While this ambiguity allowed for the systemic discrimination against and disenfranchisement of many Latinx people, it also shaped one key resistance strategy: asserting a Spanish identity. Latinx individuals strategically shored up their claims to citizenship by emphasizing their European ancestry and downplaying their native heritage. This racial reframing, what Carey McWilliams calls the "fantasy heritage" and Raymund Paredes the "hacienda syndrome," was a survival mechanism.[21] As Martha Menchaca explains, "Given the nature of the U.S. racial system and its laws, the conquered Mexican population learned that it was politically expedient to assert their Spanish ancestry."[22] For these Mexicans, appealing to their Spanish identity allowed them to affirm their access to US citizenship and all the rights and privileges that it afforded.[23] In this sense, Reavis's plan to base his wife's land claim on a highly manipulated appeal to Spanish ancestry is not unique. Though Peralta-Reavis's claim to a specific Spanish lineage was necessary to claim ownership of the Peralta Land Grant, it alludes to a wider strategic response employed by many Latinx people who suddenly found themselves on the margins of citizenship in the aftermath of US expansion.

Though this so-called Spanish fantasy heritage has often been cited as evidence of Latinx people's desire to claim a white racial identity, its invocation is much more complex than an appeal to a binary division between black and white.

As Anthony Mora argues, "Spanish identity was a quadrangulation, itself an empty signifier, created in the discursive interstice opened up through the triple negation of 'Indian,' 'Mexican,' and 'Anglo/white,' identities."[24] When Hopkins's testimony is read alongside the reality of Peralta-Reavis's fraudulent claim to Spanish ancestry, his defense of her invented heritage calls attention to the hollowness of Spanish as a racial category. Hopkins's testimony in fact attests to the emptiness of Spanish as a signifier, as his affirmation consists of a series of negations: that he "do[es] not now remember anything to the contrary" and "ha[s] no recollection of any suggestion that she was an Indian."[25] Though Peralta-Reavis's blatantly false claim to Spanish ancestry is an extreme example of "an empty signifier," it points to the gaps and fissures that plagued the relationship among Spanish, Indian, Mexican, and Anglo/white racial categories in the late nineteenth-century borderlands, underscoring how racial categories are largely empty signifiers that must be litigated into fixity.

The fragility of the quadrangulation of Spanish, Indian, Mexican, and Anglo/white racial categories is readily apparent in the opposing testimony of Jennie Mack, a key witness for the government who professed to have known Peralta-Reavis as a child and disputed her claim to Spanish ancestry in general and her connection to a Peralta family in particular. The repeated questions Mack answered in her deposition regarding Peralta-Reavis's parentage, the relationship between her mother and her father, and the character of her mother reveal the persistent anxieties surrounding mixed-race children, illegitimacy, and female sexuality in the late nineteenth-century borderlands. Mack insisted that Peralta-Reavis was the daughter of an Anglo man named John A. Treadway and "an Indian woman" named Kate.[26] Through repeated questions about their relationship, it becomes clear that Treadway and Kate were not married. Instead, Mack asserted that Kate had lived with Treadway through Peralta-Reavis's birth and then "ran off," after which time Mack had "not seen her."[27] This information discredits not only Kate but also Peralta-Reavis. If what Mack said was true, then Peralta-Reavis was a mixed-race child who had been born out of wedlock and was abandoned by her mother, a heritage that clearly negated the authentically pure "Spanish" identity that formed the basis of her property claim.

Because Kate was crucial to the government's case to discredit Peralta-Reavis's claim, the control of female sexuality became a central focus of Mack's testimony. From Spanish colonial times this control extended beyond taboos against sexual relationships between people of different races to the offspring of those relationships, who were seen as a threat to the "hierarchical and racialized social order."[28] To neutralize this threat and maintain a strict social order, these children were denied "access to economic resources and political rights and offices."[29] US expansion into the borderlands added another layer of complexity to ethnically mixed relationships and the offspring they produced. According to Miroslava Chávez-García, during the years that Peralta-Reavis/Treadway claimed to have been born in California, "the records indicate that . . . 954 Spanish-speaking women and 231 native women (20 to 30 percent of the women in those ethnic groups) formed intimate relationships with men of various ethnic backgrounds and social classes to whom they were not married."[30] The many impetuses for these relationships included an imbalance in the ratio of women to men in California and the decimation of the native population by disease and forced displacement.[31] Moreover, "among ethnically mixed couples—particularly those consisting of indigenous women and Euro-American or Spanish-speaking men—the rate of illegitimacy was even higher than among couples made up of a man and a woman from the same or similar ethnic backgrounds."[32] Though the impact of illegitimacy varied greatly, it undoubtedly complicated the lives of all people involved, disproportionately affecting economically and socially marginalized women of color.[33]

Mack's deposition therefore points to the long roots of the marginalization of native and mixed-race women in the borderlands. Though the specific currency changed over time, the sexual economy of the Americas always positioned women who were not white as highly vulnerable. The remainder of Mack's deposition describes precisely the vulnerability that a mixed-race or Native American woman would experience in a relationship with an Anglo man after US expansion, giving some clues for Kate's departure. Mack was familiar with Peralta-Reavis's parentage because she too was a Native American woman who was living in the same community as Kate with a man named Alfred Sherwood "as his wife" and who saw Peralta-Reavis "when she was born."[34] Further questioning reveals that Mack "was a little girl" when she lived with Sherwood and that other women were living with him as well. She declares, "He got my sister first, Ann," and "He got another one by the name of Ellen."[35] Her age when she was with Sherwood and her description of how he "got" the other women reveal that their relationship was more predatory than partnership. That the questioner did not appear to react to Sherwood's status as not only a polygamist but also a child molester clearly indicates how little value was ascribed to the life of native or mixed-race women like Mack. It is hardly surprising, then, that despite having children with Mack, Sherwood eventually left her to marry "a white woman."[36]

As the testimonies of Hopkins and Mack demonstrate, the credibility of Peralta-Reavis's claim to the Peralta Land Grant hinged on her ability to prove the authenticity of her Latinx identity. The terms each used to settle her identity, however, expose such claims to authenticity as socially constructed at best and as dubious forgeries at worst. The contradictions in their testimonies reveal that the racialized and gendered delimitations of Latinx identity were anything but stable. Mora affirms that racial categories at the time were marked by ambivalence, as "the Euro-American representatives of the U.S. nation-state never secured absolute control over the contours of racial and national identification, despite their having erected and policed those borders themselves."[37] The debates surrounding the racial and national identification of Peralta-Reavis, embodied by the incongruous statements made by Hopkins and Mack at the trial, reveal the very real lack of control and coherence when it came to US policing of Latinx identities at the turn of the century. This uncertainty often facilitated the legal and extralegal disenfranchisement of Latinx people in general, and women in particular, but as Peralta-Reavis's own testimony at the trial indicates, it also opened up new possibilities for survival and resistance.

Archival Silences, Borderlands Possibilities:
The Impossible Recovery of Sofia Peralta-Reavis

How complicit was Peralta-Reavis in the invention of her forged identity? Did she know and actively participate in the creation and performance of her husband's scheme? Or did she truly believe his story about her family genealogy? Such questions are impossible to answer, as the archive is largely silent on Peralta-Reavis's own thoughts. The transcripts of her testimony on the stand during the 1895 trial are the only part of the archive to record her exact words, and those remarks are highly mediated both by the questioning of Reynolds and the interruptions and objections of Reavis. Beyond these few indirect glimpses, any deep exploration of who Peralta-Reavis was or what she thought about the case and her relationship to it is plagued by abundant and frustrating silences.

Still, those silences speak volumes about the hemispheric crossroads that determined racial identity in the US Southwest. Heeding Ann Laura Stoler's call to read "along the archival grain," what the archive does say about Peralta-Reavis can be read as what Stoler calls a "condensed [site] of epistemological and political anxiety."[38] In the post-1848 US Southwest the epistemological and political anxieties surrounding the hemispheric relocation of borders, both physical and cultural, were great. At the trial Peralta-Reavis came to embody those anxieties as a living representation of the threats those new borders created, including the threat to expose and perhaps even alter the exclusionary racial foundation on which US citizenship was built, as well as the imaginary nature of racial categories themselves.

Furthermore, Peralta-Reavis's trial testimony, though mediated, is an important part of the Peralta Land Grant archives. As Deena González cautions, "To suggest that the evidence is scanty or impossible to find, as many historians do to justify excluding women or gender, is to ignore the sources or the women in them."[39] Looking specifically at land grants, Karen Roybal likewise looks to the interstices of the archival record to locate Mexican-American women's voices and "contribute to an expanding alternative archive of the Borderlands that challenge nineteenth- and twentieth-century male-centric narratives of land grants and the male bias in more generalized treatments of land issues."[40] Following the example set by González and Roybal, in an effort to comb the interstices of the Peralta Land Grant archives and acknowledge the woman in the source, I conclude with Peralta-Reavis, in her own words.

The climax of the Peralta Land Grant trial came on June 17, 1895, when Peralta-Reavis herself took the stand. Reynolds grilled her about her childhood, her relationship with her husband, and her awareness of the large inheritance she now claimed. After an intense back-and-forth in which she became increasingly agitated, Reynolds finally asked her directly:

> Q: In other words, all you know about [the Peralta Land Grant] is what [James Reavis] told you?
> A: I have looked at [the documents], as I say, but I have never looked them all over, to study them.
> Q: You have never read it, to know of your own knowledge?

A: No, sir; because, if you want to know, I have never gone to school but three months in my life; everybody has been jumping on me and keeping me from everything—(Witness here burst into tears).[41]

At this point, Reavis interjected: "It seems to me the government ought to be more considerate. The government insists upon repeating questions that we think she has answered fully enough."[42] The court agreed, but Peralta-Reavis did not shrink back: "I want to get through to-day; I am not coming back here again."[43]

Resolute, Peralta-Reavis braced herself for Reynolds's final question:

Q: There is one more question, under my duty as United States Attorney, I deem it necessary to ask. I desire to ask the witness whether or not she does not know that she is personating, as claimant here, a person who does not exist, and never did exist, to wit, the great-granddaughter of the original grantee, Don Miguel Nemecio Silva de Peralta, and so-forth.[44]

The court immediately intervened: "We think she is entitled to be protected from answering that question, unless she voluntarily wants to do it. She is under no obligation to answer it."[45] Reavis affirmed that while his wife had nothing to hide, she did "not wish to stay in the court room any longer than is necessary to answer the government" and should not be required to answer.[46] Reynolds maintained that he had "not mistreated the lady" and only "wanted her statement" on the record.[47] The court concluded that she could "answer the question, or decline to do so, as she sees fit."[48]

Decades of careful plotting and planting of evidence all led to this one moment. For Reavis, a scheme that he had spent the better part of twenty years planning was on the line. The vast and valuable territory of the Peralta Land Grant would either finally be his or stay firmly in the hands of the federal government. For Peralta-Reavis, even more was at stake. Her very existence hung in the balance. With that, she uttered her last recorded words: "No, sir; I did not know that I was personating anybody but myself."[49]

Perhaps she knew that the narrative Reavis told her of her extraordinary inheritance was false, but played along away. Referring to the testimony of Spanish-Mexican women in court, González affirms that

> women . . . adjusted their behavior to achieve the results they desired.
> Whether they were consciously or unconsciously manipulating powerful
> structures or the men who controlled them is unclear, but in the majority of
> cases in which women appear as plaintiffs or defendants, both women and men
> repeatedly resurrected the notions of modesty, honor, and reputation. In this
> way, women codified their behavior to suggest the resolutions they desired.[50]

Perhaps Peralta-Reavis codified her behavior to usher along the resolution that both she and her husband desired: the confirmation of the Peralta Land Grant. Or, perhaps after years of hearing her husband repeat the extraordinary story of her identity and inheritance, she had begun to believe it. Regardless of what she believed or why she believed it, reading along the archival grain of her statement reveals an extraordinary image: that of a mixed-race woman from a poor family in California confidently and unapologetically claiming to be a Spanish baroness and the rightful owner of a large amount of valuable property.

Discounting the boldness behind Peralta-Reavis's statement due to the unanswerable questions surrounding the context in which it was uttered risks missing its remarkable implications. Peralta-Reavis's words reveal the real threat that her husband's invented Peralta Land Grant posed: not that his story about her identity was false but that it couldn't be disproved. When Peralta-Reavis claimed that she was not "personating anybody but myself," she left unresolved the question of who she really was, foreclosing the possibility of absolutely and conclusively determining her racial identity. As a result, the lingering ambiguity of her statement resonated beyond the confines of the late nineteenth-century Santa Fe courtroom, casting doubt on not only the validity of the Peralta Land Grant but also the salience of the mutually constitutive conceptions of race, gender, and authenticity on which it depended.

ANITA HUIZAR-HERNÁNDEZ is assistant professor of border studies in the Department of Spanish and Portuguese at the University of Arizona. Her work has appeared in *Aztlán*, *MELUS*, and *SAIL*. Her book, *Forging Arizona: A History of the Peralta Land Grant and Racial Identity in the West*, is forthcoming.

Acknowledgments
This essay is based on my forthcoming book, *Forging Arizona*. I am grateful to the editors of this special issue, Maria Windell and Jesse Alemán, as well as the anonymous reviewers for their careful and generative feedback.

Notes

1   Amended Answer and Cross-Petition of the United States, June 1, 1895, rolls 62–63, Coll. 1972-007, Spanish Archives of New Mexico I, Bureau of Land Management, RG 49, National Archives and Records Administration, New Mexico State Records Center and Archives, Santa Fe, x.

2   Montoya, *Translating Property*, 4.

3   For example, the most exhaustive study of the Peralta Land Grant to date, Powell, *Peralta Grant*, does not consider these broader ramifications.

4   See, e.g., Coronado, "Historicizing Nineteenth-Century Latina/o Textuality."

5   Lazo, "Introduction," 10–11.

6   Here Reavis meant to say "Treadway," a reference to John A. Treadway, the Anglo man with whom Sofia lived as a child. According to Reavis, Treadway was merely her caretaker. During the trial, however, witnesses who knew Sofia as a child testified that Treadway was in fact her father. See Powell, *Peralta Grant*, 66, 126–27.

7   Transcript of testimony, June 12, 1895, Spanish Archives of New Mexico I, 624–25.

8   Transcript of testimony, June 12, 1895, 624–25.

9   Transcript of testimony, June 12, 1895, 624–25.

10   Ginsberg, *Passing*, 2.

11   Ginsberg, *Passing*, 2.

12   Alemán, "Crossing the Mason-Dixon Line in Drag," 122.

13   Powell, *Peralta Grant*, 130, 50–51.

14   Powell, *Peralta Grant*, 131.

15   Transcript of testimony, June 15, 1895, Spanish Archives of New Mexico I, 868.

16   US Congress, Treaty of Guadalupe Hidalgo.

17   John Nieto-Phillips notes that when the United States expanded into the Southwest, "federal and territorial officials reinstated the legal distinction between 'Indians' and non-Indians, a distinction that had formed the basis of Spanish colonial society and that [had] been

legally abolished in 1821 by the Plan de Iguala" (*Language of Blood*, 54).

18 John-Michael Rivera defines the "Mexican Question" as "a European American inquiry into the very constitution of Mexican peoplehood that found its rhetorical dimensions within the perimeters of democratic expansion and racialization of the Mexican peoples who lived in the 'frontier.'" That is to say, "the Mexican Question found its roots in the period of expansion into the western and southwestern lands of Mexicans and Native Americans, the period when both the promise of terra incognita and the savage other emerged in the consciousness of the American public" (*Emergence of Mexican America*, 54).

19 Martha Menchaca explains that the Treaty of Guadalupe Hidalgo did not grant citizenship to "Mexican Indians" and gave Congress the power "to validate or extinguish all land grant agreements that Spain and Mexico had made with Mexican Indians, including the mission Indians" (*Recovering History*, 234).

20 Gómez, *Manifest Destinies*, 3.

21 McWilliams, *North from Mexico*, 36; Paredes, "Evolution of Chicano Literature," 52.

22 Menchaca, "Chicano Indianism," 587.

23 Significantly, only wealthy and phenotypically lighter-skinned Mexican-Americans could employ this strategy effectively, resisting their individual disenfranchisement at the cost of affirming a US racial hierarchy based on the marginalization of poor nonwhite people. See Alemán, "Historical Amnesia."

24 Mora, *Border Dilemmas*, 187.

25 Transcript of testimony, June 15, 1895, 868.

26 Deposition of Jennie Mack, December 18, 1894, Spanish Archives of New Mexico I.

27 Deposition of Jennie Mack, December 18, 1894.

28 Martínez, *Genealogical Fictions*, 158.

29 Martínez, *Genealogical Fictions*, 158.

30 Chávez-García, *Negotiating Conquest*, 156.

31 Chávez-García, *Negotiating Conquest*, 155–56.

32 Chávez-García, *Negotiating Conquest*, 160.

33 Chávez-García, *Negotiating Conquest*, 172–73.

34 Deposition of Jennie Mack, December 18, 1894.

35 Deposition of Jennie Mack, December 18, 1894.

36 Deposition of Jennie Mack, December 18, 1894.

37 Mora, *Border Dilemmas*, 4–5.

38 Stoler, *Along the Archival Grain*, 20.

39 González, *Refusing the Favor*, 105.

40 Roybal, *Archives of Dispossession*, 25.

41 Transcript of testimony taken on trial of the case before the Court of Private Land Claims at Santa Fe, New Mexico, June 17, 1895, rolls 62–63, Coll. 1972-007, Spanish Archives of New Mexico I, New Mexico State Archives, 940–41.

42 Transcript of testimony, June 17, 1895, 941.

43 Transcript of testimony, June 17, 1895, 941.

44 Transcript of testimony, June 17, 1895, 941.

45 Transcript of testimony, June 17, 1895, 941.

46 Transcript of testimony, June 17, 1895, 942.

47 Transcript of testimony, June 17, 1895, 942.

48 Transcript of testimony, June 17, 1895, 942.

49 Transcript of testimony, June 17, 1895, 942.

50 González, *Refusing the Favor*, 24.

Works Cited

Alemán, Jesse. "Crossing the Mason-Dixon Line in Drag: The Narrative of Loreta Janeta Velazquez, Cuban Woman and Confederate Soldier." In *Look Away! The U.S. South in New World Studies*, edited by Jon Smith and Deborah Cohn, 110–29. Durham, NC: Duke University Press, 2004.

Alemán, Jesse. "Historical Amnesia and the Vanishing Mestiza: The Problem of Race in *The Squatter and the Don* and *Ramona*." *Aztlán* 27, no. 1 (2002): 59–93.

Chávez-García, Miroslava. *Negotiating Conquest: Gender and Power in California, 1770s to 1880s.* Tucson: University of Arizona Press, 2004.

Coronado, Raúl. "Historicizing Nineteenth-Century Latina/o Textuality." In *The Latino Nineteenth Century: Archival Encounters in American Literary History*, edited by Rodrigo Lazo and Jesse Alemán, 44–58. New York: New York University Press, 2016.

Ginsberg, Elaine K. *Passing and the Fictions of Identity.* Durham, NC: Duke University Press, 1996.

Gómez, Laura. *Manifest Destinies: The Making of the Mexican American Race.* New York: New York University Press, 2007.

González, Deena J. *Refusing the Favor: The Spanish-Mexican Women of Santa Fe, 1820–1880.* Oxford: Oxford University Press, 2001.

Lazo, Rodrigo. "Introduction: Historical Latinidades and Archival Encounters." In *The Latino Nineteenth Century: Archival Encounters in American Literary History*, edited by Rodrigo Lazo and Jesse Alemán, 1–19. New York: New York University Press, 2016.

Martínez, María Elena. *Genealogical Fictions: Limpieza de Sangre, Religion, and Gender in Colonial Mexico.* Stanford, CA: Stanford University Press, 2008.

McWilliams, Carey. *North from Mexico: The Spanish-Speaking People of the United States.* New York: Greenwood, 1968.

Menchaca, Martha. "Chicano Indianism: A Historical Account of Racial Repression in the United States." *American Ethnologist* 20, no. 3 (1993): 583–603.

Menchaca, Martha. *Recovering History, Constructing Race: The Indian, Black, and White Roots of Mexican Americans.* Austin: University of Texas Press, 2001.

Montoya, María E. *Translating Property: The Maxwell Land Grant and the Conflict over Land in the American West, 1840–1900.* Berkeley: University of California Press, 2002.

Mora, Anthony. *Border Dilemmas: Racial and National Uncertainties in New Mexico, 1848–1912.* Durham, NC: Duke University Press, 2011.

Nieto-Phillips, John. *The Language of Blood: The Making of Spanish-American Identity in New Mexico, 1880s–1930s.* Albuquerque: University of New Mexico Press, 2004.

Paredes, Raymund A. "The Evolution of Chicano Literature." In *Three American Literatures: Essays in Chicano, Native American, and Asian American Literature for Teachers of American Literature,* edited by Houston A. Baker Jr., 33–79. New York: Modern Language Association, 1982.

Powell, Donald. *The Peralta Grant: James Addison Reavis and the Barony of Arizona.* Norman: University of Oklahoma Press, 1960.

Rivera, John-Michael. *The Emergence of Mexican America: Recovering Stories of Mexican Peoplehood in U.S. Culture.* New York: New York University Press, 2006.

Roybal, Karen R. *Archives of Dispossession: Recovering the Testimonios of Mexican American Herederas, 1848–1960.* Chapel Hill: University of North Carolina Press, 2017.

Stoler, Ann Laura. *Along the Archival Grain: Epistemic Anxieties and Colonial Common Sense.* Princeton, NJ: Princeton University Press, 2009.

US Congress. Treaty of Guadalupe Hidalgo. Articles 8–9. February 2, 1848. Library of Congress. memory.loc.gov/cgi-bin/ampage?collId=llsl&fileName=009/llsl009.db&recNum=982, and memory.loc.gov/cgi-bin/ampage?collId=llsl&fileName=009/llsl009.db&recNum=983.

Archival Excess in Latinx Print Culture

US National Latinx Literature

ALBERTO VARON

Abstract   This essay considers the Latinx archive and argues for the continued importance of the nation in understanding Latinx culture. For decades, scholars have recovered a variety of divergent forms of writing that challenge the possibility of a Latinx
literary canon. These writings operate in disparate modes and genres, do not always fit
neatly within traditional understandings of "literature," and are frequently fragmentary
or incomplete—what the essay terms "archival excess," which runs counter to the perceived lack of US Latinx literary and cultural production and is inherently unstable and
evolving. The essay asserts that an unstable Latinx archive is not only symptomatic of
but also essential to the project of contemporary *latinidad*. The US nation and its atten-
dant discourses of nationalism help contain archival excess, even as the Latinx archive
challenges national borders and narratives. For this reason and for its political urgency,
Latinx studies needs to maintain recourse to the US nation, despite the field necessarily
operating as methodologically transnational.
Keywords   archives, nation, nationalism, Latino studies

The artifacts of early Latinx culture are often fragmentary and incomplete, and many of the innumerable artifacts in academic, public, and personal holdings historically have been disregarded as what I call "archival excess," superfluous to the construction of a national narrative. The profusion of these fragments, through a logic of accretion and sheer abundance, provides compelling evidence for the complexity and fecundity of the Latinx nineteenth century. Scholars have recovered complete texts, but what defines a US Latinx national archive is precisely its impermanent and incomplete nature. Moreover, ongoing archival recovery continually shifts our understanding of the past, rendering archives that are migratory and fluid, characteristics that speak to the Latinx experience and that stand in counterpoint to a closed canon that privileges a single national narrative.

Attempting to conceptualize early Latinx archives poses several challenges, among them, how to work multilingually, what qualifies as "literature," and where

ENGLISH LANGUAGE NOTES

56:2, October 2018 DOI 10.1215/00138282-6960757

to draw the boundaries around communities marked by hemispheric movement. It is nigh impossible to do work on early Latinx culture ("early" refers to pre–civil rights era print culture by and about the group now referred to as Latinxes) without including Spanish language texts (or French, or Portuguese), but even conceding the existence of a multilingual archive—fundamental to the study of Latinx culture— is insufficient to bring together texts that circulated contemporaneously but in different languages, in different geographic locations, and out of different political and regional contexts. How, then, to manage archival excess? One solution, especially for the field of Latino studies for which transnational methodologies are fundamental, is to continue to engage with the nation.

As both cultural frame and political exigency, the nation continues to structure much of our institutional and material realities. Building on textual recovery in Latino studies (a key site for the further relevance of American and literary studies), "Latinx lives" must grapple with the US nation in defining both the field of study and its political promise, even as we challenge the boundaries and characters that make up its national narrative. The US nation provides a necessary if flawed constraint that contains the archival excess generated by the transnational or hemispheric impulse driving Latino studies and that determines its political and institutional potential.

For Latino studies or any number of relatively new fields, no single collection or monograph can fully represent the field or its population. (Although the novel provides entry into existing scholarship, it was hardly the form of choice for the bulk of Latinx writing.) The Latinx archive de-emphasizes the single-authored text, recentering on the objects that circulated within Spanish and English cultural networks.[1] The multiplicity of linguistic registers, national backgrounds, and ethnic makeup leaves Kirsten Silva Gruesz wondering if the field of Latinx literature can even have "an authoritative canon for a body of literature that doesn't yet have a literary history"; she instead invites scholars to find "points of integration" into canonical American literature.[2] Rodrigo Lazo further describes this conundrum, noting that the "concept *archive* allows for a consideration of the way knowledge is organized in relation to research agendas and fields of study," but "an inter-American geographic mapping [has] not translated convincingly to an ontology of a field."[3] Despite the excellent scholarship generated by the "transnational" turn, conceptualizing culture beyond national categorization faces persistent challenges.

The people and objects that make up *latinidad* (a more recent and elastic idea, as Marta Caminero-Santangelo explains) are enormously varied, linked variously by the processes of racialization, by historical colonialisms and imperialism, or by common language, for example, but these are refracted within a US context in which the archives of Latino studies function as a temporary tethering that unifies, dilates, and dissipates, a pulsating organ expanding and contracting in response to the needs of scholars and Latinx communities.[4] (The plural term *archives* is perhaps more descriptive, recognizing the multiplicity of its potential configurations.) While the shift to *archives* occurred concomitantly with the rise of hemispheric studies, and though, methodologically, *transnationalism* does, will, and should define the field, the nation provides an essential framework through which the Latinx archive crystallizes, by charting evolution, noting limitations, or rubbing against the limits of archival endeavors.[5]

Within a climate of diminishing institutional resources and a nativist political landscape seeking to restrict political power, demonstrating Latinx contributions to the development of US history and culture can strengthen claims for contemporary Latinx rights and political inclusion. Contradicting the false logic of cultural purity, early Latinx culture offers a demonstrable rebuttal against the contention that Latinxes were not agents of US political and cultural projects. In the current moment, when a protectionist US government seeks to renegotiate the structures regulating transnational commerce and exchange, Latinxes must be framed as participants within and as shaping the United States.[6]

An unstable archive reflects the movement or even the tenuousness that so often characterizes the experience—indeed, the legal status—of Latinxes in the United States. Throughout the nineteenth and early twentieth centuries, US immigration laws all but ignored Mexicans, Central Americans, and South Americans, but since 1965 Latinxes have become ontologically linked with the idea of immigration in the US national imaginary.[7] This connection frequently vilifies Latinx immigrants as unwanted, undesirable, and harmful to a preexisting idea of the US nation. Reshaping the national narrative around Latinx contributions to a US national project dislodges these associations, potentially disrupting contemporary understandings of who Latinxes are and how they have contributed to the growth of the US nation; the fragmentary archive reframes the national past within a more elastic conception of what it means and has meant to belong in the United States. By stressing the nation, I am not advocating for the nation-state as the final arbiter of political or cultural authority, or calling for a nationalist (or patriotic) approach to the field that sees cultural networks grinding to a halt at the territorial borders. Rather, it is imperative to emphasize Latinx contributions to, and Latinxes' roles within, US national history, politics, and culture to counter exclusionary policies that so often ostracize Latinxes.

An archive is ultimately about the objects of study, and for the field of Latino studies, hovering on the cusp between becoming and being its own disciplinary formation, it is about constituting a body of shared knowledge. Within Latino studies—the institutional inheritor of civil rights movement area studies—archival formation is about controlling participation in resources and discourses, and national boundaries still discipline institutional spaces (e.g., Title VI funding). While these categories are past due for revision, they persist. Archives are always shifting and malleable, qualities that provide flexibility to revise national narratives. Thus archival excess becomes an archive of inclusion, indexical of cultural life and alternative histories that redefine intellectual history in more inclusive terms. At least that is the promise of an unstable, contingent, and porous national archive.

ALBERTO VARON is assistant professor of English and Latino studies at Indiana University. He is author of *Before Chicano: Citizenship and the Making of Mexican American Manhood, 1848–1959* (2018).

Notes

1   Raul Coronado maintains that Latino writing requires an expanded understanding of literature and textuality (*World Not to Come*).

2   Gruesz, "What Was Latino Literature?," 336, 339.

3   Lazo, "Invention of America Again," 754–55. In his excellent assessment of the archive, Lazo concedes that "hemispheric studies must contend with the adamant persistence (if very shifty) of the nation even if it wants to bypass its demands" (762).

4   Caminero-Santangelo, *On Latinidad*.

5   Others have argued for the hemispheric origins of Latino studies, for instance, Lopez, *Chicano Nations*; Coronado, *World Not to Come*; Camacho, *Migrant Imaginaries*; Saldívar, *Borderlands of Culture*; and Saldívar, *Border Matters*.

6   President Trump's administration seeks to renegotiate the North American Free Trade Agreement and restrict immigration policies to further tip the balance of power between the United States and the hemisphere.

7   Even in our contemporary moment, when so much xenophobia is directed at Muslims and the Middle East, the discourse surrounding those national and ethnic groups tends to center on their refugee status rather than on willful migration.

Works Cited

Camacho, Alicia Schmidt. *Migrant Imaginaries: Latino Cultural Politics in the U.S.-Mexico Borderlands*. New York: New York University Press, 2008.

Caminero-Santangelo, Marta. *On Latinidad: U.S. Latino Literature and the Construction of Ethnicity*. Gainesville: University Press of Florida, 2009.

Coronado, Raul. *A World Not to Come: A History of Latino Writing and Print Culture*. Cambridge, MA: Harvard University Press, 2013.

Gruesz, Kirsten Silva. "What Was Latino Literature?" *PMLA* 127, no. 2 (2012): 335–41.

Lazo, Rodrigo. "The Invention of America Again: On the Impossibility of an Archive." *American Literary History* 25, no. 4 (2013): 751–71.

Lopez, Marissa. *Chicano Nations: The Hemispheric Origins of Mexican American Literature*. New York: New York University Press, 2011.

Saldívar, José David. *Border Matters: Remapping American Cultural Studies*. Berkeley: University of California Press, 1997.

Saldívar, Ramón. *The Borderlands of Culture: Américo Paredes and the Transnational Imaginary*. Durham, NC: Duke University Press, 2006.

Rubén Darío, Latino Poet

JOHN ALBA CUTLER

Abstract   This essay examines the circulation of works by the Latin American *modern-ista* poet Rubén Darío in US Spanish-language periodicals during the early twentieth century. These poems index the immense influence that *modernismo* had on US Latino/a literature. *Modernismo* has sometimes been understood as reflecting the conservative politics of an ascendant bourgeoisie; however, the varying contexts in which Darío's poems appeared suggest that *modernismo* acted as a flashpoint for class conflict in the US Latino/a literary field. The poems thus help clarify the emergence of US *latinidad* in relation to hemispheric *latinoamericanismo*.

Keywords   print culture, Latino/a modernism, *modernismo*

In the late nineteenth and early twentieth centuries, US Spanish-language serials reprinted hundreds of poems and stories by Rubén Darío, the preeminent figure of Latin American *modernismo*. Beginning in 1888, when the New York newspaper *Las Novedades* published a review of Darío's groundbreaking book *Azul*, Latino/a serials frequently critiqued, celebrated, and reprinted Darío's work. Some poems, such as "Sonatina" and "La caridad," appeared in a variety of publications in multiple locations, their popularity lasting for decades. After his death in 1916, Latino/a serials also published dozens of homages to Darío by both well-known Latin American poets and local poets. Darío was not the most frequently reprinted *modernista* poet. That distinction likely belongs to either of the Mexican poets Manuel Gutiérrez Nájera or Amado Nervo. However, given Darío's centrality to *modernismo*, his poetry provides a way to investigate the hemispheric ligatures of US Latino/a modernism.

Modernismo's influence on Latino/a literature has been occluded, perhaps because *modernismo* does not fit easily into the paradigm of political resistance that drives Latino/a studies. Mary Pat Brady articulates this difficulty with trademark clarity in her essay "Borderlands Modernism." Brady describes *modernismo* and Anglo modernism alike as movements that fetishized a break from tradition and depended "upon an ambivalent theatricality that would adore centralized figures and centralized spaces."[1] This description aligns with accounts that emphasize *modernistas*' desire to lay claim to European literary cultural capital.[2] As Gerard Aching has shown, *modernista* poetry, emblematized in Darío's work, crystallized social

ENGLISH LANGUAGE NOTES

56:2, October 2018 DOI 10.1215/00138282-6960768
© 2018 Regents of the University of Colorado

conflict between "monopolistic oligarchies and a bourgeoisie that had begun to reap benefits from economic liberalism and international trade."[3] The social conflict Aching describes is configured differently from the class conflicts we generally imagine Latino/a literature to engage. To oversimplify, whereas there is a strong tradition of understanding Latino/a literature as rooted in a commitment to working-class politics *against* the exploitative machinations of bourgeois capitalism, *modernismo* represents the interests of a newly ascendant bourgeoisie against the elite Creole oligarchies of nineteenth-century Latin American republics. Little wonder that Brady asserts that "the modernism of the borderlands would offer an obscure and disdainful disinterest" toward *modernismo*'s pursuit of literary cultural capital.[4] In Brady's reading, borderlands modernism—represented by such works as Mariano Azuela's *Los de abajo* (1915) and Américo Paredes's *George Washington Gómez*—is the true precursor of contemporary Latino/a literature.

Borderlands modernism stands as a powerful paradigm of opposition literature; however, in this essay I make the case that we should reconsider how *modernista* writing may have signified within US Latino/a reading communities. Spanish-language serials put *modernismo* to many uses; encountering a Darío poem reprinted in a Texas newspaper in the 1920s was an aesthetic experience distinct from encountering it in a book or a literary magazine like Venezuela's *El Cojo Ilustrado*. As I argue in what follows, Latino/a serials were heterogeneous spaces in which bourgeois dominance was anything but assured and in which *modernista* verse signified in multiple ways. Darío's poems rubbed shoulders with advertisements, labor solicitations, and other forms of discourse that hailed both working-class and middle-class readerships. They appeared in newspapers with explicitly conservative, middle-class politics, such as San Antonio's *La Prensa*, but also in anarchist and socialist magazines like New York's *Pueblos Hispanos*. Darío's poems never meant just one thing for Latino/a readers.

Reconsidering *modernismo* allows us to see, among other things, how the spirit of *latinoamericanismo* underwrote Latino/a identity long before a corporatized Latino/a identity emerged to replace the ethnonationalism of 1960s activist movements. Most Latino/a serials in the late nineteenth and early twentieth centuries had specific national or regional commitments, but *modernismo* provided the aesthetic framework by which those commitments were articulated through hemispheric solidarity. As Laura Lomas has argued in relation to José Martí's writing, "Although the adjective 'Latino/a' did not denote in the late nineteenth century what it does today . . . it did point to an incipient form of this major cultural formation in the Americas."[5] Indeed, *latinoamericanismo* provided a cohesive force for Spanish-language literary publishing throughout the United States for decades. When I refer to Darío as a Latino poet, I hope to index this connection between *latinoamericanismo* and US *latinidad*, pressuring the national boundedness that has come to characterize US Latino/a studies.

Attending to *modernismo* also means attending to the Latino/a culture of reprinting, too long neglected. Meredith McGill has argued that the practice of reprinting texts in the antebellum United States "helped to produce a distinctive literary culture that cannot adequately be perceived through the optics of national literary study" because that culture was "regional in articulation and transnational in scope."[6] Like US literary studies, Latino/a literary studies has for the most part followed the model of the national literary tradition, and recovery of texts from before the 1960s has focused on finding exceptional individual texts and authors that establish or advance the project of that tradition.[7] The value of the scholarship produced by this strategy is immense; without it, we would not know about such landmark texts as María Amparo Ruiz de Burton's *Squatter and the Don* (1885) or Paredes's *George Washington Gómez* (1990). However, a narrow focus on these texts comes at the expense of neglecting the expansive literary culture nurtured in Spanish-language serials in the decades preceding and following the turn of the twentieth century. Daily and weekly newspapers, cultural digests, and literary magazines circulated thousands of poems, short stories, and *crónicas* within and between Latino/a communities during this period, but we have up to this point only the barest sense of how editors, publishers, and readers encountered these texts.

I will unfold this argument by examining Darío's poems reprinted in five Latino/a serials across several decades. I found these poems by searching the Readex Newsbank Hispanic-American Newspapers online database, which contains digitized runs of over two hundred serials published between 1888 and 1950. In all, I found 208 instances of reprinted poems by Darío, as well as 30 more homages or tributes to Darío by other writers. It is worth emphasizing that this is only a partial portrait of an incomplete archive.[8] Nevertheless, these reprintings illustrate the thorough saturation of Latino/a print culture in *modernismo*. I show in the first half of the essay how poems reprinted in *Las Dos Repúblicas* and *El Tiempo* imply a more extensive system of transnational textual circulation than we have yet envisioned, and I challenge assumptions about the rigidity of some regional and nationalist ideological investments. As the second half of the essay explores, these reprinted poems demand that we revise our narratives of *modernismo*'s political meaning in Latino/a literary history. *Modernismo* was not merely the expression of an ascendant bourgeoisie or elite exile class; poems reprinted in *La Prensa*, *El Defensor*, and *Pueblos Hispanos* demonstrate how it acted as a crossroads of class conflict. I conclude by briefly investigating an homage to Darío, "Requiescat in pace!" by J. Restrepo Gómez (1916), which appeared in *La Prensa*. Restrepo Gómez's poem hinges on a critique of bourgeois values, signaling the conflicted, sometimes contradictory class politics of both *modernismo* and the small middle class that controlled Latino/a literary production during the early twentieth century. It suggests that Darío's poetry resonated with Latino/a readers most forcefully when it expressed anxiety about the scale and speed of change in modern life, particularly changes in the organization of global capital. *Modernismo* thus played a crucial role in the unfolding of US Latino/a modernism.

Darío and the Latino/a Culture of Reprinting
Tracking Darío poems through the archive of US Latino/a serials shows the dynamism and scope of the Hispanophone culture of reprinting. In their bibliography of Hispanic periodicals, Nicolás Kanellos and Helvetia Martell document the existence of over a thousand Spanish-language serials in the United States between

1888 and 1950.[9] The vast majority of these serials included literary texts as part of their regular publication agenda, reprinting poems, short stories, and *crónicas* alongside the original works of local writers. For example, San Antonio's *La Prensa*, the daily newspaper founded by the Mexican journalist Ignacio Lozano in 1913, published poetry in each of its daily issues for decades, as well as poems, *crónicas*, and short stories in its weekly cultural magazine, *Suplemento Dominical* (*Sunday Supplement*). The literary texts in the archive of *La Prensa* alone number in the tens of thousands. At a time when the market for Spanish-language books in the United States was limited, these serials were the most important literary institutions for Latino/a communities.

The routes Darío's poems took to arrive in Latino/a serials were sometimes surprising. Consider, for example, "Sinfonía," which appeared in the Los Angeles semiweekly newspaper *Las Dos Repúblicas* in July 1892. "Sinfonía" is actually a well-known Darío poem titled "Tarde del trópico," which was eventually included in *Cantos de vida y esperanza* in 1905. In 1892 Darío was not yet the literary titan he would become, and nothing about the poem's republication in *Las Dos Repúblicas* suggests that the editors regarded Darío as exceptional. Nevertheless, the republication of the poem in *Las Dos Repúblicas* is revealing, since "Tarde del trópico" was originally published in *El Diario de Centro América*, the most important newspaper in Guatemala, on June 4, 1892, only a month before it appeared in *Las Dos Repúblicas*.

In general, the time line of Darío's reprintings in Latino/a newspapers makes *modernismo* appear slightly belated in the United States in comparison to the rest of Latin America, but this publication of "Tarde del trópico" bucks that trend. The Readex database shows only two publications of Darío poems in Latino serials before 1905, when *Cantos de vida y esperanza* was published in Madrid. While *modernismo* was at its apex in Latin America, it seems barely to have appeared on the US Latino/a literary scene in the first decade of the twentieth century. *Las Dos Repúblicas* is before its time in this respect, but it's worth pointing out why. A repeated advertisement in the newspaper promises that *Las Dos Repúblicas* "is the only Spanish paper published in the State of California twice a week devoted to the interests of the United States, Mexico, and all the Central and South American countries. It has correspondents in Madrid and Barcelona besides those of the United States, Central and South America, and Mexico."[10] Rather than maintaining actual correspondents, it seems more likely that Antonio Cuyas, the editor of *Las Dos Repúblicas*, or Antonio J. Flores, the newspaper's business manager, subscribed to newspapers from Central and South America and Mexico. As far as I can determine, "Tarde del trópico" was not reprinted in Mexico in the month between its appearance in *El Diario de Centro América* and its republication in *Las Dos Repúblicas*, which suggests that the newspapers editors subscribed to the Guatemalan newspaper and encountered the poem there.[11] The poem's republication in Los Angeles signals how enmeshed the Los Angeles Spanish-speaking community was in hemispheric networks of circulation. The editors of *Las Dos Repúblicas* (or other Latino/a serials) did not even need to know who Darío was. Simply by virtue of subscribing to Latin American newspapers, editors welcomed the wave of *modernismo* into US Latino/a reading communities.

It is worth noting how the persistence of such transnational circulation in the early twentieth century resists portraits of Latino/a print culture as regionalist and/or nationalist in scope. For example, A. Gabriel Meléndez and Doris Meyer have characterized the lively fin de siècle New Mexican print culture as regionalist. Meyer observes that "in the 1880s, seventeen new periodicals were begun [in New Mexico], and in 1890, forty-four followed suit," asserting that "overall, New Mexico produced more Spanish-language newspapers than any other region of the Southwest."[12] Meyer and Meléndez agree that New Mexican print culture—as emblematized in the formation in 1892 of the Hispano-American Press Association—was regional in its articulation and political commitments. Meléndez writes that "many *periodiqueros* aimed to create a literary tradition to reflect the sociohistorical experience of *Nuevomexicanos* and other *Mexicano*-origin communities of the Southwest."[13] Examples of this *nuevomexicano* literary tradition include the poems of José Escobar, the short novels of Eusebio Chacón, and the *costumbrista* sketches of Manuel C. de Baca.[14]

For good reason, Meyer and Meléndez emphasize the work of New Mexican writers in their scholarship, referring only in broad strokes to the relationship of those writers to hemispheric literary currents. In her discussion of José Escobar's poetry, Meyer writes: "To classify Escobar's poetry as postromantic or premodernist would be to follow a literary taxonomy which, as has often been suggested, might better be ignored. . . . But it is important to note that he was aware of the innovative poetic trends in neighboring Mexico and was an admirer of the modern poets there."[15] Meyer's discussion avoids naming the Mexican poets she has in mind in order to reserve the spotlight for Escobar. At the same time, she makes a point of securing Escobar's bona fides by describing his familiarity with the "innovative poetic trends" current in Mexico during his journalistic career. Meyer's description is not wrong, but *modernismo* did not only occur elsewhere. Instead, as the case of Darío shows, these currents moved through New Mexican and other US Latino/a print cultural contexts.

The publication of Darío's poem "Caso" in the January 28, 1911, issue of the Las Cruces weekly *El Tiempo* suggests how Latino/a texts worked intimately with hemispheric contemporaries. This issue of *El Tiempo* is particularly fruitful, since it was the first issue published after the New Mexican populace approved a state constitution on January 21, 1911. New Mexican statehood had been one of the rallying cries of *nuevomexicano* cultural production for the previous thirty years, so one might expect the editors of *El Tiempo* to devote the entire issue to celebrating this important political victory. However, the small literary section on the third page of the newspaper goes in a different direction. In addition to Darío's "Caso," the section reprints a fictional vignette by the Honduran writer Froylán Turcios and a lyric prose fragment by Isabel Elías. Evidence suggests that the fragment by Elías was an original publication.[16] Juxtaposing Elías's contribution to the reprinted writings of Turcios and Darío lends her some of the more esteemed writers' cultural capital. She literally inhabits the same textual space as the *modernista* icons.

All three literary texts published by *El Tiempo* in this issue center on existential anxiety, though they approach that anxiety from different angles. "Caso" begins as the story of "un cruzado caballero" (a star-crossed knight) who is wounded when the tip of a lance pierces him near his heart. A doctor tells the knight that he will die if the lance tip is removed, but the knight dies anyway. The poem then pivots as the speaker addresses his lover, Asunción, to tell her that he is like the knight:

> Pues el caso es verdadero:
> Yo soy el herido, ingrata,
> Y tu amor es el acero;
> Si me lo quitas, me muero,
> Si me lo dejas me mata!

> [Well, the story is true:
> I am the wounded, O ingrate,
> And your love is the lance;
> If you take it away, I'll die,
> And if you leave it, it will kill me!][17]

Darío's poem thus uses the inevitability of death as a lever for the speaker's romantic overture. This fits well with Turcio's contribution, a fictional vignette titled "Los años lentos que pasan." The vignette appears to be excerpted from a longer work of fiction, as the first paragraph uses pronouns with no antecedents to describe a couple who feel "una sombra mortuoria" (a morbid shadow) fall over them one evening. The vignette amounts to a short conversation between the man and woman in which the man laments the march of time, using an image that resonates strongly with the lance that pierces the knight's heart in "Caso": "A veces el recuerdo se clava como un áspid sobre el corazón y prende una nueva tiniebla en la noche de mi tedio profundo" (Sometimes memory cleaves to my heart like an asp and spurs a new darkness in the night of my deepest ennui).[18] The woman agrees and the two sit in silence, reflecting on the futility of existence. "Caso" and "Los años lentes que pasan" mark an existential turn in *modernismo*, in which form and beauty cannot fully compensate for the threat of annihilation.

Turcio's and Darío's texts animate and highlight the existential anxiety of Elías's "Como el rio"—sandwiched between the other two texts—even as Elías's lyric allegory departs in important ways from its *modernista* neighbors. "Como el rio" is a lyric description of a river that begins as a spring at the summit of a mountain: "Cuatro gotas, que más tarde se convierten en un hilillo cristalino que con delicadeza suma cae primero y luego se arrastra, como si temiera romperse, formando un riachuelo que crece y crece como vida que nace, con su misma variedad, con sus mismas alternativas" (Four drops, which later become a crystalline thread, which with supreme delicacy rushes at first and then drags, as if afraid of breaking itself, forming a creek that grows and grows like a life being born, with the same variety, with the same alternatives).[19] The sentence's syntactic abundance mimics the birth and growth of the river, flowing through restrictive clauses and participial constructions and announcing the conceit subtly, as if life were the metaphor for the river, rather than the other way around. Eventually the *riachuelo* becomes a mighty river, but at the point where it is widest, and its current strongest, the river is like a man who arrives at old age only to realize that his journey is almost done, and there is no way to change the course of past events: "Las aguas se suceden, y como vidas de su vida, siguen y siguen el mismo derrotero y hacen el mismo derrubio que él hiciera, terminando al fin su vida, muy corta, aunque parezca larga, en el mar, en ese mar insondable y en donde como en una eternidad desaparece una vida á todas igualada por la muerte" (The waters pass, and like lives of his life, they follow and follow the same course and carve the same track that he has made, finally finishing their life, so short, though it appears long, in the sea, in that fathomless sea where, as in eternity, one life and all others equalized by death disappear).[20] In contrast to Turcios's and Darío's texts, in which the relationship of two individuals heightens the threat of death, Elías's lyric depicts death as the great leveler and the confrontation with death as ultimately isolating.

To see Latino/a serials as one node in a hemispheric network of textual circulation is to counterpoint the historically nationalist organization of Latino/a studies. Elías's allegory implies a moral lesson, that individuals should not be deceived by self-importance, but, as in "Caso," the formal beauty of the lyric is just as important as the theme or content. "Como el rio" is, in fact, a stunning piece of writing, one that stands on its own. But setting Elías alongside Turcios and Darío gives readers a curated sense of a literary zeitgeist. "Como el rio" is successful not only because of its singular refinement but also because of how it taps into that zeitgeist. Cultural capital is at play here; the editors of *El Tiempo* (Marcial and Luis Valdez) would have counted on Darío and, to a lesser extent, Turcios to lend some of the prestige of their names to legitimize Elías's text. But the formal and thematic resonances of the three texts suggest that recognition is as important here as cultural capital: both the readers' recognition of shared human experiences and the texts' implicit recognition of each other as interlocutors.[21] Appearing in Las Cruces, Elías's text could be construed as an example of borderlands modernism, but the more capacious field designation of Latino/a modernism helps make sense of its hemispheric affiliations.

Darío, *Modernismo*, and Class Consciousness

The class politics of *modernismo* must be considered alongside the geographic scale of field designations. As a paradigm, Latino/a modernism allows us to see how hemispheric consciousness informed Latino/a critiques of US capitalism. One interesting place to test this hypothesis is in Mexican exile and immigrant newspapers fomenting the ideology known as *México de afuera* or "Mexico from abroad." Kanellos has described *México de afuera* as essentially a conservative antiassimilationist stance promulgated by "cultural elites" whose "cultural and business entrepreneurship exerted leadership in all phases of life in the colonia."[22] One of the most important of those cultural elites was Ignacio E. Lozano, the founder of *La Prensa*, the Spanish-language daily in San Antonio that became the preeminent Mexican newspaper of the Southwest. Yet even as the frequent appearance of Darío's poetry in *La Prensa* might invite us to reconsider the nature of Mexican immigrant nationalism, it might also reaffirm a portrait of Spanish-language print culture as essentially a bourgeois institution disconnected from the interests of the working-class masses that predominated in Latino/a communities.

I want to argue that this is an accurate, but not fully sufficient, account of *modernismo*'s place in Latino/a print culture, taking as a case study the appearance of "Sonatina" in *La Prensa* in 1914. One of the most important poems of Darío's 1896 book *Prosas profanas*, "Sonatina" distills Darío's vision of *modernista* poetry into its purest form. Cathy L. Jrade describes "Sonatina" as providing "a bold, far-reaching statement of the *modernista* project," writing that the poem captures Darío's ambivalent attempt to incorporate wealth and luxury into his poetry while rejecting them in favor of the aesthetic realm.[23] The poem centers on a princess who feels imprisoned by her wealth and position:

> ¡Pobrecita princesa de los ojos azules!
> Está presa en sus oros, está presa en sus tules,
> en la jaula de mármol del palacio real.

> [Poor blue-eyed princess!
> She is imprisoned by her gold, imprisoned by her tulles,
> in the marble cage of the royal palace.][24]

In the poem's final stanza, however, the princess's fairy godmother comforts her with the promise of salvation:

> —Calla, calla, princesa—dice el hada madrina
> En caballo con alas hacia acá se encamina,
> En el cinto la espada y en la mano el azor,
> El feliz caballero que te adora sin verte,
> Y que llega de lejos, vencedor de la Muerte
> A encenderte los labios con un beso de amor!

> ["Quiet, quiet, Princess," says the fairy godmother.
> "He is riding here on a winged horse
> With a sword by his side and a goshawk on his wrist,
> That happy knight who loves you sight unseen,
> And may he come soon, that vanquisher of Death
> To inflame your lips with love's kiss!"][25]

Jrade observes: "The linking of the hero-savior with Pegasus, the horse of the Muses, identifies the hero as an artist. His ability to lead his love, and his readers, out of the imperfect present into a paradisiacal future recalls the Christlike attributes that become a recurrent feature of Darío's later poetry about poetic responsibility."[26] The power of the aesthetic to provide escape or refuge from the imperfections of the material world is emphasized through the poem's form, the layered rhymes and sing-song rhythms of the dactylic alexandrines. The princess's "jaula de mármol" also corresponds to an important feature of *modernista* poetics that

Aching has identified. Noting the recourse of *modernista* poets to portraying "salons, drawing-rooms, cells in castles and monasteries, alcoves, medieval or preindustrial work-rooms, and other private niches," Aching writes that "the *modernistas'* idealization of these exclusive sanctuaries also emblematized and hence captured the aspirations of the monied classes to cultivate the art of leisure away from the 'debasing' commercial and industrial labor upon which they depended for their own economic welfare."[27] In its Latin American context, then, the poem already has complex class commitments. Its implicit celebration of art over and against the spiritual emptiness of the princess's possessions could be taken as a critique of bourgeois materialism. Yet its appropriation of the beauty of the princess's possessions and its vision of private contemplation suggest a deep investment in bourgeois subjectivity.

The poem's signification in *La Prensa* is equally complex. "Sonatina" may appear to bolster *La Prensa's* elitist values, offering its presumably middle-class readers a sense of their cultural superiority. However, the poem's republication in the newspaper transforms its material appearance. *Modernismo's* frequently noted drive toward aesthetic autonomy was a function of the material circulation of its texts as much as it was of the content or form of those texts. As Julio Ramos has shown, autonomy for Martí, Darío, and other *modernistas* was a decades-long process of leaving the constraints of the newspaper and mass culture *behind.*[28] But because uneven capitalist development constrained the publication and circulation possibilities in the Latino/a literary field, the newspaper was precisely the place where *modernismo* found its primary home in the United States. Darío published *Prosas profanas* in 1896 in Buenos Aires under the prestigious imprint Pablo Coni e Hijos, with a print run of just five hundred copies. He issued another limited edition in Paris in 1901. In both cases, the poem was marked by both the prestige of the publisher and the bibliographic codes that signaled the imprimatur of the Latin American literary elite.[29] By contrast, when "Sonatina" appears in *La Prensa*, it does so divorced from the full weight of Darío's cultural capital. Rather than inhabiting the pure, autonomous realm of the aesthetic, a poem dwelling among other poems, it inhabits the more constrained, porous aesthetic space of the newspaper's literature page, planted among *avisos económicos* (classified ads), short stories, an editorial notice, and several commercial advertisements (fig. 1).

It would be a mistake to exaggerate the differences in poetic circulation in Latin America and the United States, as well as the influence on readers of the strange juxtapositions often created by newspaper publishing. The development of literary book and magazine publishing in Latin America did not happen all at once, and many of Darío's poems found homes in newspapers throughout the Americas in the early twentieth century. Nevertheless, as emblematic of a larger trend, the central role that newspapers played in circulating Darío's poetry to US Latinos marks the difference between a Latin American bourgeoisie becoming newly ascendant through fin de siècle liberal modernization and a Latino/a petty bourgeoisie whose economic and cultural influence was constrained by its structural marginalization and the increasing proletarianization and racialization of Latinos nationwide. Kanellos is not wrong to label Lozano and other Spanish-language

Figure 1. "Literatura y Variedades" page in *La Prensa*, San Antonio, TX, October 31, 1914. Page image created from the archives of the Recovering the U.S.-Hispanic Literary Heritage Project.

newspaper owners "cultural elites," but that designation is a relative one. He notes that "the defense of the community was also important to the immigrant press. Hispanic newspapers in particular were sensitive to racism and abuse of immigrant rights."[30] *La Prensa* fits this description. The same issue that reprints "Sonatina" contains front-page headlines criticizing the US Marine occupation of Veracruz and a proposed Arizona law requiring Mexican immigrants to naturalize in order to maintain employment. Mexican nationalism meant that Lozano's conservatism existed in a balance with the sense that all Mexicans, regardless of class, belonged together in a common cause.

Moreover, the relationship of "Sonatina" to its surroundings in *La Prensa* suggests the constraints that the newspaper as a medium put on *modernista* literary autonomy. This includes the advertisements on the same page, and news, editorials, and other notions of the literary in play in the issue. In addition to the multiple advertisements encouraging subscriptions, the October 31, 1914, issue includes three book lists for titles sold at the Librería Lozano, the bookstore operated by Lozano out of the same building as the newspaper press. Kanellos observes that "large commercial newspapers were founded to serve broad segments of the transmigrant communities, with articles that appealed to workers as well as to middle- and upper-class readers and, through the fashion and food pages, even to middle-class women."[31] The heterogeneity of the newspaper audience is suggested by competing notions of the literary circulating in the paper. Contrast the literature page—featuring Darío alongside Nervo, the avatar of Mexican *modernismo*—with the list of "Libros de Aventuras" that appears a few pages earlier, advertising "*Aventuras de Sherlock Holmes*, el terror de los criminales" (*Adventures of Sherlock Holmes*, the bane of all criminals) for forty cents each.[32] In fact, the Librería Lozano carried very little *modernista* poetry. Among the three book lists in this issue, only one carries a recognizably *modernista* title, *El parnaso español contemporáneo*, and at $1.25 it was considerably more expensive than the standard adventure novel.

To see the newspaper as a heterogeneous space implies holding out the possibility that Darío's poetry might be put to more than one use. Jrade's reading of "Sonatina," for example, is perfectly in keeping with the *modernista* ethos of literary autonomy that scholars have described. But if Latino/a bourgeois subjectivity evolved as culturally bound to Latino/a working-class subjectivity, then we might read "Sonatina" differently. In fact, another reading is provocatively implied by the poem's appearance more than a decade later in the Edinburg weekly newspaper *El Defensor*, where it was reprinted as "Sonatina a la desconacida [*sic*]."[33] The modified title is transformative. Whereas "Sonatina" indicates an autonomous musical form, the newly transitive "Sonatina *a* la desconacida" indicates a song sung *to* another person. The term *desconacida*—either a typographical error or a colloquial rendering of *desconocida*—is provocatively ambiguous. *Desconocida* could indicate someone who is unknown, anonymous, or someone who is a stranger because she is foreign or exotic.

Presumably the *desconocida* is the princess, but in a conventional reading of the poem, the princess's primary problem isn't that she is unknown; it's that her material wealth and luxury fail to provide spiritual sustenance. One way of explaining the transformation to "Sonatina a la desconocida" is to look at how *El Defensor* frames the poem. Unlike *La Prensa*, which reprints the poem on a page devoted to literature, *El Defensor* puts its literature section, which amounts to two columns, in the center of its "Pagina del Hogar" ("Page of the Home") (fig. 2). The poem is flanked by "Sección para Damas" ("Section for Ladies") on one side and "Para los Niños" ("For Children") on the other, effectively feminizing and infantilizing

Figure 2. "Pagina del Hogar" page in *El Defensor*, Edinburg, TX, March 20, 1931. Page image created from the archives of the Recovering the U.S.-Hispanic Literary Heritage Project.

literary discourse. This bourgeois gesture is different from simple literary autonomy. It corresponds to what Georg Lukács describes as reification, the "rational objectification" of society under capitalism.[34] Moving literature to the domestic, feminine realm implies that it has little use value beyond moral refinement. At the same time, the transformation of the poem's title suggests how the editor of the "Pagina del Hogar" might have pushed back against the marginal place of women's culture in the newspaper. What was once a poem about the power of the aesthetic embodied in a masculine figure—the knight who comes to the princess's rescue at the end of the poem—is now a poem centering more fully on the unknowability of the woman. That unknowability might be a function of her gender or, if we take *desconocida* to indicate foreignness, a result of her doubly marginal place as an immigrant woman in the United States.

A more potent example of a Latino/a serial using a Darío poem for decidedly nonbourgeois ends is the publication of "Marina" in the New York leftist magazine *Pueblos Hispanos* in 1944. Like "Sonatina," "Marina" was originally published in *Prosas profanas*, part of a group of poems that Darío added for the 1901 Paris edition. Also like "Sonatina," "Marina" can be taken as an expression of *modernista* poetics in its celebration of French symbolist poets. The poem depicts a speaker about to embark on a journey to the island of Cythera, the mythical home of Aphrodite. As he departs the speaker bids farewell to his homelands:

> "Adiós—dije—países que me fuisteis esquivos;
> adiós peñascos enemigos del poeta."
> . . . .
> Mi barca era la misma que condujo a Gautier
> y que Verlaine un día para Chipre fletó,
> y provenía de
> el divino Astillero del divino Watteau.

> ["Goodbye—I said—you lands who rejected me;
> goodbye, treacherous enemies of the poet."
> . . . .
> My ship was the same one that carried Gautier
> and that Verlaine once chartered for Cyprus,
> and it came from
> the divine Shipyard of the divine Watteau.][35]

The speaker depicts himself as departing lands inhospitable to the practice of poetry and setting out in the same ship as his French precursors Théophile Gautier and Paul Verlaine. The reference to the eighteenth-century French painter Jean-Antoine Watteau associates the aesthetic refinement of symbolism with the ornamentation of rococo style. For the speaker of the poem, these are the purest forms of aesthetic expression, and such a speaker corresponds precisely to the dictum of "art for art's sake" often associated with *modernismo* (first credited, in fact, to Gautier). Darío thus sets up a central tension in "Marina" between the implicit backwardness of Latin America and true modern expression as embodied in French poetry.

Yet "Marina" dramatically pivots away from this opposition in the end, and as it does so, it points toward the kind of *latinoamericanismo* that *Pueblos Hispanos* promoted. As he departs, seemingly happy in his quest, the speaker hears a phantom crying out on the beach:

> Entonces, fijo del azur en lo infinito,
> para olvidar del todo las amarguras viejas,
> como Aquiles un día, me tapé las orejas.
> Y les dije a las brisas: "Soplad, soplad más fuerte;
> soplad hacia las costas de la isla de la Vida."
> Y en la playa quedaba desolada y perdida
> una ilusión que aullaba como un perro a la Muerte.
>
> [Then, fixed upon the infinite blue of the horizon,
> to forget above all the old bitternesses,
> like Achilles one day, I covered my ears.
> And I said to the breezes: "Blow, blow stronger;
> blow toward the coasts of the Isle of Life."
> And on the beach the phantom remained
> desolate and lost, howling like a dog to Death.][36]

The confusion of metaphors around Achilles suggests the extent of the speaker's denial and repression. It is not Achilles whose hearing is blocked, of course, but the men aboard Odysseus's ship, whose ears their captain fills with wax to protect them from the Sirens' song. The confusion results from a clever line break; Achilles is the one who forgets his resentments after the death of Patroclus in the *Iliad* and agrees to fight once again with the Greeks. But this makes the speaker's comparison of himself to Achilles nonsensical. Rather than show courage, like Achilles, he covers his ears and flees. For all the speaker's bluster about forsaking his benighted homelands, he proves himself cowardly and naive. The poem leaves us not with the refined beauty of Gautier or Verlaine but with a decidedly untypical image for a Darío poem, the phantom howling like a dog. The speaker cannot fully repress or leave behind the "países esquivos" (disdainful countries) he denigrates earlier in the poem. "Marina" thus demonstrates a high degree of self-consciousness about the subordinated relationship of Latin American aesthetics to European aesthetics, and although Darío has often been characterized as Frenchified, the poem intimates that it is foolish to think that poetry can keep one safe from the world as it is. Like it or not, the poem suggests, you are Latin American through and through. This idea strongly resonates with the editorial vision of *Pueblos Hispanos*, reprinted in each issue in a sidebar titled "El porque de *Pueblos Hispanos*." The statement calls for the unity of "todas las colonias hispanas en Estados Unidos" (all the Hispanic colonies in the United States), including "puertorriqueños, filipinos, mexicanos, etc." (Puerto Ricans, Filipinos, Mexicans, etc.), as well as "mejores relaciones entre las Américas mediante la difusión de las culturas hispanas" (better relations among the Americas through the diffusion of Hispanic cultures).[37]

Pueblos Hispanos provides evidence that Darío's poetry could signify in vastly different ways in Latino/a print culture—for instance, by being instrumentalized for leftist politics. *Pueblos Hispanos* was printed as a sixteen-page magazine, and "Marina" sits on the right-hand side of the centerfold page, alongside an article titled "El poder soviético" ("Soviet Power") by the Reverend Hewlett Johnson, an English cleric whose socialist politics earned him the sobriquet "The Red Dean of Canterbury." (The article was translated by the Puerto Rican nationalist poet and playwright René Jiménez Malaret.) The same issue includes articles about fascist influences in England (reprinted from the *Daily Worker*), the initiation of the Bracero Program, and Nicolás Guillén and the advent of Afro-Cuban poetry. Like all issues of *Pueblos Hispanos*, which was founded in 1943 by the Puerto Rican nationalists Juan Antonio Corretjer and Clemente Soto Vélez, the issue also includes several articles calling for Puerto Rican independence and denouncing Francisco Franco's fascist government in Spain. A reading audience savvy enough to situate Corretjer, Soto Vélez, and Guillén in hemispheric literary movements would know that Darío was no revolutionary, but his status as the leading poet of the era in which *latinoamericanismo* became ascendant means that he could still be marshaled for leftist hemispheric politics.

Conclusion: Remembering Darío

In addition to the hundreds of Darío poems reprinted in Latino/a serials, Spanish-language newspapers published several dozen poems paying homage to Darío after his death in February 1916. These homages deserve their own article; the series of poems published by Gilberto Díaz in *La Prensa* in 1939 are particularly interesting. To conclude this essay, I want to highlight one of these homages as an index of the conflicted class politics of many Latino/a serials. The poem— "Requiescat in pace!," by J. Restrepo Gómez—was published in the July 10, 1916, issue of *La Prensa*, five months after Darío's death. The poem apostrophizes Darío as a new deity, addressing him as "Padre nuestro / que estás en los cielos con Hugo y Verlaine" (Our Father / who art in heaven with Hugo and Verlaine) and asking for his intervention:

> Ruega por nosotros, tú que también fuiste,
> en tu revoltosa peregrinación,
> un desengañado y un loco y un triste
> con llagas profundas en el corazón.

> Vela por nosotros, Maestro Darío,
> por piedad ampara nuestra pequeñez
> y líbranos siempre de tanto judío,
> de tanto canalla, de tanto burgués.

> [Pray for us, you who were also,
> in your rebellious wandering,
> disillusioned and crazy and sad
> with deep wounds in your heart.

> Pray for us, Master Darío,
> cover our smallness with devotion
> and free us from so much Jew,
> from so much swine, from so much bourgeois.][38]

The "us" of the poem refers to poets, but the poem's depiction of Darío as a patron saint for wandering sufferers seems apt also for the migrant readership of *La Prensa*. After all, the ethos of *México de afuera*, as Kanellos has noted, is grief at being expelled from the land of nativity, along with a desire to return. But what truly stands out in Restrepo Gómez's poem is the earnest prayer for salvation from "tanto judío," "tanto canalla," and "tanto burgués." Understanding the resonance of these terms for both Darío and the readership of *La Prensa* can help illuminate the complicated class politics of Latino/a serials as literary institutions.

The apparent disdain in the poem's invocation of "tanto burgués" would not be out of place in today's academic circles—though perhaps not amplified by the anti-Semitism implicit in "tanto judío"—but it also reflects anxieties specific to early twentieth-century hemispheric contexts. As Ericka Beckman notes in a discussion of Darío's influential short story "El rey burgués," from *Azul*: "The term 'bourgeois' . . . was not widely used in the late nineteenth century. It was *modernismo*, and perhaps even Darío's story, that put the term in greater circulation. According to the story, to speak 'bourgeois' is to speak the language of the universal equivalent, what Marx called *warensprache*, or the language of commodities."[39] The French term *bourgeois*, which Marx used to describe the capitalist class, referred to owners of industrial means of production who innovated the independent labor contract that perfected capitalist exploitation of labor. But as Beckman points out, "The bourgeois labor contract . . . had not become predominant in late nineteenth-century Spanish American societies, either in the world of writers or in Spanish American societies at large."[40] Nevertheless, Beckman argues that Darío was aware of a dramatic transformation in the economic organization of the Americas as Latin American nations became enmeshed in global circuits of capital by exporting natural resources. The introduction of the term *bourgeois* to describe such a shift is paradoxical. For Aching, Darío and the *modernistas* represent the ascendance of the Latin American bourgeoisie, yet that ascendance happens in large part through a repeated critique of bourgeois materialism, and in particular a critique of the United States as embodying bourgeois values.

That critique certainly seems active in "Requiescat in pace!," but it is also inflected with the specific conditions of migrant life in the United States, where the bourgeois labor contract was very much a part of life, and where Latinos were subject to brutally exploitative labor conditions. (It's instructive to note that several Latino/a serials reprinted "El rey burgués," including *La Prensa*, which ran the story on January 26, 1915, little more than a year before Restrepo Gómez's poem.) The small Latino bourgeois (or petty bourgeois) class found itself perpetually in danger of proletarianization, and the lack of upward mobility for working-class migrants only underscored the racial stratification of US capitalism. To be liberated from "tanto burgués" in Restrepo Gómez's poem thus signifies on multiple levels.

These multiple levels of meaning gesture at the central role that Darío and other *modernista* poets played in laying the framework for early Latino/a literature. They provided a critique of US materialism from the standpoint of a spiritualized *latinoamericanismo* that could be repurposed in the United States as an incipient Latino/a consciousness, even in places where regional or national commitments predominated. That Latino/a consciousness transforms into critiques of the exploitation experienced by Latino/a workers in such texts as Alirio Díaz Guerra's *Lucas Guevara* (1914) and Daniel Venegas's *Las aventuras de don Chipote* (1928), anarchist and socialist tracts such as Luisa Capetillo's *Influencia de las ideas modernas* (1916), and meditations on Latino/a petty bourgeois anxiety and the vanishing landed class in novels like Jovita González and Margaret Eimer's *Caballero* (1997) and Paredes's *George Washington Gómez* (1990), both written in the 1930s. Only in light of the prolific Spanish-language print culture of the early twentieth century do these texts begin to clarify as constituting the field of Latino/a modernism.

JOHN ALBA CUTLER is associate professor of English and Latina/o studies at Northwestern University and author of *Ends of Assimilation: The Formation of Chicano Literature* (2015).

Notes

1   Brady, "Borderlands Modernism," 106.
2   See, e.g., Casanova, *World Republic of Letters*; and Siskind, *Cosmopolitan Desires*.
3   Aching, *Politics of Spanish American "Modernismo,"* 6.
4   Brady, "Borderlands Modernism," 106.
5   Lomas, *Translating Empire*, 231.
6   McGill, *American Literature*, 10.
7   Notable exceptions to this trend include Gruesz, *Ambassadors of Culture*; and Coronado, *World Not to Come.*
8   To give a sense of just a few of the gaps, the Readex database contains no issues of the New Orleans literary magazine *Mercurio* or the Los Angeles daily newspaper *Opinión*, and its coverage of the New York daily newspaper *La Prensa* stops at 1930.
9   These numbers are based on my own count of Kanellos and Martell, *Hispanic Periodicals in the United States.*
10   *Las Dos Repúblicas*, "Two Republics."
11   Because there are no conveniently accessible archives of *El Diario de Centro América*, I cannot ascertain if the poem was originally published under the title "Sinfonía" and then changed when Darío included it in *Cantos de vida y esperanza* a decade later.
12   Meyer, *Speaking for Themselves*, 6. Although Meyer is probably correct that New Mexico produced more Spanish-language newspapers than any other region, that fact is slightly misleading, since many New Mexican newspapers were ephemeral projects, lasting only a few issues. While New Mexican print culture was undoubtedly lively, in terms of total production the urban centers of Los Angeles, San Antonio, and New York surpassed it.

13   Meléndez, *Spanish-Language Newspapers*, 135.
14   Chacón's writings are available in *The Writings of Eusebio Chacón.* For more on Chacón's short novels, see Cutler, "Eusebio Chacón's America."
15   Meyer, *Speaking for Themselves*, 70.
16   In contrast to Turcios and Darío, Elías's name appears directly under the title of her text in standard typeface, rather than at the end in small capitals. At least two individuals with the name Isabel Elías appear on census records in the region during this period: one born in 1879 in Arizona and residing in Tucson, and one born in 1890 in Mexico and residing in El Paso. Given El Paso's proximity to Las Cruces, the latter is the more likely candidate. See "United States Census, 1940," database with images, *FamilySearch* (familysearch.org/ark:/61903/1:1: KWV7-7TY), Isabel G. Elias in household of Juan Elias, San Elizario, Justice Precinct 4, El Paso, Texas; citing enumeration district (ED) 71-18, sheet 9B, line 65, family 159, Sixteenth Census of the United States, 1940, NARA digital publication T627, Records of the Bureau of the Census, 1790–2007, RG 29, National Archives and Records Administration, 2012, roll 4028, Washington, DC.
17   Darío, "Caso." The *El Tiempo* reprinting drops the inverted exclamation mark before the penultimate line. Unless otherwise indicated, all English translations are my own.
18   Turcios, "Los años lentos que pasan."
19   Elías, "Como el rio."
20   Elías, "Como el rio."
21   Rita Felski describes recognition as a fundamental practice of reading: "Reading may offer a solace and relief not to be found elsewhere, confirming that I am not entirely alone, that there are others who think or feel

like me. Through this experience of affiliation, I feel myself acknowledged; I am rescued from the fear of invisibility, from the terror of not being seen" (*Uses of Literature*, 33).

22   Kanellos, *Hispanic Immigrant Literature*, 40.

23   Jrade, *Modernismo*, 81.

24   Darío, "Sonatina."

25   Darío, "Sonatina."

26   Jrade, *Modernismo*, 78.

27   Aching, *Politics of Spanish American "Modernismo,"* 28.

28   Ramos argues that "the newspaper was a condition of possibility for literary modernization, although it also brought into being the limits of literature's autonomy" (*Divergent Modernities*, 102).

29   As Lawrence Rainey has shown relative to Anglo modernism, the limited edition was a brilliant strategy for maintaining the illusion of aesthetic autonomy while taking advantage of the principle of scarcity to increase the exchange value of the book commodity (*Institutions of Modernism*).

30   Kanellos, *Hispanic Immigrant Literature*, 36.

31   Kanellos, *Hispanic Immigrant Literature*, 39.

32   *La Prensa*, "Libros de Aventuras."

33   Darío, "Sonatina a la desconacida [sic]."

34   Rationalization is the attempt to systematize life through the regulation of time, maximizing efficiency. Objectification refers to the instrumentalization of both things and people (Lukács, *History and Class Consciousness*, 92).

35   Darío, "Marina."

36   Darío, "Marina."

37   Corretjer, "El porque de *Pueblos Hispanos.*" This reading of "Marina" runs counter to a common narrative positing that Darío embraced *latinoamericanismo* in *Cantos de vida y esperanza* only after 1898. Surely Corretjer knew Darío's work intimately enough to understand the implications of framing "Marina" this way.

38   Restrepo Gómez, "Requiescat in pace!"

39   Beckman, *Capital Fictions*, 48–49.

40   Beckman, *Capital Fictions*, 49.

Works Cited

Aching, Gerard. *The Politics of Spanish American "Modernismo": By Exquisite Design.* New York: Cambridge University Press, 1997.

Beckman, Ericka. *Capital Fictions: The Literature of Latin America's Export Age.* Minneapolis: University of Minnesota Press, 2013.

Brady, Mary Pat. "Borderlands Modernism." In *The Cambridge Companion to the American Modernist Novel*, edited by Joshua Miller, 106–21. New York: Cambridge University Press, 2015.

Casanova, Pascal. *The World Republic of Letters*, translated by M. B. Debevoise. Cambridge, MA: Harvard University Press, 2004.

Chacón, Eusebio. *The Writings of Eusebio Chacón*, edited and translated by A. Gabriel Meléndez and Francisco A. Lomelí. Albuquerque: University of New Mexico Press, 2012.

Coronado, Raúl. *A World Not to Come: A History of Latino Writing and Print Culture.* Cambridge, MA: Harvard University Press, 2014.

Corretjer, Juan Antonio. "El porque de *Pueblos Hispanos.*" *Pueblos Hispanos*, January 22, 1944.

Cutler, John Alba. "Eusebio Chacón's America." *MELUS* 36, no. 1 (2011): 109–34.

Darío, Rubén. "Caso." *El Tiempo*, January 18, 1911.

Darío, Rubén. "Marina." *Pueblos Hispanos*, January 22, 1944.

Darío, Rubén. "Sonatina." *La Prensa*, October 31, 1914.

Darío, Rubén. "Sonatina a la desconacida." *El Defensor*, March 20, 1931.

Las Dos Repúblicas. "The Two Republics." Advertisement. July 19, 1892.

Elías, Isabel. "Como el rio." *El Tiempo*, January 28, 1911.

Felski, Rita. *Uses of Literature.* Malden, MA: Wiley-Blackwell, 2008.

Gruesz, Kirsten Silva. *Ambassadors of Culture: The Transamerican Origins of Latino Writing.* Princeton, NJ: Princeton University Press, 2002.

Jrade, Cathy L. *Modernismo, Modernity, and the Development of Spanish American Literature.* Austin: University of Texas Press, 1998.

Kanellos, Nicolás. *Hispanic Immigrant Literature: El Sueño de Retorno.* Austin: University of Texas Press, 2011.

Kanellos, Nicolás, and Helvetia Martell. *Hispanic Periodicals in the United States, Origins to 1960: A Brief History and Comprehensive Bibliography.* Houston: Arte Público, 2000.

Lomas, Laura. *Translating Empire: José Martí, Migrant Latino Subjects, and American Modernities.* Durham, NC: Duke University Press, 2008.

Lukács, Georg. *History and Class Consciousness*, translated by Rodney Livingstone. Cambridge, MA: MIT Press, 1971.

McGill, Meredith. *American Literature and the Culture of Reprinting, 1834–1853.* Philadelphia: University of Pennsylvania Press, 2003.

Meléndez, A. Gabriel. *Spanish-Language Newspapers in New Mexico, 1834–1958.* Tucson: University of Arizona Press, 2005.

Meyer, Doris. *Speaking for Themselves: Neomexicano Cultural Identity and the Spanish-Language Press, 1880–1920.* Albuquerque: University of New Mexico Press, 1996.

La Prensa. "Libros de aventuras." Advertisement. October 31, 1914.

Rainey, Lawrence. *Institutions of Modernism: Literary Elites and Public Culture*. New Haven, CT: Yale University Press, 1998.

Ramos, Julio. *Divergent Modernities: Culture and Politics in Nineteenth-Century Latin America*, translated by John D. Blanco. Durham, NC: Duke University Press, 2001.

Restrepo Gómez, J. "Requiescat in pace!" *La Prensa*, July 10, 1916.

Siskind, Mariano. *Cosmopolitan Desires: Global Modernity and World Literature in Latin America*. Evanston, IL: Northwestern University Press, 2014.

Turcios, Froilán. "Los años lentos que pasan." *El Tiempo*, January 28, 1911.

Telephonic *Modernismo*
Latinidad and Hemispheric Print Culture in the Age of Electricity

KELLEY KREITZ

Abstract   This essay analyzes the Havana-based literary weekly *La Habana Elegante* to consider the hemispheric dimensions of late nineteenth-century media change and the role that writers of Latin American descent played in it. As new electric media and improved print technology powered an expanding and interconnected world of print, *La Habana Elegante* mediated a hemispheric, Spanish-speaking print culture, especially through its foreign correspondence from New York City. The periodical defined that print culture through a notion of *latinidad* that bridged Latin America and the United States—and by envisioning a two-way flow of ideas between writers and readers. As US-based English-language newspapers developed emerging mass cultural forms that starkly divided producers and consumers, *La Habana Elegante* tapped into notions of simultaneity inspired by the telegraph and, especially, the telephone to promote a more interactive modern media system meant to circulate Latin American culture throughout the hemisphere.

Keywords   *modernismo*, *La Habana Elegante*, Julián del Casal, Nicanor Bolet Peraza, Spanish-language press

Writing from New York City in 1887 for the Cuban literary weekly *La Habana Elegante* (*Elegant Havana*), the Venezuelan writer and editor Nicanor Bolet Peraza announced the launch of the *New York Herald*'s Paris edition (later known as the *International Herald Tribune* and, more recently, the *International New York Times*), which took advantage of the new transatlantic telegraph cable to deliver news from New York City to Paris with a delay of only a few hours. Displaying an enthusiasm for the period's new media technologies that is characteristic of the articles he published in his better-known roles as the editor of the New York–based *La Revista Ilustrada de Nueva York* (*New York Illustrated Magazine*) from 1886 to 1890 and as the founding editor of *Las Trés Américas* (*The Three Americas*) from 1893 to 1896, Bolet Peraza casts the *Paris Herald* as much more than a new business endeavor by a leading member of New York's English-language popular press: "Esa hoja puede atravesar en segundos el Atlántico, volar de un hemisferio á otro

ENGLISH LANGUAGE NOTES
56:2, October 2018 DOI 10.1215/00138282-6960779
© 2018 Regents of the University of Colorado

hemisferio . . . y unir á dos mundos en el pensamiento" (That sheet can cross the Atlantic in seconds, fly from one hemisphere to another . . . and join two worlds in thought).[1] Powered by the century's new telegraphic technology, print put what had long been considered the hemisphere of the future on a level playing field with the hemisphere that housed the world powers of the writer's present: "El producto de los cerebros se difunde como atmósfera por todas las latitudes, no existiendo ya el pasado, siendo todo presente, viviendo toda la creación en un solo día" (Mental production spreads like an atmosphere across all latitudes, with the past no longer existing, everything being the present, all creation living in a single day).[2]

This new world of simultaneous experience that enables the exchange of ideas in all directions, Bolet Peraza notes, does not belong to the *Herald* alone: "Parecería de magia si no estuviésemos familiarizados con los fenómenos de la electricidad, si no perteneciéramos como pertenecemos á esta centuria de titanes que han subido á los cielos" (It would appear to be magic if we were not familiar with the phenomenon of electricity, if we did not belong as we do belong to this century of Titans who have risen to the heavens).[3] The *Herald*'s expansion to Paris appears not as a magical feat at which to marvel but as an inspiration—indeed, an invitation—to consider the possibilities afforded by the changing world of print. This media context, in which anything seemed possible, constitutes an important and understudied factor in Latinx lives of the nineteenth century—especially for understanding the contributions of cultural producers like Bolet Peraza, who participated in the literary and media innovation of the 1880s and 1890s.[4]

This essay analyzes the Havana-based periodical *La Habana Elegante*—an elite, illustrated, Spanish-language literary weekly that featured poetry, prose, and cultural news from Europe, Latin America, and the United States—as a window on the hemispheric dimensions of nineteenth-century media change and on the role that cultural producers of Latin American descent played in it. At the very moment when newspapers like the *Herald* were developing in the English-language daily press emerging forms of mass entertainment that drew a stark line between producers and consumers, *La Habana Elegante* engaged with the period's prevalent discussions of simultaneity inspired by the telegraph and, especially, the telephone to explore the possibility of hemispheric, Spanish-language, modern media centered on ideas and on a less passive form of consumption.[5] In conversation with a network of Hispanophone cultural periodicals—especially those of the Spanish-language press in New York City, which *La Habana Elegante* featured in frequent foreign correspondence from that city—the magazine envisioned a new kind of relationship between writers and readers, characterized by a two-way flow of ideas between them. Rewiring the encounter between *La Habana Elegante* and late nineteenth-century notions of simultaneity provides fresh perspectives on a periodical that scholars have primarily understood in relation to the transnational Latin American literary movement of *modernismo*. In addition, my analysis sheds light on the hemisphere as a conceptual framework—or, as Claire Fox described it, "a field for locating particular trajectories."[6] The hemisphere provided the conceptual space in which *La Habana Elegante* generated an emerging idea of *latinidad* through its articulations of a Hispanophone print culture centered on more inclusive cultural production and communication.[7]

Throughout its run from 1883 to 1896 *La Habana Elegante* engaged with new ideas of time and space that circulated widely in the age of electricity. Stephen Kern notes that in the late nineteenth century cultural arenas from psychology to physics to literature developed new ways of conceptualizing the past, the present, and the future, but it was "the sense of the present [that] was the most distinctively new, . . . expanded spatially to create the vast, shared experience of simultaneity."[8] This "ability to experience many distant events at the same time" captured the imaginations of many cultural producers, as Bolet Peraza's reflection on the telegraph illustrates.[9] As *La Habana Elegante* engaged in the conversation about the synchronization of experience in far-flung places that followed the invention of the telegraph earlier in the nineteenth century, its writers' ideas about what simultaneity might ultimately achieve through the printed page also contributed to the surge of speculation that followed the invention of the telephone in 1876.[10] According to William Uricchio, "Although the telegraph before it [the telephone] had transformed Western notions of time and space, the telephone offered something even more radical—the live transmission of voice, the opportunity to direct point-to-point encounters with the simultaneous."[11] This "directable simultaneity," in a sense, made it possible for anyone who had access to a telephone to do what required vast resources like those of the *Herald* to accomplish by telegraph.[12] In Kern's words, "Telephones break down barriers of distance—horizontally across the face of the land and vertically across social strata."[13] That potential to level existing hierarchies and facilitate greater exchange appears in groundbreaking, if also incomplete, ways in *La Habana Elegante*'s most ambitious moments.

In studies of the Latin American literary movement known as *modernismo*, in which most of the research on the period's Spanish-language cultural periodicals like *La Habana Elegante* resides, scholars have long noted the strategic engagement of leading writers and editors with the period's changing world of print.[14] Recently, Andrew Reynolds, Rielle Navitski, and others have situated *modernista* experimentation with new media technologies (especially photography and early film) in relation to periods of media change—a notion that media scholars have employed to challenge teleological approaches to media history and to theorize the role of culture in determining the uses of new technologies.[15] As Lisa Gitelman and Geoffrey Pingree explain, "When new media emerge in a society, their place is at first ill defined, and their ultimate meanings or functions are shaped over time by that society's existing habits of media use . . . , by shared desires for new uses, and by the slow process of adaptation between the two."[16] Periods of media change, in this sense, constitute theaters in which cultural producers wage the type of "war of competing social imaginaries," to borrow Raúl Coronado's words, evident in many nineteenth-century Spanish-language texts.[17] In the case of *La Habana Elegante*, what was at stake was determining whose publications, media practices, ideas, and culture would define hemispheric print culture in the age of electricity.[18]

As they explored where the period's new electric media might lead, *La Habana Elegante*'s editors and contributors constructed a notion of hemispheric *latinidad* that demonstrates Robert McKee Irwin's insight that nineteenth-century *latinidad* is "an unstable, sometimes volatile, and often incomplete transnational process."[19]

Scholars have located some of the earliest notions of pan–Latin American identity, along with the origins of the term *Latin America*, in mid-nineteenth-century French efforts to gain influence in areas colonized by Spain and Portugal.[20] Although those French foundations clearly influenced writers associated with *modernismo* as they made their own attempts to conceive "a Spanish American cultural space," neither the terminology for describing the region and its people nor the sense of common experience that such terminology was meant to evoke had found solid ground by the end of the nineteenth century.[21]

In *La Habana Elegante* and its community of Spanish-language cultural periodicals, the language showed the variability of a still inchoate idea. At times, writers employed phrases such as an 1895 *La Habana Elegante* article's appeal to "nuestra raza, la noble raza hispano-americana" (our people, the noble Spanish American people).[22] As in that example, writers at times made use of the adjective *hispano-americano/a* (which was sometimes spelled without the hyphen). The adjective *latino/a* also appeared somewhat less often. None of these words or phrases evoked the subject positions that exist today, nor did they draw the same lines that now separate Latin American and Latinx cultural traditions. On the contrary, as one of Bolet Peraza's editorial notes published in *La Revista Ilustrada de Nueva York* makes explicit, the point was to find new ways to unite and empower "los pueblos de nuestra raza en este hemisferio" (the people of our race in this hemisphere).[23] *Latinidad*, in this context, thus constitutes a possibility that was still unfolding—one inseparable from *La Habana Elegante*'s attempts to establish a more interactive media system meant to circulate Latin American culture throughout the hemisphere.

La Habana Elegante's Hemispheric *Latinidad*

Throughout its run *La Habana Elegante* exhibits a tension between its status as a Cuban publication, which catered its literary selections and cultural news to an elite Cuban audience, and its participation in a network of Spanish-language editors and writers united by a "hemispheric ethos."[24] An 1888 self-promotional article transports us into *La Habana Elegante*'s discursive landscape through a description of the magazine as a dear friend who drops by the reader's home each week around sunset: "A esa hora, os supongo, bella lectora, regando las escogidas plantas que ornan y perfuman con sus pintadas flores vuestro patio, vuestro azotea ó vuestro balcón" (I imagine you at that hour, lovely reader, watering the arranged plants that adorn and perfume with their painted flowers your patio, your terraced roof, or your balcony).[25] Employing the exquisite imagery and invocations to an imagined female readership that were characteristic of *modernismo*, the article locates *La Habana Elegante* in an exclusive Cuban context—in the elite homes of central Havana. The magazine enters that comfortable setting as a cultivated connoisseur, who offers "un juicio crítico concienzudo y noticias artísticas de todas partes" (a thorough review and artistic news from everywhere) to a cultural world whose center is Havana.[26]

Although Havana typically appears in the weekly as a lively literary capital, it takes on a very different form in the expressions of frustration with the Spanish colonial administration that occasionally burst through *La Habana Elegante*'s bookish scenery. One editor laments that in Havana "todo es desorden, desidia y desaseo" (all is disorder, carelessness, and uncleanliness).[27] The article casts blame surprisingly directly, given the censorship laws that governed the Cuban press at the time: "Censuramos, con justicia, al Municipio" (We censure, justly, the municipality), whose "deber de implantar en la Habana . . . puerto comercial" (duty of establishing in Havana . . . a commercial port) prioritizes Spain's economic interests over the city's well-being.[28]

While some lamentations about "las calles [que] no pueden ser peores" (the streets [that] could not be worse) seem to mimic *modernista* malaise, others display the periodical's characteristic humor.[29] An 1887 article called "Una nevada en La Habana" ("A Snowfall in Havana") tells the story of a nearsighted correspondent who, having lost his glasses and recently arrived in Havana from Ecuador, mistakes all the dust in the city for snow: "Los techos de las lindas y elevadas casas, sus barandas, vidrieras, todo estaba blanco. Los asientos de los parques, las flores, las fuentes, los árboles ¡qué espectáculo tan hermoso! ¡blanco, blanco, todo cargado de purísima nieve!" (The rooftops of the tall and beautiful houses, their handrails, stained glass—all was white. The park benches, flowers, fountains, trees—what a beautiful spectacle! White, white, all filled with the purest snow!).[30] With bitter irony, the article turns the conditions that plague precisely the central Havana neighborhood that houses *La Habana Elegante*'s most privileged class of readers into cause for celebration. When the narrative ultimately reveals that the so-called snowfall "no es más que una broma que quieren dar los Padres del pueblo á los inocentes corresponsales de las naciones extranjeras" (is nothing more than a prank that the fathers of the town want to play on the innocent correspondents of foreign nations), it is clear that the real joke is on the colonial administrators responsible for the city's deteriorating infrastructure.[31]

As Havana decays under colonial rule, New York figures in the magazine as an idealized Cuban space. The periodical's correspondence from that city regularly features "lo que ocurra por acá en la colonia cubana" (what is happening here in the Cuban community), whose members included José Martí, as well as the writer, publisher, and Spanish-language bookstore owner Nestor Poncé de León and the novelist Cirilio Villaverde.[32] In *La Habana Elegante*'s Cuban New York City, for example, "Coney Island en todo su esplendor" (Coney Island in all its splendor) is "lleno de familias cubanas" (full of Cuban families).[33] The correspondent Luis A. Baralt portrays New York's iconic modern attraction as a haven for Cubans, including two leading figures of the city's Spanish-language press: "Ayer tuve el gusto de ver allí á los amigos José Martí y Enrique Trujillo, que piensan pasar todo el verano en ese pueblo" (Yesterday I had the pleasure of seeing there friends José Martí and Enrique Trujillo, who are thinking of spending the whole summer in that town).[34] *La Habana Elegante*'s New York becomes, as Baralt writes in another letter from New York, the "Centro Cubano en los Estados Unidos" (Cuban center of the United States)."[35]

But in New York City it becomes harder for *La Habana Elegante* to focus exclusively on "los escritores cubanos de más reputación" (the most reputable Cuban writers), especially in reports on the publishing activities of that city's Spanish-language press.[36] Announcing that Martí's children's magazine *La Edad de Oro* (*The Golden Age*) "debe salir de las prensas hoy mismo" (should come off the presses today), Baralt describes the periodical's intended audience as "los niños de América latina" (the children of Latin America).[37] He pictures, in contrast to the Cuban cultural space constructed by some of *La Habana Elegante*'s articles, a transnational audience, which he refers to again as that of "la América española" (Spanish America).[38] A similar notion of a Spanish-speaking transnational audience appears in an 1888 editorial note announcing the publication of Martí's translation of Helen Hunt Jackson's novel *Ramona*: "Aplaudimos la idea de su versión á un idioma que habla la mitad de América tanto más también cuanto el asunto es completamente americano" (We applaud the idea of its translation into a language spoken by half of America—even more so because its subject matter is fully American).[39] The passage exhibits the leading role that language plays in characterizing the periodical's transnational community of readers. The new translation speaks to the "half of America" for which English is a foreign language. At the same time, the language barrier that the description constructs does not prevent access to something "more fully American" that, the editors seem to hope at least, unites the hemisphere's parts.

Indeed, in most of *La Habana Elegante*'s reflections on its Hispanophone print community, the hemisphere appears as an undivided site of circulation and exchange—as in an editorial notice called "Nuestros huéspedes" ("Our Guests"), which mentions "los ilustrados colegas que nos han honrado con su visita" (the illustrious colleagues who have honored us as our guests).[40] The notice lists the Hispanophone periodicals with which *La Habana Elegante* has connections, organized by the following locations: "Estados Unidos, Méjico, Venezuela, Isla de Trinidad, Colombia, Santo Domingo, Rep. Argentina, Curaçao, Jamaica, Guatemala, Ecuador, Honduras."[41] On display here is a Hispanophone print culture that stretches from the United States (where *La Revista Ilustrada de Nueva York*, which was then edited by Bolet Peraza, appears first on the list), to the Caribbean, to South America—including countries that are not predominantly Spanish-speaking.

La Habana Elegante's articulations of a hemispheric, Hispanophone audience put the magazine in conversation with—and also set it apart from—contemporaneous efforts to envision new audiences for a changing media landscape. As mentioned previously, within the New York–based English-language popular press, the *Herald* found itself competing (through endeavors like its *Paris Herald* mentioned at the outset of this article) with Joseph Pulitzer's efforts to circulate new stories with mass appeal through the *New York World*. Similarly, by the 1890s a new class of US-based English-language magazines set out to achieve what Richard Ohmann has called the first "national mass culture" by "reaching large audiences and turning a profit on revenues from advertising for brand named products."[42] During the same period *La Habana Elegante* and its peer magazines mediated their own new audience on a transnational scale.

Along with its Hispanophone peers (including many of those mentioned in "Nuestros huéspedes"), *La Habana Elegante*'s editors and writers generated an emerging notion of *latinidad* with hemispheric dimensions. That incipient *latinidad* did not replace or even compete with the notions of identity provided by the nationalities of the writers and readers who saw themselves as part of the periodical's Spanish-language print community. As it took shape in the pages of *La Habana*

Elegante, hemispheric *latinidad* represented the possibility of belonging to a common culture led by the "movimiento de la literatura hispano-americana" (Spanish American literary movement) that *La Habana Elegante* represented—as well as to a shared struggle for true democracy and, perhaps most experimentally, a hopeful effort to realize the potential of emerging modern media to increase opportunities for communication and connection.[43] In *La Habana Elegante* that latter hopefulness centered on the idea of telephonic simultaneity in ways that set the weekly apart from many of its Hispanophone and Anglophone contemporaries.

Telephonic Possibilities

Significantly and uniquely for the period, *La Habana Elegante*'s editors and writers located their ideas about telephonic simultaneity in the world of print rather than in emerging aural or visual media. As Uricchio has noted in the context of film history, "An idea of simultaneity already defined and experienced through the telephone quickly took hold in the popular imagination as a quality that could be extended in image."[44] While some cultural producers imagined the simultaneous transmission of images associated with "the televisual" long before the emergence of television, another class of fantasies focused on the transmission of sound.[45] An illustrative example is the *Telephone Herald*, a newspaper service launched by the Hungarian Tivadar Puskás in 1893, which used telephone technology to deliver daily news in a form that anticipated radio broadcasting. What gets lost in such examples, whether centered on images or sound, is the two-way directionality that constituted one of the telephone's unique characteristics. In *La Habana Elegante* telephonic possibility does not take the form of proto-broadcasting (a one-way activity by definition) of sounds and images. Instead, the magazine explores how print might blur the line between writer and reader, producer and consumer.[46]

A hint of a new kind of relationship between writer and reader appears in an 1888 article for *La Habana Elegante* by the Havana-based Julián del Casal. The article, called "La prensa" ("The Press"), assesses the city's active newspaper industry with surprising insight, especially given Casal's reputation in Latin American literary history as a poet who distanced himself from the practical concerns of a print market dominated by newspapers. Casal explains a recent proliferation of newspapers in Havana by asserting that starting a publication "no se necesita protección, ni dinero, ni se adquiere inmediata responsabilidad" (does not require protection, or money, nor does it come with immediate responsibilities).[47] From Casal's perspective (albeit as a privileged Cuban in Havana), the real challenge is not launching a publication but staying in business. Some publications "logran sostenerse a costa de grandes esfuerzos; otros desaparecen rápidamente por falta de lectores; siendo difícil que alguno prospere, toda vez que el público tiene sus diarios predilectos" (manage to sustain themselves by expending great effort; others disappear rapidly for lack of readers, since it is difficult to prosper when the public has its favorites) (LP, 291). Casal emphasizes the central role of readers in driving the content of a publication. His suggestion that a successful periodical must reflect the views of its audience, not just of its editors, lent particular cogency to his analysis of *La Lucha* (*The*

Struggle), a pro-independence daily to which he contributed and which also had had a number of run-ins with Spanish censors.

No doubt with issues of censorship in mind, Casal praises *La Lucha* as a periodical that "no sirve directamente a ningún partido político, sino a los intereses generales del país" (does not directly serve any political party, but rather the general interests of the country) (LP, 293). The ideas that Spanish colonial authorities might find objectionable, he suggests, come not from the paper but from the people themselves: "Tanteando el pulse de la muchedumbre, es su primer cortesano y su más ardiente defensor. El pueblo compensa a su periódico, consumiendo diariamente numerosos ejemplares" (It [the paper] feels the pulse of the crowd, which is its primary adviser and most ardent champion. The people repay their newspaper, consuming numerous copies daily) (293). By asserting that readers drive the paper's content, Casal reverses the direction of the flow of ideas typically associated with a periodical.

Even more surprisingly, Casal characterizes these contributing readers as a crowd. The vision he offers is not the one of refined consumption conducted within the confines of a privileged interior space (such as a library or personal study) that is typically associated with *modernismo*. Nor does the article describe the kind of one-way transmission of print from a privileged (and increasingly professionalized) class of producers to passive consumers. Instead, Casal describes *La Lucha* as a paper that, although it does not draw content directly from readers, accesses their sentiments and passions. In hindsight, his vision of the newspaper might be considered an alternative blueprint for the mass press and its related "new category of person: the consumer."[48] While his idea certainly does not reject consumption, Casal gestures toward a more active readership whose consumption of the paper is a means of communicating with its editors, rather than an end in itself.

Another version of a two-way exchange between writers and readers appears in Bolet Peraza's "Carta de Nueva York" ("New York Letter"), dedicated to the festivities that surrounded the arrival of the Statue of Liberty. Describing the flags representing many nations at the event, Bolet Peraza does not situate the idea of liberty represented by France's gift in a US context (as one might expect in a piece of foreign correspondence written from New York) but styles it as something within reach of all humanity: "Los colores de todas las naciones del globo flotaban alegres, como si la humanidad entera hubiese querido asociarse á aquellos festejos de la Libertad" (The colors of all the nations of the globe floated happily, as if all humanity had wanted to associate itself with those festivities of Liberty).[49] Beyond the clear attempt to evoke a sense of hope for Cuba's own independence struggle, Bolet Peraza's words also offer another glimpse of a print culture that enables two-way exchange between writers and readers: "El rasgo distintivo de esta rumbosa fiesta ha sido el de su carácter eminentemente popular" (The distinctive feature of this magnificent party has been its eminently popular character).[50] Despite the "ostentosa pompa oficial" (ostentatious official pomp), he explains, the celebration ultimately exhibits and thrives on "la efusión de almas libres" (the outpouring of free souls).[51] Like the mass of readers whose interests and beliefs determine the content of *La Lucha*, the crowd celebrating the arrival of the Statue of Liberty—and not its official planners—ultimately shapes the celebration. While Casal's readers exercise their influence as consumers, Bolet Peraza's crowd acts as a public empowered by the democracy that Cuba—and many newly independent nations of Latin America—then longed to establish.

Although Casal's and Bolet Peraza's articles never mention the telephone directly, a series of articles offering a variation on the periodical's weekly update on local cultural and social events indicates that the telephone resided within the imaginative horizon of *La Habana Elegante*'s editors and writers. The series narrates the city's cultural news "por teléfono" (by telephone) through flirtatious exchanges between a female caller and a male editor. Recalling the stories of romances between female telephone operators and male callers that were popular during the period, the articles parody the magazine's typical society news and explore further what two-way exchange might look like in print.

One such article published on February 13, 1893, begins with a call to *La Habana Elegante*'s editorial office from an unnamed female reader who seeks to "darle algunas noticias para su semanario" (give you some news for your weekly paper).[52] In the exchange that follows, the caller replaces the editor as the narrator of the article's news. Speaking for "La Junta auxiliar de señoras que tiene á su cargo remitir á la Exposición de Chicago los productos de la mujer cubana" (the Ladies Auxiliary Board, which has been charged with sending goods produced by Cuban women to the Chicago Exposition), the caller conveys "un llamamiento por medio de la prensa, á las señoras y las señoritas de la Isla para que si quieren presentar trabajos en la Exposición, los remitan á la morada de la presidenta, Prado 90" (a call by way of the press to the single and married ladies of the island announcing that, if they want to submit their work to the exhibition, they should send it to the home of the president, at Prado 90).[53] The caller's message thus echoes the work achieved by her own narration of that message in the article—that of engaging female readers in representing themselves, in this case not just in *La Habana Elegante* but on the world stage provided by the Chicago Exposition. Although the text was in fact written by one of the publication's male editors, the article's byline seems to uphold the potentiality signaled by its female caller; the author, who elsewhere in the magazine uses the pen name Ignotus, signs off here with an ambiguous single letter, I. Ultimately, the lighthearted exchange depicted in the article raises the serious possibility of increasing the voices included in the magazine's male-dominated contributor list.

In the context of a magazine whose editors sought to advance a hemispheric, Hispanophone print culture, each of these examples suggests the inseparability of *La Habana Elegante*'s hemispheric *latinidad* and the possibilities its editors saw in the world of print in the age of electricity. Even in this Cuban publication that—with its weekly updates on Havana's cultural society news—clearly spoke to a readership largely centered on the island, the telephonic possibility explored in its most ambitious articles belongs to a larger community of people of Latin American descent throughout the hemisphere. In this way, *La Habana Elegante* represented a bold vision of where the changing world of print might lead—and of a proud new form of *latinidad* meant to help describe that print culture's media practices, its geographic reach, and the people whose ideas and sentiments would circulate freely within it.

Lost Connections

It is from the vantage point of an innovator poised to transform a print culture with hemispheric dimensions that *La Habana Elegante*'s editor, Enrique Hernández Miyares, recounts his "primeras impresiones" (first impressions) of New York City on June 24, 1894. In that issue Hernández Miyares describes what at first appears as a minor miscommunication with a man he mistakes for "un *reporter* del *Herald* que deseaba *intervieviarme* [sic] como director de *La Habana Elegante*" (a *Herald* reporter who wished to interview me as editor of *La Habana Elegante*).[54] When Hernández Miyares replies affirmatively to the North American's incomprehensible English, the man "comenzó á limpiarme los zapatos" (began to polish my shoes).[55] Like so many instances in *La Habana Elegante*, the humor of this scene—including Hernández Miyares's amusing deployment of Spanglish to highlight the practice of interviewing that was then a not entirely trusted innovation of the English-language press—veils a sentiment that cuts much deeper. Hernández Miyares finds himself unrecognizable to the US-based Anglophone press as a fellow media innovator.

Throughout 1894 *La Habana Elegante* exhibits a growing sense of the periodical's invisibility from the perspective of the US English-language press. The November 11 issue includes an article in which the North American translator Mary Elizabeth Springer observes, "Es tan poco conocida la literatura hispano-americana en los Estados-Unidos, que hasta algunas personas ignoran que existe" (Spanish American literature is so little known in the United States that some people are unaware that it exists at all).[56] Even Springer's own laudatory comments limit *La Habana Elegante*'s lofty ambitions: "Nuestros vecinos del Sur pueden lisonjearse de poseer una literatura espléndida, digna de estudio, y muchos autores renombrados, cuya fama se ha extendido por Europa é Hispano-América" (Our neighbors to the south can delight in having a splendid literature, worthy of study, and many renowned authors whose fame has stretched throughout Europe and Spanish America).[57] Springer's well-meaning praise contains Spanish-language cultural writing within the southern half of the hemisphere.

The sense of novelty and possibility so evident throughout most of the magazine's run gives way in its final years to frequent expressions of frustration. In another installment of "La Habana elegante por teléfono," which appeared on February 3, 1895 (two years after the example considered earlier), another female caller asks, "Por qué no escribe ya las crónicas?" (Why don't you write *crónicas* any more?), to which the editor answers, "¡Es tan pesado escribir sobre el mismo tema en *El Fígaro*, *La Discusión*, *La Primavera*, de Guanabacoa y *La Habana Elegante*!" (It is so annoying to write about the same thing in *El Fígaro*, *La Discusión*, *La Primavera*, of Guanabacoa, and *La Habana Elegante*!).[58] In contrast to the active field of periodicals representing diverse interests and new possibilities evident in Casal's "La prensa," this text portrays a world of repetition and excess. Moreover, the telephone's potentiality here is superficial compared to that of the earlier installment in this series. In this article (which the author signs this time as Ignotus), the phone call merely provides a means of venting frustration in a print landscape on the verge of becoming obsolete—and also on the verge of war. Later that February uprisings around the country started Cuba's third independence war with Spain. *La Habana Elegante* ceased publication the following year.

Hemispheric Afterlives

La Habana Elegante's experimental idea of a telephonic relationship between writer and reader—as well as its corresponding hemispheric *latinidad*—has been difficult to recognize through the notions of literary value, the forms of mass media, and the formations of Latin American and Latinx identity that solidified after *La Habana Elegante*'s heyday. Certainly, the emerging notions of literature as a privileged, autonomous sphere of literary writing, as well as the ideas of pan–Latin American identity and resistance to US imperialism that have become defining characteristics of *modernismo* are in evidence in *La Habana Elegante*. At the same time, in light of the magazine's explorations of telephonic simultaneity, one might think of *modernismo* as containing multiple scenes that come into view if one looks back on the period through something like the lens of a kaleidoscope. Rotate the cylinder, and the key terms in the previous scene (*Latin America, literature*) end up reconfigured into a new pattern. There the defining features are a hemispheric form of *latinidad* and an idea of the literary that, rather than elevate the cultural producer to a separate sphere, put writers and readers in communication with each other—or even, at times, engaged everyone as creators.[59]

As we gaze on that new scene, the term *modernismo*, often dated back to Rubén Darío's 1888 book of prose poems, *Azul* (*Blue*), brilliantly foreshadows what was to come as literature became an elite, specialized category in the context of twentieth-century mass media. By defining *modernismo* through an idea of literature as a privileged class of writing, Darío helped secure the movement's value in the eyes of those who interpreted it later from the perspective of the twentieth-century literary field in Latin America. But such a notion of what one might call canonical *modernismo* also foreclosed some of the possibilities of the movement's most visionary texts. A far less familiar (and also less fully formed) telephonic *modernismo* evident in *La Habana Elegante* might have led to different notions of the literary—and to corresponding ideas of modern media and of *latinidad*. Those ideas centered on leveling hierarchies and on increasing the exchange of ideas across the divides created by writer and reader, producer and consumer, and perhaps also Hispanophone and Anglophone America.

Viewed in such terms, the hemisphere itself—as the conceptual space in which the period's writers and editors formed their new notions of print culture, literature, and *latinidad*—appears as another one of those "dreams that failed to cohere" of the Latinx nineteenth century.[60] No wonder, then, that the hemisphere has recently proved so generative for scholars seeking to reanimate the possibilities that shaped Latinx lives of the nineteenth century and inspired their media innovations.

KELLEY KREITZ is assistant professor of English and affiliate faculty member in the Latinx Studies program at Pace University in New York City. She is also codirector of the university's digital humanities center, Babble Lab. Her research on print and digital cultures of the Americas has appeared or is forthcoming in *American Literary History, Educational Media International*, and *Revista de Estudios Hispánicos*. She is completing a book tentatively called *Electrifying News: A Hemispheric History of the Present in Nineteenth-Century Print Culture*.

Acknowledgments

Thank you to Katerina González Seligmann and Cara Kinnally, who reviewed drafts of this article, and to the Centro de Estudios Martianos for providing a research base in Havana.

Notes

1   Bolet Peraza, "Carta de Nueva York" (1887). All translations are mine. Scholars have generally dated *La Habana Elegante*'s print run from 1883 to 1896. As this issue of *ELN* was in production, I found in the New York–based *Cacara Jícara*, edited by *La Habana Elegante*'s Enrique Hernández Miyares after he had left Havana for New York, an indication that the periodical may have continued clandestinely for a few years after 1896.

2   Bolet Peraza, "Carta de Nueva York" (1887).

3   Bolet Peraza, "Carta de Nueva York" (1887).

4   I use this term following this special issue's focus on "Latinx lives in hemispheric context," although I recognize that applying the word *Latinx* to a nineteenth-century context adds complexity to recent efforts to "test out the possibility of a meaningful commonality of the idea of Latino expression, even before the term was invented" (Gruesz, *Ambassadors of Culture*, xi). My purpose here is to locate *La Habana Elegante* within a longer history of the development of notions of *latinidad*, especially to show how some ideas of *latinidad* emerged as responses to the possibilities that writers of Latin American descent saw in modern media. In that context, Raul Coronado's explanation of his use of the word *Latino* in his seminal study of nineteenth-century Spanish-language texts in Texas applies to the use of *Latinx* in this article: "'Latino,' in this sense, refers less to a subject-position than it does to a literary and intellectual culture that emerges in the interstices between the United States and Latin America" (*World Not to Come*, 30).

5   In New York's popular press, the *Herald* represented an older guard of newspapers challenged by a "new journalism" with mass appeal led by Joseph Pulitzer's *New York World*. See Schudson, *Discovering the News*.

6   Fox, "Commentary," 643.

7   Gretchen Murphy has shown that a hemispheric imaginary powered by US imperialism also took shape during the same period. She also notes that "Californio, Tejano, and Latin American writers . . . offered alternatives to dominant formulations of hemispheric interconnection and difference" (*Hemispheric Imaginings*, 9). I would argue that *La Habana Elegante* provides one such example. Kirsten Silva Gruesz has demonstrated in her analysis of the New York–based *El Mundo Nuevo/La América Ilustrada* that at least as early as the 1870s Spanish-language literary periodicals were constructing notions of a hemispheric community of print (*Ambassadors of Culture*, chap. 5). My point here is to show how *La Habana Elegante* mediated a hemispheric community that took on particular characteristics in the context of the emerging mass press and expanding ideas of simultaneity in the 1880s and 1890s.

8   Kern, *Culture of Time and Space*, 314.

9   Kern, *Culture of Time and Space*, 67.

10   It took several decades for the telephone to reach widespread use throughout the Americas, but phones did have a novel presence in Cuba in the 1880s and 1890s, as we will see, with the first telephone network established in Havana in 1895.

11   Uricchio, "Storage," 129.

12   Uricchio, "Storage," 129.

13   Kern, *Culture of Time and Space*, 316.

14   The foundational studies include Ramos, *Divergent Modernities*; González, *La crónica modernista hispanoamericana*; and Aching, *Politics of Spanish American "Modernismo."*

15   See Reynolds, "'La lente indiscreta'"; and Navitski, "'Ese pequeño arte que tanto amamos.'"

16   Gitelman and Pingree, "Introduction," xii.

17   Coronado, "Historicizing," 66.

18   I make a similar claim in my reading of *La Revista Ilustrada de Nueva York* in "American Alternatives." There I am interested in that publication's ambitions to increase access to the production of print. Here I discuss *La Habana Elegante*'s own ideas centered on telephonic possibility, which I see as the publication's unique contribution to a transnational effort (in which both publications played key roles) to advance a new Spanish-language print culture throughout the hemisphere. Many of the texts analyzed herein belong to the genre of *crónica modernista* (modern chronicle), an experimental literary genre associated with *modernismo*. Although I do not discuss the *crónica* in this essay, I have considered the genre as a vehicle for media innovation in "Networked Literature."

19   Irwin, "Almost-Latino Literature," 122.

20   See, e.g., Holloway, "Introduction."

21   Aching, *Politics of Spanish American "Modernismo,"* 115.

22   Bolet Peraza, "La influencia americana." The word *raza* is difficult to translate in this context, as it can mean "race," "people," or "nation."

23   *La Revista Ilustrada de Nueva York*, "Importante para hispano-américa."

24 Cutler, "Reading Nineteenth-Century Latina/o Short Fiction," 128.
25 *La Habana Elegante*, "La Habana Elegante" (March 11, 1888).
26 *La Habana Elegante*, "La Habana Elegante" (March 11, 1888).
27 *La Habana Elegante*, "Urbanidad pública."
28 *La Habana Elegante*, "Urbanidad pública." On censorship in nineteenth-century Cuba, see Basail Rodríguez, *El lápiz rojo*.
29 Chic, "La Habana en 1893."
30 *La Habana Elegante*, "Una nevada en La Habana."
31 *La Habana Elegante*, "Una nevada en La Habana."
32 Baralt, "Carta de Nueva York" (July 7, 1889).
33 Baralt, "Carta de Nueva York" (July 7, 1889).
34 Baralt, "Carta de Nueva York" (July 7, 1889).
35 Baralt, "Carta de Nueva York" (July 21, 1889).
36 *La Habana Elegante*, "La Habana Elegante" (April 29, 1888).
37 Baralt, "Carta de Nueva York" (July 21, 1889).
38 Baralt, "Carta de Nueva York" (July 21, 1889).
39 *La Habana Elegante*, "Ramona."
40 *La Habana Elegante*, "Nuestros huéspedes."
41 *La Habana Elegante*, "Nuestros huéspedes."
42 Ohmann, *Selling Culture*, vi.
43 *La Habana Elegante*, "A nuestros suscriptores."
44 Uricchio, "Storage," 130.
45 Uricchio, "Storage," 129.
46 Navitski locates a similar potentiality in discussions of film in the 1920s in the Mexican periodical *El Universal Ilustrado*, which "blurred the distinction between passive consumers and active participants in film culture" ("'Ese pequeño arte que tanto amamos,'" 315).
47 Casal, "La prensa," 291 (hereafter cited as LP).
48 Ohmann, *Selling Culture*, 8.
49 Bolet Peraza, "Carta de Nueva York" (1885).
50 Bolet Peraza, "Carta de Nueva York" (1885).
51 Bolet Peraza, "Carta de Nueva York" (1885).
52 I., "Por teléfono."
53 I., "Por teléfono."
54 Hernández Miyares, "New York."
55 Hernández Miyares, "New York."
56 Springer, "Semblanzas de escritores hispano-americanas."
57 Springer, "Semblanzas de escritores hispano-americanas."
58 Ignotus, "La Habana elegante por teléfono."
59 I argue that this latter possibility powered the editorial strategy of *La Revista Ilustrada de Nueva York* in "American Alternatives."
60 Coronado, "Historicizing," 51.

Works Cited

Aching, Gerard. *The Politics of Spanish American "Modernismo": By Exquisite Design*. Cambridge: Cambridge University Press, 1997.

Baralt, Luis A. "Carta de Nueva York." *La Habana Elegante*, July 7, 1889.

Baralt, Luis A. "Carta de Nueva York." *La Habana Elegante*, July 21, 1889.

Basail Rodríguez, Alain. *El lápiz rojo: Prensa, censura e identidad cubana (1878–1895)*. Havana: Centro Juan Marinello, 2014.

Bolet Peraza, Nicanor. "Carta de Nueva York." *La Habana Elegante*, July 5, 1885.

Bolet Peraza, Nicanor. "Carta de Nueva York." *La Habana Elegante*, November 6, 1887.

Bolet Peraza, Nicanor. "La influencia americana." *La Habana Elegante*, September 1, 1895.

Casal, Julián del. "La prensa." In *Poesía completa y prosa selecta*, edited by Álvaro Salvador, 290–93. Madrid: Verbum, 2001.

Chic, Fleur de. "La Habana en 1893." *La Habana Elegante*, January 22, 1893.

Coronado, Raúl. "Historicizing Nineteenth-Century Latina/o Textuality." In *The Latino Nineteenth Century*, edited by Rodrigo Lazo and Jesse Alemán, 49–70. New York City: New York University Press, 2016.

Coronado, Raúl. *A World Not to Come: A History of Latino Writing and Print Culture*. Cambridge, MA: Harvard University Press, 2013.

Cutler, John Alba. "Reading Nineteenth-Century Latina/o Short Fiction." In *The Latino Nineteenth Century*, edited by Rodrigo Lazo and Jesse Alemán, 124–45. New York City: New York University Press, 2016.

Fox, Claire. "Commentary: The Transnational Turn and the Hemispheric Return." *American Literary History* 18, no. 3 (2006): 638–47.

Gitelman, Lisa, and Geoffrey Pingree. "Introduction: What's New about New Media." In *New Media, 1740–1915*, edited by Lisa Gitelman and Geoffrey Pingree, xi–xxii. Cambridge, MA: MIT Press, 2003.

González, Aníbal. *La crónica modernista hispanoamericana*. Madrid: Porrúa Turanzas, 1983.

Gruesz, Kirsten Silva. *Ambassadors of Culture: The Transamerican Origins of Latino Writing*. Princeton, NJ: Princeton University Press, 2002.

La Habana Elegante. "La Habana Elegante." March 11, 1888.

La Habana Elegante. "La Habana Elegante." April 29, 1888.

La Habana Elegante. "A nuestros suscriptores." July 15, 1894.

La Habana Elegante. "Una nevada en La Habana." May 9, 1887.

La Habana Elegante. "Nuestros huéspedes." July 3, 1887.

La Habana Elegante. "Ramona." September 23, 1888.

La Habana Elegante. "Urbanidad pública." December 25, 1887.

Hernández Miyares, Enrique. "New York.—
Primeras impresiones." *La Habana Elegante*,
June 24, 1894.

Holloway, Thomas. "Introduction." In *A Companion
to Latin American History*, edited by Thomas
Holloway, 1–9. Oxford: Wiley-Blackwell, 2011.

I. [Ignotus]. "Por teléfono." *La Habana Elegante*,
February 12, 1893.

Ignotus. "La Habana Elegante por teléfono."
La Habana Elegante, February 3, 1895.

Irwin, Robert McKee. "Almost-Latino Literature:
Approaching Truncated Latinidades." In *The
Latino Nineteenth Century*, edited by Rodrigo
Lazo and Jesse Alemán, 110–23. New York
City: New York University Press, 2016.

Kern, Stephen. *The Culture of Time and Space, 1880–
1918*. Cambridge, MA: Harvard University
Press, 1983.

Kreitz, Kelley. "American Alternatives: Participatory
Futures of Print from New York's Nineteenth-
Century Latina/o Press." *American Literary
History*, forthcoming.

Kreitz, Kelley. "Networked Literature: The *Crónica
Modernista* and Nineteenth-Century Media
Change." *Revista de Estudios Hispánicos* 50, no.
2 (2016): 321–46.

Murphy, Gretchen. *Hemispheric Imaginings: The
Monroe Doctrine and Narratives of U.S. Empire*.
Durham, NC: Duke University Press, 2005.

Navitski, Rielle. "'Ese pequeño arte que tanto
amamos': Remediating Cinema in *El
Universal Ilustrado*." *Revista de Estudios
Hispánicos* 50, no. 2 (2016): 293–320.

Ohmann, Richard. *Selling Culture: Magazines,
Markets, and Class at the Turn of the Century*.
London: Verso, 1996.

Ramos, Julio. *Divergent Modernities: Culture and
Politics in Nineteenth-Century Latin America*,
translated by John D. Blanco. Durham, NC:
Duke University Press, 2001.

La Revista Ilustrada de Nueva York. "Importante para
hispano-américa." October 1890.

Reynolds, Andrew. "'La lente indiscreta': Visuality
and Mediality in *Modernista* Literary
Expression." *Revista de Estudios Hispánicos* 50,
no. 2 (2016): 347–70.

Schudson, Michael. *Discovering the News: A Social
History of American Newspapers*. New York:
Basic, 1978.

Springer, Mary. "Semblanzas de escritores hispano-
americanas." *La Habana Elegante*, November
11, 1894.

Uricchio, William. "Storage, Simultaneity, and the
Media Technologies of Modernity." In
*Allegories of Communication: Intermedial
Concerns from Cinema to the Digital*, edited by
John Fullerton and Jan Olsson, 123–38.
Bloomington: Indiana University Press, 2004.

Why I Still Believe in Chicanx Studies

MARISSA LÓPEZ

Abstract　While an inclusive Latinx studies has real intellectual justification, the move to craft Latinx rather than specifically Chicanx scholarly questions relies on presentism and adumbrates conflicts over class and citizenship. Drawing on her personal experience justifying the use of *Chicano* in her first book to her academic press editors, the author meditates on the politics of Latinx versus Chicanx, the pitfalls and promises of nationalist discourse, and the need to nurture and cultivate a vibrant Chicanx studies as a counter to the neocolonial tendencies of academic multiculturalism.

Keywords　Chicanx, Latinx, disciplines, academic publishing

After my first book, *Chicano Nations*, was under contract, but before it had been published, I received some revision notes from my editor—phrased mostly in the form of questions rather than commands—the main thrust of which was: Why cling to this term *Chicano* if what you're really sketching out is a transnational *latinidad*? Why not call this book *Latino Nations*? Moreover, he wondered, doesn't expanding the historical scope and breadth of *Chicano* diffuse its historical force as a marker of *el movimiento*? A book with *Latino* in the title would have broader appeal.[1]

I had fielded questions like this before, and I held my ground. True, in the 1960s *Chicano* came to be associated with a specific political and cultural subjectivity that has been critiqued and revised since. The word was not invented in the 1960s, though, and the problematic politics of *el movimiento* do not justify abandoning the term altogether in favor of *Latinx*.[2] *Latinx* can be strategically useful, but I am always suspicious when I'm encouraged to substitute it for *Chicanx*. *Latinx* makes it too easy to consolidate difference and erase history, and I bristle at the presumed novelty of the transnational turn it's meant to connote. Late eighteenth- and early nineteenth-century Latinxes had, like many of us in the twenty-first century, transnational, transamerican perspectives that grounded visions of progressive social change. Thinking of these writers balancing their national and pan-American aspirations challenges our parochialism and shows how the desire to contain *chicanidad* in space and time is part of a larger story about partitioning the hemisphere.

ENGLISH LANGUAGE NOTES

56:2, October 2018　DOI 10.1215/00138282-6960790
© 2018 Regents of the University of Colorado

In *Chicano Nations* I wanted more than anything else to make a place for early writers. I wanted to construct a genealogy of Chicanx literature that rested on the ambivalence resulting from a nation's desire to hide the political, cultural, and historical reality of its global interconnection. But this is a counterintuitive way of talking about Chicanx nationalism, which is usually seen as part of a progress narrative that moves from the heteronormative patriarchy of *el movimiento* to the enlightened transnationalism of the era since the North American Free Trade Agreement in which Chicanx subjectivities correlate to hybrid Chicanx spaces, or border zones. That story, however, is much too neat. Chicanx nationalism develops well before the 1960s, in other times and other spaces that are also transnational and multivalent, not newly so but historically and constitutively.

Acknowledging this complicates the relationship between our present and earlier periods of Chicanx history. As scholars, we must remain invested in the nation as both political reality and abstract imaginary. We must seek a balance between transamerican potential and national realities. We must develop an approach to Chicanx literary history that realizes the fundamental contradiction between the heterogeneity of a Mexican-American past and historiographical tendencies toward homogenization. We must, that is, recognize the exclusionary potential of asserting difference even as we remain wary of celebratory attempts to fold disparate Latinx groups into a unifying category like *transnational latinidad*.

If there's so much debate and ambivalence, though, why, to return to my editor's question, keep using *Chicanx*? Simply put, to move toward a rubric of *transnational latinidad* makes it possible to avoid—or at least downplay—history, and I want to keep history alive and kicking. The United States absorbed nearly half of Mexico in 1848, and the essence of *chicanidad* lies in negotiating that engulfment. Insisting on *Chicanx* illuminates the local's imbrication with the global. The Chicanx struggle in the United States is intimately connected with the global struggle against oppression, and Chicanx studies must understand its globality to parse the ever-changing dimensions of *chicanidad*.

In the 2010s more than ever, as nativism and historical amnesia threaten to hijack US democracy, we must nurture *Chicanx* as a living, breathing term with a past, a present, and a future. I still believe in Chicanx studies because to lock *Chicanx* into a static past, to say that it can only ever mean one thing, refer to one historical moment, is to vitiate its political and cultural import for the present. Especially for writers in the early periods, for whom the word *Chicanx* effectively didn't exist, we must recognize their philosophical affinities with *chicanidad* even as we are building long histories of *latinidad*. We must understand their intellectual conflicts and cultural debates as constitutive of the debates and tensions characteristic of contemporary *chicanidad*.

MARISSA LÓPEZ is associate professor of English and Chicana/o studies at UCLA. She studies Chicanx literature from the nineteenth century to the present with an emphasis on nineteenth-century Mexican California. Her first book, *Chicano Nations* (2011), is about nationalism and Chicanx literature from the early 1800s to the post-9/11 era. Her second book, *Racial Immanence: Chicanx Bodies beyond Representation*, is forthcoming.

Notes

1   López, *Chicano Nations.*
2   Since I wrote *Chicano Nations, Chicanx* and *Latinx* have emerged as terms that refuse the gendered binaries of *Chicana, Chicano, Chicana/o,* and even *Chican@*, offering scholars a more elegant way, in my opinion, of navigating the thorny politics of language.

Work Cited

López, Marissa K. *Chicano Nations: The Hemispheric Origins of Mexican American Literature.* New York: New York University Press, 2011.

Borderlands *Letrados*

La Crónica, the Mexican Revolution, and Transnational Critique on the US-Mexico Border

YOLANDA PADILLA

Abstract   Angel Rama's concept of the *letrado* refers to Latin American lettered individuals who used writing to consolidate the nation. But what might it have meant to be a *letrado* in the geopolitical context of the US-Mexico border in the early twentieth century, one that combined territorial dispossession, migration, and revolution? This essay examines the contributions of border Mexicans to *La crónica*, an influential Laredo, Texas, newspaper that appeared at least from 1910 to 1914. These "borderlands *letrados*" engaged the Mexican nation from positions of opposition during the Mexican Revolution while contending with Anglo-American nativist imperatives, which shaped their cultivation of an ethnic identity in the United States. Mobilizing the concept of the *letrado* in the context of these borderlands writers makes them legible within larger Latin American currents while elucidating their place at the center of issues encompassing ethnic, national, and transnational concerns.
Keywords   Mexican Revolution, *letrado*, *La crónica*, US-Mexico border

I n her memoir of the Mexican Revolution (1910–20), written during the 1920s and entitled *La rebelde*, Leonor Villegas de Magnón strove to provide a distinct perspective from the one that was already congealing in official versions of the war, one that commemorated a group of politically and socially engaged border Mexicans whose contributions to Mexican history were in danger of erasure: "La historia se ha encargado de relatar los hechos, pero se ha olvidado del importante papel de Laredo, Texas, Nuevo Laredo, Tamaulipas y otros pueblos fronterizos que en esos momentos se unieron en un fraternal acuerdo" (History has assumed responsibility for documenting the facts, but it has forgotten the important role played by the communities of Laredo, Texas, and Nuevo Laredo, Tamaulipas and other border cities which united themselves in a fraternal agreement).[1] In speaking about the border region, Magnón often singles out her adopted hometown of Laredo, as she elaborates on the rich intellectual and political culture produced by the city's ethnic

ENGLISH LANGUAGE NOTES

56:2, October 2018 DOI 10.1215/00138282-6960801

Mexicans, especially through their Spanish-language newspapers. She details their active participation in the revolution, both as direct participants in the war and as intellectuals passionate in their belief that their insights should carry weight despite their marginalized positions north of the border. Of particular importance were Nicasio Idar and his children, especially Clemente and Jovita. They published *La crónica*, a weekly newspaper that ran at least from 1910 to 1914 and that stood alongside Los Angeles's *Regeneración* and San Antonio's *La prensa* in terms of circulation and influence.[2] While the Idars provided coverage of worldwide affairs, they focused on Mexico and the local Texas-Mexican border community, devoting great attention to the Mexican Revolution. Alongside Magnón, who also published in the newspaper, they challenged Mexican narratives that either ignored the border region or disdained its people. Refusing to honor the international line as a division, they understood Mexicans in the United States to constitute the continuation of Mexican history north of the border.

Mexicans in the United States were not unified in their responses to the revolution. They were a diverse group marked by differences in key elements of identity formation, such as class, race, and regional background, and comprising an array of subject positions as migrants, immigrants, exiles, and deeply rooted residents who traced their family lines back to when the US Southwest was still the Mexican North. Accordingly, they spanned the political spectrum, ranging from radical anarchists to conservative counterrevolutionists.[3] The Idars and their circle were Tejana/o "progressives," a term used by Benjamin Heber Johnson to describe Tejanas/os who supported the revolution and were active in an array of social justice causes but were more moderate than border anarchists such as Ricardo and Enrique Flores Magón.[4]

La crónica challenged modernist imperatives that take as their starting point the hierarchical relations between center and periphery, hierarchies constitutive of Western modernity.[5] In the postrevolutionary Mexican context, such imperatives took the form of an aggressive nation-building project that was predicated on the appropriation of the revolution's meanings through centralization, exclusion, and the drive to achieve modernity and that was shaped through narratives such as the official histories Magnón identifies. The *Crónica* writers did not reject notions of nationhood or modernity; rather, their understanding of the nation was more capacious than the geopolitically defined nation at the heart of Western modernity. They accepted this definition in dealings with the United States, mobilizing it as a basis for their demands for civil and political rights. However, when they used their writings to make demands on Mexico, they did so by mobilizing the nation in a second sense, that of a cultural nation that we now recognize as "Greater Mexico," a term coined by Américo Paredes to refer to "all the areas inhabited by people of Mexican culture—not only within the present limits of the Republic of Mexico but in the US as well—in a cultural rather than a political sense."[6] For these writers, then, the nation was not an "either/or" but a "both/and" proposition: their understanding of nationhood was flexible, and they refused the idea that they could claim membership in only one. Thus they used their writings to engage the Mexican Revolution in ways that grappled with Western modernity's exclusionary imperatives, doing so by foregrounding lived experiences and forms of knowledge from the periphery and, consequently, by challenging paradigms of social identity as necessarily contained within a unified national culture strictly delimited by political borders.

While *La crónica* and other *fronterizo* newspapers consistently provided sophisticated analysis of the war and weighed in on the Mexican nation's future, they have remained relatively invisible in Mexican and Latin American scholarship. Despite the increasing attention to the revolution's transnational dimensions, this neglect persists even in studies aimed at bringing to light ignored elements of the war.[7] The field that does attend to *fronterizo* newspapers from this period, borderlands studies, has a different blind spot, in that it tends to emphasize the relatively autonomous cultural practices developed by border Mexicans with respect to national centers, and it underexamines the commitment that many of these writers felt toward the ideal of the nation. I suggest addressing these issues by framing the *Crónica* writers through Angel Rama's concept of the "opposition *letrado*." This concept follows from Rama's elaboration of the Latin American *ciudad letrada* (lettered city), which names the nexus of lettered culture, state power, and urban location through which first Iberian monarchs and, later, state bodies imposed order. The *letrados* were an urban lettered elite who used their mastery of and access to the written word to sustain the institutions of the state and consequently maintain their proximity to power.[8] In the final chapter of his book, titled "The City Revolutionized," Rama argues that the cycle of revolutions that took place throughout Latin America in the early twentieth century—including the Mexican Revolution— "unleashed truly transformative forces in successive waves, ever widening the circle of political participation with the inclusion of new social groups."[9] Thus lettered men for the first time had the opportunity to make lives of prestige and power for themselves without having to be part of a governmental bureaucratic machine. Modern *letrados* no longer had to be descended from the "best" families, no longer even had to hail from the city (*LC*, 94). The result was the rise of "opposition *letrados*," lettered men who engaged in intellectual and political activities not only independent of the state but in opposition to it (112).

Rama presents a bleak view of the efficacy of these new *letrados* in challenging the lettered city's totalizing power; their attempts, he argues, were either absorbed by the power structure or simply unequal to the task of "alter[ing] the relationship between power and signification."[10] Ultimately, "opposition *letrados*" is something of a misnomer, as they revert to the position of conventional *letrados*, wittingly or not. Nevertheless, the idea that there was an opening for opposition sheds light on the commitments and strategies of the *fronterizos* that concern me here, while allowing an analysis of the significant ways in which they differed from Rama's *letrados*. The benefit of considering the *Crónica* writers as opposition *letrados* comes in Rama's emphasis on revolution, spatialization, and the nation. Like the opposition *letrados* he identifies, the *Crónica* writers used the technology of the written word to engage the revolution as participants and chroniclers, doing so very consciously from the peripheral spatial positions that explicitly challenged the "centrifugal" force funneling all power to the Mexican center.[11] Yet, and again like Rama's opposition *letrados*, they did so even as they valued the project of the nation itself, for while they actively sought the overthrow of the Mexican government during the revolution, their impassioned opinion pieces charted a course for the nation to follow in anticipation of the war's end. Mobilizing Rama's theorization of the opposition *letrado* in the context of these borderlands writers, then, makes them legible within larger Latin American currents, as Rama argues that similar processes occurred throughout the region. Morever, for borderlands studies, the concept of the opposition *letrado* directs more emphasis on the importance of the nation.

At this point, however, the *Crónica* writers—whom I conceptualize as borderlands *letrados*—diverge from Rama's paradigm, for reasons stemming from their positions in the geopolitical context of the US-Mexico border. One significant difference is the extent to which women acted as borderlands *letradas*, as suggested by my references to Villegas de Magnón. As Anne Lambright and Elisabeth Guerrero point out, the lettered city belonged to men; the few Latin American women in a position to use the technology of the written word wrote "*against* this lettered city of a privileged few."[12] Yet women in the borderlands had a long history of creating and shaping print culture in the region. It is difficult to pinpoint exactly why *fronterizas* could access the written word. It is possible that being in a liminal space between nations created opportunities for women to break out of traditional molds, and that the struggles and uncertainties of the revolution accelerated such possibilities. In their writings these women were motivated by many of the same objectives as their male counterparts, but they used distinct discursive strategies that were deemed gender appropriate.[13]

Another divergence is that whereas *letrados* worked to build and consolidate the nation, even if they did so from a position of opposition, those in the borderlands did it in a context that combined territorial dispossession and (im)migration. As such, I understand borderlands *letrados* to engage the Mexican nation in ways that both reflect and shape their positions as subjects of the United States. This has at least two implications. First, because they understood themselves to mark a vital and ongoing aspect of Mexican history, one that they placed at the center of Mexico's national narrative, they were deeply cognizant of the relationship between local conflicts and national projects; in fact, addressing the former often meant framing the problem in terms of the latter. Second, understanding their stories as part of Mexican history meant that they often elaborated on their local situations in terms of a larger context of dispossession, with a resulting emphasis on and critique of the neocolonial relationship between Mexico and the United States. Through their engagements with the nation, then, the Mexican-American *letrados* contributed to Greater Mexico's history as a site of knowledge production, as they elucidated the place of Mexicans in the United States at the center of issues encompassing ethnic, national, and transnational concerns.

The Santayanas of the Borderlands

In elaborating on his concept of the opposition *letrado*, Rama chooses as his paradigmatic example José Vasconcelos (1881–1959), the Mexican writer, philosopher, and politician regarded as the chief architect of Mexico's postrevolutionary system of mass education, a system that grew out of a vision for nation building that Vasconcelos helped formulate. Rama continually returns to the example of Vasconcelos because of the Mexican thinker's prominent involvement with aspects of the revolution that are central to Rama's conceptualization of the transformations that took place in twentieth-century Latin American politics and culture. Rama argues that the Mexican Revolution was characterized by issues and debates—including those of nationalism and mass education with which Vasconcelos is identified—that would endure throughout the century and from country to country. Thus "the impact of the early revolutions on the lettered city takes on the larger implications of the period as a whole" (*LC*, 100).

Moreover, Vasconcelos came of age in the US-Mexico borderlands and thus exemplifies Rama's contention that the conditions of early twentieth-century Latin America allowed for the emergence of the first *letrados* from outside the capital cities. In making this point about Vasconcelos, Rama acknowledges that the borderlands were important to the revolution and that many of Mexico's most famous *letrados* spent much time there while composing their positions on the war and what it meant for the nation. However, he offers no analysis of the geopolitical specificities of the region and the role they might have played either in the emergence of these *letrados* or in shaping their particular perspectives. Nor does he attend in any way to the importance of those we might call *fronterizos*, or border dwellers, to the story he tells. For while he attaches great significance to the emergence of *letrados* from outside the capital, ultimately his interest is in those who identified with and were oriented toward the Mexican interior.

Vasconcelos was one of these. Born in Oaxaca, he was raised in the border town of Piedras Negras, Coahuila, while attending school in Eagle Pass, Texas, and eventually made his way to Mexico City to attend law school. In the first volume of his memoir, *Ulises criollo* (1935), he recalls with great ambivalence his time in the border region. In a theme familiar in Latin American letters more generally, he lauds the modern accoutrements of life in the United States while bemoaning what he views as the profound lack of spirituality and culture there. Moreover, he asserts that those US qualities have left a deep mark on the areas immediately south of the border as well, so that northern Mexico is unrecognizable to him as part of his homeland. Such themes are implicit when he recalls the hostility he and his Mexican classmates faced in their Texas school, an experience that fostered the nationalist pride that shaped his early writings: "En la frontera se nos había acentuado el prejuicio y el sentido de raza; por combatida y amenazada, por débil y vencida, yo me debía a ella. En suma: dejé pasar la oportunidad de convertirme en filósofo yanqui. ¿Un Santayana de México y Texas?" (In the frontier our sense of prejudice and race pride had been accentuated; because I was embattled and threatened, and because I was weak and defeated, I came into my own. In sum: I let pass the opportunity to convert myself into a Yankee philosopher. A Santayana of Mexico and Texas?).[14] Vasconcelos's brief consideration of a life for himself as a *letrado* of the border is tinged with derision from the outset, as he smirks at his own suggestion that he might have been the Santayana of the borderlands. George Santayana, the early twentieth-century philosopher, literary and cultural critic, and Harvard professor, was born in Madrid and, although he immigrated to the United States at nine, retained his Spanish citizenship throughout his life. That "foreignness" is commonly thought to have informed his pointed commentaries on American culture.[15] It could be that Vasconcelos is making an analogy between Santayana's "outsider" position and his own interloper status as a Mexican schoolboy in the Texas borderlands. What is more certain is that he means for the idea that someone akin to the urbane Harvard philosopher would have inhabited the borderlands to strike the reader as ridiculous.

This fleeting moment hints at the long history of disdain with which the Mexican center has held the region. Numerous scholars have noted this view of the Mexican North as a "cultural desert" and, even more, as an untameable zone of rebellion unassimilable into the national body.[16] María Socorro Tabuenca Córdoba notes that the "barbaric" cultural desert in the Mexican imaginary includes the US Southwest along with northern Mexico. She identifies this deeply rooted attitude, "North of the Borderism," as in part the result of a "Mexican centralist necessity to possess a 'national identity' inherited from the nineteenth century. In the wake of the loss of more than half of Mexico's territory, 'national unity' urgently erected a retaining wall of *mexicanidad* (Mexicanness) at the border."[17] North of the Borderism, then, combines a historical disdain of *fronterizos* with an anti-imperial impulse to look inward, to sever the story of the Mexican nation from that of Mexicans who were sacrificed to US imperial expansion.

Vasconcelos had a complicated relationship with the United States and the inhabitants of the border, at times embracing both when it suited him politically.[18] But he largely shared in and propagated North of the Borderism, even expanding its geographic reach, writing in the second volume of his memoir that everything from the northern Mexican environs to New York was a "no man's land of the spirit, a desert of the soul."[19] Vasconcelos eventually left the border region to pursue greatness in the Mexican capital. But what and whom did he leave behind? What if he had stayed in the region to become, in his words, a "yanquí philosopher," focusing his attention on the revolution from the perspective of Mexicans north of the border?

In the same early scene from *Ulises criollo* in which he elaborates on the prejudice he and his fellow Mexicans faced in Texas schools, Vasconcelos provides a tantalizing glimpse of the proto–Mexican-Americans he left behind, those border philosophers who might have become, in his terms, Santayanas of the borderlands. Discussing how the class would naturally divide itself into Anglo versus Mexican students when tense issues such as the Alamo or the US-Mexico War were raised, he clarifies whom he counts as "Mexican": "Al hablar de mexicanos incluyo a muchos que aun viviendo en Texas y teniendo sus padres la ciudadanía, hacían causa común conmigo por razones de sangre. Y si no hubiesen querido era lo mismo, porque los yanquis los mantienen clasificados" (In speaking of Mexicans, I include many who, while living in Texas and with parents who were citizens of the United States, made common cause with me for reasons of blood. And if they had not wanted to, it would not have mattered, for the Yankees classified them as such).[20] This passage elucidates the double outsider status occupied by Mexicans in the United States: the *yanquís* refused to distinguish among Mexicans of different citizenship statuses and with differing relationships to the Mexican nation, lumping them together and treating them with the same prejudice, yet there was a strong awareness of such differences among Mexicans themselves. Vasconcelos's parents worked to keep him oriented southward, where the "authentic" heart of

Mexico resided,[21] and it is clear throughout his memoir that he views these "other" Mexicans either as oddities or as imposters.

However, as the writings of Magnón and others attest, they rejected the idea that they should be discounted as true Mexicans because of their distance from the capital, their proximity to the United States, or their identification with the borderlands. For them, there was nothing problematic, amusing, or inauthentic about their positions either as cultural Mexicans with a profound commitment to the future of the Mexican nation or as members of an emerging ethnic group north of the border. Magnón highlights this very issue in an early draft of her memoir, praising Clemente Idar—one of the *La crónica* contributors I discuss below—for his efforts both in the revolution and in support of Mexican workers established in the United States. She then chastises those Mexicans who viewed the border with contempt, asserting that *fronterizos* such as Idar were "ejemplos de los llamados 'Pochos' que tanto desprecian en la capital y que guardan en ambos puños fuertemente apretados el honor y el decoro internacional de una psicología incomprensible y grandiosa" (examples of the so-called Pochos, who are so scorned by the Mexican capital and who guard with tightly held hands the honor and international decorum of an incomprehensible and grand psychology).[22] The term *pocho* was an insult directed at border dwellers to indicate that they were tainted by their proximity to the United States and thus were not "real" Mexicans.

While both the US and Mexican centers saw them as peripheral, Magnón and many other politically active Mexicans of the borderlands understood themselves to mark the continued unfolding of Mexican history in the United States, a point Magnón insistently and repeatedly makes in her memoir. While she could never publish *La rebelde* in her lifetime, she joined other *fronterizos* in employing the Spanish-language newspapers that dotted the border to counter Mexico's disdain as they plotted a course for the revolution and wrote themselves into Mexican history. This point brings me back to Rama's idea of the opposition *letrado*. Rama overlooks the significance of the border region to the culture and politics of the revolution, perhaps due to a too narrow focus on national boundaries in his thinking. But his stipulation that *letrados* had to make their way to the city—in this case Mexico City—repeats the omission of border Mexicans from Mexican and more broadly Latin American history that Villegas de Magnón and others fought against. It also neglects the severe political persecution so many opposition *letrados* faced in the Mexican interior, as well as the more constant regulation and censorship of the written word that had always been a hallmark of the lettered city.

While my focus is on how Mexican-American engagements with the revolution shaped Mexican-Americans' understandings of their positions as subjects of the United States, I want to take a moment to underscore the central role played by Mexicans north of the border in shaping what is now the Mexican literary canon through their newspaper stewardship. Despite generally oppressive living conditions, Mexicans in the United States enjoyed some advantages, chief among them a relative political freedom compared to revolutionaries to the south. As a result, hundreds of novels of the revolution were published in Spanish-language newspapers throughout the US side of the border, including many of the most celebrated.

When one considers the heightened stakes of regulation and persecution in the lettered city during the revolution, in conjunction with the extensive Spanish-language print culture that had developed on the US side of the border and that so many Mexican revolutionaries made use of, it becomes possible to imagine the border region as a locus of oppositional lettered activity of the period. This also suggests that, despite the friction and deeply felt differences of identity between *fronterizos* and Mexicans who were of or oriented toward the interior, these *letrados* worked together to produce a textual culture of opposition, a process largely led by the inhabitants of the borderlands who had developed the necessary infrastructure. One implication of this is that if, as Rama and others have argued, the Mexican Revolution established some of the issues and political currents that would mark Latin America as a whole throughout the century, and if border Mexicans played a significant role as opposition *letrados* in the revolution, then they were important figures in the development of twentieth-century Latin American politics and culture.

La Crónica and the Borderlands Letrados

Having established the importance of these *fronterizos* as opposition *letrados*, I now want to attend to their significance as what I am conceptualizing as "borderlands *letrados*." Throughout 1910 and 1911 *La crónica* consistently expressed two chief concerns: first, it decried racism against Mexicans in the United States, and second, it supported the political reforms of the Mexican Revolution.[23] As Richard Griswold del Castillo has argued, *La crónica* often explicitly brought the two issues together, such as when it "asserted similarities between Mexican dictator Porfirio Díaz's corruption and the venality of Anglo-American politicians in Texas."[24] Such comparisons suggest that the periodical understood Mexican and Mexican-American issues in mutually informing ways and that responding to the revolution also meant responding to situations faced by Mexicans in the United States.

The revolution's promise gave Mexican-Americans a language through which to press their cases for social justice. For example, in an article dated December 24, 1910, and thus published a mere month after the breakout of the war, Nicasio Idar mobilized the rebellion's rhetorical commitment to agrarian land reform in his exhortations to *Mexicanos*—by which he meant recent immigrants and native-born Mexican-Americans—to fight for civil and economic equality. "*This is the time*," he writes, "when the *Mexicanos* of today should begin to interest themselves in the reconquest of their lands and liberty."[25] As Griswold del Castillo points out, the idea that the "revolution should motivate" Mexican-Americans "to organize and unite their communities" to fight for their civil rights was a recurrent theme.[26] *La crónica*'s commitment to the revolution's ideals, then, became an important framework for the adaptation and negotiation of an ethnic identity, one predicated on ideas of rights and resistance.

At the same time, and like Magnón's memoir, *La crónica*'s engagements with the revolution produced a nationalism that simultaneously placed border Mexicans at the center of the revolutionary project and thus attempted to reshape a Mexican national narrative that had rendered them either invisible or a threat to Mexican cultural and national integrity. Like many Mexicans who ended up north of the border, the *letrados* of Laredo refused to be cut loose by the Mexican nationalist project, insisting on writing themselves into the story of the nation in ways that combined an emerging ethnic history with the larger history of US-Mexican relations. One finds this logic operating in the Idar quote referenced above, in which Idar uses the national project of the revolution to spur the Mexican-American fight for social justice, doing so through the language of "reconquest" and thus invoking the larger history of US imperial aggression against Mexico. Consequently, in fighting for their rights as ethnic subjects of the United States, Mexican-Americans would also be the protagonists in fighting to right a historical wrong between nations.

The Laredo *letrados* also strategically joined their histories to those of the Mexican migrant laborers who streamed into the United States as a result of the violence of the revolution. One consequence of the revolution was the migration of over 1 million Mexicans to the United States in pursuit of economic and social stability. For Texas Mexicans who lived along the border, the migrants who crossed the river were a daily reminder both of the failures of the revolutionary project and of the contempt with which many Anglo-Americans regarded the migrants. At the 1911 Primer Congreso Mexicano, a conference organized in Laredo by the publishers of *La crónica* in response to the heightened climate of violence and nativism faced by Texas Mexicans, a letter sent by one of the delegates addressed this issue: "Día a día se ve cruzar el Río Bravo por grandes grupos de mexicanos que ansiosos de mejor salario para el sostenimiento de la familia van a Texas, y si bien es cierto que consiguen comer y vestir mejor . . . también es cierto que con frequencia son tratados con un vergonzoso desprecio de parte de los americanos tratandolos como a raza degenerada o oculta" (Day by day one sees large groups of Mexicans cross the Río Bravo and, anxious for a better salary with which to support their families, go to Texas, and if it is true that they attain better living conditions . . . it is also true that the Americans frequently treat them with shameful disregard, as if they were dealing with a degraded or hidden race).[27] It did not take long for the politically active *Tejanos*, deeply cognizant of the relationship between local conflicts and national projects, to place the everyday subjection of migrant laborers within the context of the history of US dominance over Mexico. Nicasio Idar's son, Clemente, would do just that in an article that shows his bristling at the exploitation of Mexican workers to be rooted in a broader nationalist sensibility: "Texas-Mexicans have produced with the sweat of their brow the bountiful agricultural wealth known throughout the country, and in recompense for this they have been put to work as peones on the land of their forefathers."[28] Such passages illustrate David Gutiérrez's argument that Mexican-Americans have engaged in a constant process of defining and redefining themselves against more recent Mexican (im)migrants.[29] In this way, the increasing visibility of recent Mexican (im)migrants informed how the Laredo *letrados* conceptualized their identities as Mexican-Americans, especially as they tried to make sense of the relationship between the positions occupied by both groups in the United States.

Clemente Idar makes similar, though more explicit, connections. In a 1910 article in *La crónica*, he protests the segregation of and discrimination against Mexican students in the US education system:

Una completa aclaración de los hechos vendrá á demostrar, por una parte, que los mexicanos que hemos nacido en este país y á pesar de nuestra nacionalidad Americana, no disfrutamos en toda su extension de los privilegios y garantías que nos ofrece la Constitución Federal; y, por otra, que á los individuos netamente mexicanos, también se les niegan derechos y prerogativas que los Tratados de Guadalupe Hidalgo entre México y los Estados Unidos, mutuamente les concedieron, resultando, que mexicanos y méxico-americanos, estamos en igual situación. . . . Únicamente reclamamos un derecho. A los japoneses, á los irlandeses, á los escoceses, á los ingleses, á los italianos y á tantas otras razas que en grande afluencia inmigran á este país, no se les pone ninguna traba para que concurran á las escuelas públicas de todos los Estados de la República Americana. ¿Por qué se le pone al mexicano y al méxico-americano? . . . ¿Ya se olvidaron los tratados de Guadalupe Hidalgo?

[A complete clarification of the facts will prove on the one hand that we, the Mexicans born in this country, even though we have American citizenship, do not fully enjoy the privileges and guarantees that the Federal Constitution offers. On the other hand, it will prove that those individuals who are fully Mexican have also been denied privileges and prerogatives that the Treaty of Guadalupe Hidalgo between Mexico and the United States mutually conceded. This results in the fact that Mexicans and Mexican-Americans are in the same situation. . . . We simply reclaim a right. Japanese, Irish, Scottish, English, Italians and other races that immigrate to this country in such a great number do not meet with any obstacles to attend public schools in any state of the American Republic. Why do the Mexican and the Mexican-American meet with these problems? . . . Did [American educators] already forget the Treaty of Guadalupe Hidalgo?][30]

Like his father Nicasio, Clemente Idar combines ethnic grievance with the history of Mexican imperial subjection in ways that position the border subject at the center of US-Mexico relations. Drawing parallels between the injustices endured by Mexican-Americans and newcomer Mexican (im)migrants, he highlights the interconnections between local and international conflicts, arguing that the second-class citizenship experienced by Mexican-Americans indicates the unequal power relations between Mexico and the United States. That inequality is repeatedly made manifest by the continuous waves of migrants who enter the United States and are denied their rights under the Treaty of Guadalupe Hidalgo, a situation that indicates disregard not only for the migrants themselves but also for the Mexican state. When Idar concludes that "Mexicans and Mexican-Americans are in the same situation," he gestures toward a collapsing of the distinctions between them and suggests that all Mexicans in the United States, whether long or newly settled, citizen or not, act as an index of the US-Mexico relationship. Thus, in keeping with his father's line of argument, Clemente ultimately claims that the fight for group rights is a fight to rectify Mexico's neocolonial relation to the United States while also suggesting that Mexican-Americans mark the continued unfolding of Mexican history north of the border.

Idar's intertwining of local, national, and international concerns demonstrates a sophisticated understanding of the inextricability of the plights of Mexican migrants from those of Mexican-Americans. For while they made up a variety of legal status categories in the United States, they tended to be lumped together in a single "outsider" category. The lack of differentiation imposed on Mexicans in the United States is a situation that Idar embraces in this instance, as he draws a parallel between the problems of Mexican-Americans and the disregard for the terms of the Treaty of Guadalupe Hidalgo. His yoking together of local and international conflicts makes discrimination in US schooling policies reverberate with the history of US imperialism while positioning Mexican-American dispossession as central to that history, and as the basis for resistance. Moreover, juxtaposing these issues—whether in a single article or in an array of articles appearing side by side and page by page in *La crónica*—implicitly promotes a similarly transnational view of the revolution itself, as the linking of discrimination and violence against Mexican-Americans with the struggles of Mexican (im)migrants and the revolutionary upheaval causes all to become intertwined with and shaped by a long history of US domination.

Yet while Idar asserts the similarities of the situations faced by Mexican-Americans and Mexican (im)migrants, and insists on infusing his critiques of the issues that bind them with the history of imperial conquest, he does not lose sight of the local parameters of the nation-based projects that most immediately affect Mexican-Americans as subjects of the United States, in this case the project of citizenship. Here Idar dramatically shifts from considering Mexican-American history as international history, to situating that story within the classic American immigrant narrative, and then returning to the international perspective of military and diplomatic conflict with which he began. Consequently, he suggests that disrespect for the Mexican nation feeds discriminative practices against Mexican-Americans and that full inclusion into the national polity for the latter will be predicated on respect in the international arena for the former. One sees this in the plaintive end to his article, where, after commenting on the smooth entry of other immigrants into the US education system (and showing a clear lack of understanding of the hostilities faced by those groups), he wonders why Mexicans and Mexican-Americans face so many obstacles: "Did [American educators] already forget the Treaty of Guadalupe Hidalgo?"

By examining these men and women of the border through the concept of the opposition *letrado*, I hope to make at least two broad critical interventions in the fields of Latin American studies, transnational American studies, and border studies. Generally speaking, US hemispheric scholarship has focused on US economic and political dominance in the hemisphere, resulting in an exciting body of work that has oriented American studies toward transnational analyses. However, that work has also been criticized from a Latin Americanist perspective because it tends to treat Latin America as little more than a recipient site of US policies and aggressions.[31] By focusing on Mexican-American engagements with the revolution, I foreground Mexico's role as a protagonist in the story of Mexican-Americans, not simply as a victim of US aggression. Even more central to the story I am telling is the fact that Mexican-Americans were not simply acted on by these Mexican ideologies; on the contrary, they actively responded to the revolution, attempting to shape many of its most important political and social currents in ways that subsequently informed their struggles for social justice in the United States. In so doing, they asserted themselves as active agents in Mexican history even as they attempted to make lives for themselves north of the border. The concept of the *letrado* enables the recognition of their role as active agents not only within Mexican history but also within hemispheric history. Situating segments of Mexican-American culture in this way has implications for border studies, a field that rightly emphasizes Mexican-American cultural autonomy in the borderlands as well as the local conflicts that give rise to them. As invaluable as this focus on the local is, it can obscure the continuing persistence of state-national power in communities that are resistant toward national centers, while overlooking the relationships among local conflicts, national projects, and transnational currents. In this case, the Laredo *letrados'* responses to their local conditions as subjects of the United States were shaped by national projects emanating from both Mexico and the United States and were a local manifestation of a hemispheric movement of limited opposition. This approach allows for a continued examination of how Mexican-Americans have been excluded from the United States, but it adds a focus on how they operate as dynamic parts of multiple nations and of transnational phenomena.

YOLANDA PADILLA is on the faculty of the School of Interdisciplinary Arts and Sciences at the University of Washington, Bothell. She is completing a book tentatively titled *Revolutionary Subjects: The Mexican Revolution and the Transnational Emergence of Mexican American Literature and Culture, 1910–1959*. She has published essays related to this project in *CR: New Centennial Review* and in the volume *Open Borders to a Revolution*. She is coeditor of two volumes: *Bridges, Borders, and Breaks: History, Narrative, and Nation in Twenty-First-Century Chicana/o Literary Criticism* (2016) and *The Plays of Josefina Niggli: Recovered Landmarks of Latina Literature* (2007).

Acknowledgments
I thank Bianet Castellanos, Adriana Estill, Lourdes Gutiérrez Nájera, and Desirée Martín for reading and commenting on an earlier draft of this essay.

Notes

1   Magnón originally wrote her memoir in Spanish. When she could not find a publisher, she translated her account into English in the hope that a US press would publish it, but without success. Clara Lomas published the English version of *The Rebel* in 1994 and the Spanish version in 2004. The English version of the quotation is from Lomas's introduction to *The Rebel*, xxxix. The Spanish is from Villegas de Magnón, *Le rebelde*, 52.

2   Kanellos, "Brief History," 100.

3   Among the many works that examine the role played by Mexicans in the United States in the Revolution, see Griswold del Castillo, "Mexican Revolution"; García, *Desert Immigrants*; Montejano, *Anglos and Mexicans*; Zamora, *World*; Pérez, *Decolonial Imaginary*; Lomas, "Transborder Discourse"; and Marroquín

Arredondo, Franco, and Mieri, *Open Borders to a Revolution*. For an engaging microhistory of the revolution in El Paso, Texas, see Romo, *Ringside Seat to a Revolution*.

4   Johnson, *Revolution in Texas*, 42. For more on the women of this circle, especially in terms of their roles as educators, see Enoch, *Refiguring Rhetorical Education*.

5   See Pratt, "Modernity and Periphery."

6   Paredes, *Texas-Mexican Cancionero*, xiv.

7   For example, the important edited collection *Sex in Revolution* focuses on gender yet mentions none of the dozens of *fronterizas* who actively engaged the war as writers and in other capacities. See Olcott, Vaughan, and Cano, *Sex in Revolution*.

8   Chasteen, Introduction, vii–viii.

9   Rama, *Lettered City*, 105 (hereafter cited as *LC*).

10 De la Campa, *Latin Americanism*, 132.

11 In describing the Mexican center, I borrow the term *centrifugal* from Leal, "Mexico's Centrifugal Culture," 111–12.

12 Lambright and Guerrero, *Unfolding the City*, xix.

13 I examine the gender dynamics of these borderlands *letrados* in my manuscript in progress, tentatively titled *Revolutionary Subjects: The Mexican Revolution and the Transnational Emergence of Mexican American Literature and Culture, 1910–1959*.

14 Vasconcelos, *Memorias*, 1:65.

15 Tiller, "George Santayana."

16 Zuñiga, "El norte de México"; Alonso, *Thread of Blood*, 18.

17 Tabuenca Córdoba, "Sketches of Identities," 498.

18 Skirius, "Vasconcelos."

19 Vasconcelos, *Memorias*, 1:554, quoted in Zuñiga, "El norte de México," 19.

20 Vasconcelos, *Memorias*, 1:31.

21 Vasconcelos, *Memorias*, 1:54.

22 Quoted in Lomas, Introduction, xli.

23 Griswold del Castillo, "Mexican Revolution," 44.

24 Griswold del Castillo, "Mexican Revolution," 46.

25 Quoted in Griswold del Castillo, "Mexican Revolution," 46. Italics mine.

26 Griswold del Castillo, "Mexican Revolution," 46.

27 Quoted in Limón, "El Primer Congreso Mexicanista de 1911," 96. My translation.

28 *La crónica*, "El león despierta," July 13, 1911, quoted in Zamora, *World*, 97.

29 Gutiérrez, *Walls and Mirrors*, 6.

30 Idar, "Tanto los niños Mexicanos." Jessica Enoch, from whom I quote the English translation (*Refiguring Rhetorical Education*, 139), attributes the translation to Raquel Moran Tellez and Malena Florin.

31 Sadowski-Smith and Fox, "Theorizing the Hemisphere," 7.

Works Cited

Alonso, Ana María. *Thread of Blood: Colonialism, Revolution, and Gender on Mexico's Northern Frontier*. Tucson: University of Arizona Press, 1995.

Chasteen, John Charles. Introduction to *The Lettered City*, edited and translated by John Charles Chasteen, vii–xiv. Durham, NC: Duke University Press, 1996.

de la Campa, Roman. *Latin Americanism*. Minneapolis: University of Minnesota Press, 1999.

Enoch, Jessica. *Refiguring Rhetorical Education: Women Teaching African American, Native American, and Chicano/a Students, 1865–1911*. Carbondale: Southern Illinois University Press, 2008.

García, Mario T. *Desert Immigrants: The Mexicans of El Paso, 1880–1920*. New Haven, CT: Yale University Press, 1981.

Griswold del Castillo, Richard. "The Mexican Revolution and the Spanish-Language Press in the Borderlands." *Journalism History* 4, no. 2 (1977): 42–47.

Gutiérrez, David G. *Walls and Mirrors: Mexican Americans, Mexican Immigrants, and the Politics of Ethnicity*. Berkeley: University of California Press, 1995.

Idar, Clemente. "Tanto los niños Mexicanos como los Mexico-Americanos, son excluidos de las Escuelas Oficiales." *La crónica*, December 24, 1910.

Johnson, Benjamin Heber. *Revolution in Texas: How a Forgotten Rebellion and Its Bloody Suppression Turned Mexicans into Americans*. New Haven, CT: Yale University Press, 2003.

Kanellos, Nicolás. "A Brief History of Hispanic Periodicals in the United States." In *Hispanic Periodicals in the United States, Origins to 1960: A Brief History and Comprehensive Bibliography*, edited by Nicolás Kanellos with Helvetia Martell, 3–136. Houston: Arte Público, 2000.

Lambright, Anne, and Elisabeth Guerrero, eds. *Unfolding the City: Women Write the City in Latin America*. Minneapolis: University of Minnesota Press, 2007.

Leal, Luis. "Mexico's Centrifugal Culture." *Discourse* 18, nos. 1–2 (1995–96): 111–21.

Limón, José E. "El Primer Congreso Mexicanista de 1911: A Precursor to Contemporary Chicanismo." *Aztlan* 5, nos. 1–2 (1974): 85–117.

Lomas, Clara. Introduction to *The Rebel*, by Leonor Villegas de Magnón, xi–lvi. Houston: Arte Público, 1994.

Lomas, Clara. "Transborder Discourse: The Articulation of Gender on the Borderlands in the Early Twentieth Century." *Frontiers* 24, nos. 2–3 (2003): 51–74.

Marroquín Arredondo, Jaime, Adela Pineda Franco, and Magdalena Mieri, eds. *Open Borders to a Revolution: Culture, Politics, and Migration.* Washington, DC: Smithsonian Institution Scholarly Press, 2013.

Montejano, David. *Anglos and Mexicans in the Making of Texas, 1836–1986.* Austin: University of Texas Press, 1987.

Olcott, Jocelyn, Mary Kay Vaughan, and Gabriela Cano, eds. *Sex in Revolution: Gender, Politics, and Power in Modern Mexico.* Durham, NC: Duke University Press, 2006.

Paredes, Américo. *A Texas-Mexican Cancionero: Folksongs of the Lower Border.* Urbana: University of Illinois Press, 1976.

Pérez, Emma. *The Decolonial Imaginary: Writing Chicanas into History.* Bloomington: Indiana University Press, 1999.

Pratt, Mary Louise. "Modernity and Periphery: Toward a Global and Relational Analysis." *Beyond Dichotomies: Histories, Identities, Cultures, and the Challenge of Globalization,* edited by Elisabeth Mudimbe-Boyi, 21–47. Albany: State University of New York Press, 2002.

Rama, Angel. *The Lettered City,* edited and translated by John Charles Chasteen. Durham, NC: Duke University Press, 1996.

Romo, David Dorado. *Ringside Seat to a Revolution: An Underground Cultural History of El Paso and Juárez, 1893–1923.* El Paso, TX: Cinco Puntos, 2005.

Sadowski-Smith, Claudia, and Claire F. Fox, "Theorizing the Hemisphere: Inter-Americas Work at the Intersection of American, Canadian, and Latin American Studies." *Comparative American Studies* 2, no. 1 (2004): 5–38.

Skirius, John. "Vasconcelos and *México de Afuera* (1928)." *Aztlán* 7, no. 3 (1976): 479–97.

Tabuenca Córdoba, María Socorro. "Sketches of Identities from the Mexico-US Border (or the Other Way Around)." *Comparative American Studies* 3, no. 4 (2005): 495–513.

Tiller, Glenn. "George Santayana: Ordinary Reflection Systematized." In vol. 1 of *The Oxford Handbook of American Philosophy,* edited by Cheryl Misak, 125–44. Oxford: Oxford University Press, 2008.

Vasconcelos, José. *Ulises criollo: La vida del autor escrita por él mismo.* Mexico City: Botas, 1935. Repr. as *Memorias.* Vols. 1–2. Mexico City: Fondo de Cultura Económica, 1982.

Villegas de Magnón, Leonor. *La rebelde,* edited by Clara Lomas. Houston: Arte Público Press, 2004.

Zamora, Emilio. *The World of the Mexican Worker in Texas.* College Station: Texas A&M University Press, 1993.

Zuñiga, Victor. "El norte de México como desierto cultural: Anatomía de una idea." *Puentelibre* 1 (1995): 18–23.

Reading the Contingencies of Print on the Borderlands

ELISE BARTOSIK-VÉLEZ

Abstract   One of the most vivid accounts in the historical record of the Pueblo Revolt of
1680 was written by Antonio de Otermín, Spanish governor of the province of Santa Fe
de Nuevo México, who fled the uprising with his life intact, unlike four hundred of his
countrymen. Due to a series of decisions by scholars, editors, and grant agencies in the
twentieth century, this letter is today best known in an English translation and within the
frame provided by the popular *Heath Anthology of American Literature*. The appropriation of Otermín's letter by the discipline of American (US) literature, because its subject matter involves territory that more than two hundred years later became part of the
United States, merits scrutiny. One approach, outlined here, is to follow the traces of
the publication history of this document and to interrogate the unique story it tells about
the contingencies of print on the borderlands.

Keywords   borderlands, canon, American literature, translation, book history

In his letter dated September 8, 1680, to Francisco de Ayeta, the Spanish governor of the province of Santa Fe de Nuevo México, Antonio de Otermín, reported on the revolt of the Pueblo Indians. That letter describes how, after more than eighty years of Spanish rule in the region, Puebloans rebelled on August 10, killing four hundred Spaniards. Since 1990 an English translation of Otermín's account (first published in the 1930s) has been included in the popular *Heath Anthology of American Literature*.[1] Since then two other anthologies of American literature have also included that same translation.[2] Each year scores of undergraduates taking American literature classes in the United States now read the English translation of Otermín's letter, a text whose inclusion in these anthologies amounts to its being claimed by early "American" (read: US) literary history.

Meanwhile, the original manuscript *in Spanish* remained unpublished in Seville's Archivo General de las Indias until 2017, when Jerry Craddock and Barbara De Marco transcribed and published it on the University of California, Berkeley, Cíbola Project website.[3] This partly explains why the Latin Americanists and borderlands scholars whom I asked about Otermín's letter had never heard of it (as I had not),

ENGLISH LANGUAGE NOTES

56:2, October 2018   DOI 10.1215/00138282-6960812
© 2018 Regents of the University of Colorado

yet my English Department colleague with whom I recently cotaught a class on literature of the early Americas suggested we include it in our syllabus.

Our class engaged in a fascinating discussion on my failure to provide Otermín's letter in Spanish for students taking the course for Spanish credit. Could it not be argued, we asked, that Otermín's letter had more to do with Spanish imperialism and New Spain—even modern Mexico—than with the prehistory of the future United States? Or did Otermín's text fit in our course simply because it refers to events that occurred in territory that later became part of the United States?

The *Heath* instructor's guide encourages us to teach Otermín's letter as an example of local resistance to global colonialism.[4] My students certainly wanted to read the Puebloans as prenational protestors against the Spanish powers that be. I recalled Claire Fox's critique of "literature of the Americas" courses during my class discussions. She has called them "the fashionable Anglo-American *mea culpa* that strives to think globally while controlling the terms, and language, of the debate."[5]

An alternative approach is to follow the trail created by the publication history of Otermín's letter. Two key moments shape that history, the first in 1937 when only the English translation of Otermín's letter was published in volume 3 of *Historical Documents Relating to New Mexico, Nueva Vizcaya, and Approaches Thereto, to 1773* by Charles W. Hackett. The previous two volumes included both Spanish transcriptions and English translations. It appears that financial considerations—and Hackett's desire to quickly finish a project that he originally began more than ten years prior—dictated this change in volume 3.[6] The second key moment was some fifty years later when the late Chicano studies scholar Juan Bruce-Novoa selected the English translation published in Hackett's book for inclusion in the *Heath Anthology*. In the first edition Otermín's letter was oddly placed at the end of a section called "Seventeenth-Century Wit," which featured the work of Edward Taylor and Cotton Mather. The instructor's guide suggests that students "write on what this event signifies in U.S. history." This framing, perpetuated in later editions and different anthologies that included the document, prevents a full appreciation of Otermín's letter either as a document of Spanish imperialism or as a source illuminating indigenous history. But explicitly tracing the publication history of this letter allows us to uncover the process by which it has been claimed by early American literature, and it provides an opportunity to address the contingencies that influence how scholars interpret primary texts.

ELISE BARTOSIK-VÉLEZ is professor of Spanish at Dickinson College. Her book, *The Legacy of Christopher Columbus in the Americas: New Nations and a Transatlantic Discourse of Empire*, appeared in 2014. She is most recently author of "Simón Bolívar's Rome" in the *International Journal of the Classical Tradition* (2016) and "Recovered Possibilities: Moving the Seats of Empire from England and Spain to America" in *Atlantic Studies: Global Currents* (2018). Her current scholarship focuses on the legacy of the classical world in British and Spanish America.

Notes

1   This English translation was published in Hackett, *Historical Documents*, 3:327–35.

2   Mulford et al., *Early American Writings*; Castillo and Schweitzer, *Literatures of Colonial America*.

3   De Marco and Craddock, "Documents from the Early Days."

4   "The central issue raised by these selections revolve[s] around the opposing forces of colonialism and native resistance to it" (Bruce-Novoa, "Hypertext Instructor Guide").

5   Fox, "Comparative Literary Studies of America," 871.

6   Charles W. Hackett to A. V. Kidder, Carnegie Institute of Washington, June 17, 1933, and August 22, 1935, Adolph and Fanny Bandelier file, box 2, folder 39, Carnegie Institute of Science, Washington, DC.

Works Cited

Bruce-Novoa, Juan. "Hypertext Instructor Guide: Tales of Incorporation, Resistance, and Reconquest in New Spain." In *The Heath Anthology of American Literature*. 3rd ed. college .cengage.com/english/lauter/heath/3e /instructors/syllabuild/iguide/puebrev.html.

Castillo, Susan, and Ivy Schweitzer, eds. *The Literatures of Colonial America: An Anthology*. Malden, MA: Blackwell, 2001.

De Marco, Barbara, and Jerry R. Craddock, eds. "Documents from the Early Days of the Pueblo Revolt of 1680: Archivo General de Indias, Audiencia de Guadalajara, legajo 138, fols. 199r–265r, 470v–558v." Research Center for Romance Studies. escholarship.org/uc/item /4v34d0nw.

Fox, Claire. "Comparative Literary Studies of the Americas." *American Literature* 76, no. 4 (2004): 871–86.

Hackett, Charles W. *Historical Documents Relating to New Mexico, Nueva Vizcaya, and Approaches Thereto, to 1773*. 3 vols. Washington, DC: Carnegie Institution of Washington, 1937.

Mulford, Carla, Angela Vietto, and Amy E. Winans, eds. *Early American Writings*. New York: Oxford University Press, 2002.

Latin Place Making in the Late Nineteenth and Early Twentieth Centuries

Cuban Émigrés and Their Transnational Impact in Tampa, Florida

KENYA C. DWORKIN Y MÉNDEZ

Abstract   Starting in the mid-1880s and becoming fully effective by the 1930s, the "curriculum of culture" that Tampa's Latin immigrant, cigar-making enclaves experienced circulated in the spaces they and others occupied regularly—the cigar factory, mutual aid society, the coffeehouse, and the theater (also homes and the union hall). These Cuban (and Spanish and Italian) cultural and social values were passed on from one generation to the next within the community, and even to non-Cubans, via reverse assimilation. The outcome was an ethnic American social identity whose impact thoroughly transformed living and working spaces in a segregated, Jim Crow space and fundamentally reshaped its landscape, foodways, and identity. The brand of "Americanism" that Tampa's Latin community practiced did not typically display the competitive individualism often associated with traditional Americanism, instead emphasizing living as a community and fostering cooperation and affiliations among numerous sociocultural groups.
Keywords   Hispanic, Latino, immigration, theater, community of place

Tampa Latins and Their "Curriculum of Culture"

This article discusses what I call a "curriculum of culture," a phenomenon whose impact then and even now in Tampa, Florida, is a culturally situated set of values that convey knowledge, beliefs, and behaviors.[1] It is contingent on community-defined and redefined competencies regarding how not only to survive and thrive in the host society but also to be agents of their own lives and mediate social class and cultural differences. In Tampa's Latin enclaves, this "course of instruction" was experienced or, more accurately, circulated in primary spaces cigar makers and others occupied regularly—the cigar factory, mutual aid society, the coffeehouse, and the theater (it also circulated at home and in the union hall). The outcome of this curriculum was a situated social identity. These immigrants culturally and

ENGLISH LANGUAGE NOTES
56:2, October 2018 DOI 10.1215/00138282-6960823
© 2018 Regents of the University of Colorado

architecturally transformed a city whose dominant population, identity, and culture were white, southern, and segregationist. In the twentieth century, it even impacted the government-sponsored Federal Theater in Tampa. Edward Hale Bierstadt's research on immigrants to this country and efforts to Americanize them focuses almost entirely on what was and continues to be done to promote their assimilation, but seldom on how the immigrants themselves affected the nation and their communities.[2] My intention here is to demonstrate the extremely important role that this curriculum of culture had in allowing Tampa Latins to "stage" their identities, concerns, attitudes, and values over many decades, and of particular interest, between 1887 and 1930, the community's formative years and a period of significant US expansion into the Spanish-speaking Caribbean.[3]

Before *Latino*: When "Latin Community" Took On a New Meaning of Its Own

Immigrants transformed the American urban landscape through their participation in agriculture, manufacturing and related industries, transportation, communications and utilities, wholesale and retail trade, and services between 1880 and 1920, during the Second Industrial Revolution. In Tampa, Florida, the situation was no different during that same period, except that the manufacturing that literally put the city on the map did not involve new technologies but a tradition that required individual and collective expertise and workmanship—cigar making.

In 1886 Ybor City, a small enclave in Tampa, became home to thousands of immigrants escaping difficult economic and political circumstances in their homelands—Cuba, Spain, and later Sicily. Motivated by investment opportunities and production problems, a select number of Spanish and Cuban businessmen, among them Martínez Ybor, for whom the enclave was named, brought to Tampa the one manufacturing industry that almost single-handedly fueled the city's economic boom—the hand-rolled cigar business.[4] The relocation of this industry, first from Cuba to Key West, then from Key West to Tampa, fueled immigration of hundreds and then thousands of highly skilled Cuban workers (and Spaniards and Sicilians) to a small town of under eight hundred people. In ten years the population had grown sixfold; by 1900 it was fifteen thousand, thanks largely to the influx of Cubans, Spaniards, and Sicilians, in that order of importance. By 1930 the city's population was over one hundred thousand, 25 percent of which was Cuban (prior to the 1930s, the black Cuban population was roughly 15 percent of the total Cuban population, but it dwindled significantly from the 1930s on).[5]

This transnational workforce brought with it its cultures, languages, foods, social and familial practices, politics, music, and, of particular interest, a highly developed tradition of popular performance. These immigrants did not come in search of work but brought it with them, a relatively unusual circumstance in US immigration history. That the industry established in Tampa was Cuban, and a large percentage of the workers were too, essentially guaranteed that Cuban culture would end up being the de facto *cultura franca*. Spaniards maintained their specific culture through their own networks and organizations, as did Sicilians, who also had to learn Spanish.[6] Some of the almost daily elements typical of the lives of cigar workers that made it very easy for them to remain predominantly Spanish-speaking and connected to their cultures included being able spend the day speaking Spanish and conversing with *lectores* or fellow *tabaqueros* as they worked. In addition, most if not all of the food and other supplies they and their families needed were purchased at bodegas or other Spanish-speaking stores. However, it is imperative to also include key aspects of working in a Cuban-style factory town that ensured the survival of Cuban and other immigrant cultures: living in delimited ethnic enclaves; constantly receiving new immigrants from the home countries; creating vibrant, multifaceted mutual aid societies; having myriad coffeehouses of their own at which to share ideas; and creating and promoting popular theater and other cultural activities couched in their cultures and values.[7]

This "habitus" could be seen as a milieu through which individuals and groups of individuals learned through mimesis or imitation.[8] Such a combination of social and cultural factors allowed Tampa Latins to reproduce their social structure, find solutions to their community's problems, and shape their futures.[9] Behavioral psychology, too, posits that people develop behaviors through social learning and then imitation, with the expectation that they will be rewarded (or punished).[10] John Bodnar argues that some immigrants promoted their unique culture, mentality, and consciousness and created a new type of culture: "This culture was not a simple extension of the past . . . or simply an affirmation of a desire to become an American . . . and posits that immigrants claimed and deployed personal and collective agency, using their knowledge of the past, to shape their futures, and stay positive about their current situations."[11] Jeffrey Mirel contends that, although immigrants to the United States were still attached to their cultural traditions after arriving, they also became attached to American democracy, explaining that although they learned about American history and patriotic allegiance to their new country, they also "put their distinctive stamp on them" and, in effect, created a new kind of America and American.[12] In Tampa the collective Latin identity became an identity-establishing manifestation of their sense of collective belonging, of being a community, with *community* signifying a form of togetherness that a group attempts to foster through a search for common ground.[13] This multiplicity of people and perspectives also recalls Kristina Wirtz's assertion regarding Mikhail Bakhtin's 1981 exploration of the carnivalesque, which she sees in Cuba *bufo* and which I see functioning as a chronotope of sorts because the genre contains a dialogic play of voices that allows for experiments with new social alignments and identifications.[14]

The Four Elements of the Tampa Latin Curriculum of Culture

What follows is an initial review of the four elements of a curriculum of culture particular to Tampa's Latin community and, to some extent, those surrounding or somehow a part of it. Each section of the article breaks down the origin, context, and impact of the activity itself, the places in which it happens, and the porous nature of the spaces dividing those places, which facilitated both circulation and cross-fertilization. Because of this curriculum of culture, what started in the 1880s as discreet immigrant group identities—Cuban, Spanish, and Italian—eventually transformed into what could be seen as an increasingly collective identity by the late 1930s, due to the Depression but especially World War II. This collective Tampa Latin identity combined elements of all three group's traditions and values, a few of those of their American equivalents, and allowed them to evolve from immigrants and exiles to ethnic Americans. Importantly, though, the brand of "Americanism" they practiced did not typically display the competitive individualism often associated with traditional Americanism, and instead they emphasized living as a community and fostering cooperation and affiliations among numerous sociocultural groups.[15]

Latin Mutual Aid: "With All, and for the Good of All"

The very people responsible for Tampa's growth began their new lives in enclaves that would remain segregated from the rest of the same city that benefited so immensely from their presence, hard work, and culture.[16] The fraternal benefit societies Tampa Latins built (known as mutual aid societies, or *sociedades benéficas*) were a product of much-needed autonomy and self-reliance.[17] With roots in mutualism and cooperativism, the many services they offered, and the philosophy behind them make them clear examples of the Tampa Latin curriculum at work.[18]

Facing a denial of medical and other services due to white Tampan discrimination, mutual aid societies fashioned after Hispano-Cuban models were built by the three major ethnic groups represented among Ybor City's population. La Iguala, started by a Cuban doctor, was the first medical establishment. Others included El Porvenir, established for Spanish residents; the Sociedad La Benéfica for Cubans; and the González and Trelles clinics for the Latin community at large. The hospitals that were built shortly after, the Sanatorio del Centro Español (Centro Español Sanatorium) and the Centro Asturiano Hospital, were full-service institutions and served most of the community for decades, even after health care became more available to Tampa Latin residents outside their ghettoes after World War II. The first, full-fledged mutual aid societies were the Círculo Cubano (founded 1902, white Cuban), Sociedad La Unión Martí-Maceo (founded 1907, black Cuban), the Centro Español (founded 1891, Spanish), Centro Asturiano (founded 1902), and the Unione Italiana (founded 1894, Sicilian/Italian).[19] There was one other institution in Ybor City, the German-American Club,[20] and similar institutions and activities in West Tampa, another immigrant enclave, like the Centro Español de West Tampa and La Sicilia.[21] At their inception, the *sociedades* were voluntary, state-chartered fraternal associations with a representative governmental structure that for a monthly fee offered benefits: for instance, in-house health services and hospitalization (functioning much like early health maintenance organizations), burial insurance, worker's compensation, instruction (even American citizenship classes), theater and other cultural events,[22] gathering places, and meeting rooms for members and community residents. Eligibility for membership in these societies was not a matter of simply belonging to the right ethnic group. "Good character," which can be interpreted as embracing the values espoused by the "community" and also as a precept in the core of the "curriculum of culture," was an important element in membership in any of these societies; one had to be sponsored by two members in good standing to join one of these organizations. They were more than safe havens for members of each ethnic group; they were also leading sites at which club members could keep up their language and culture and perform, perpetuate, and experiment with their national and new, incipient identities.

These societies also dramatically changed the city's landscape with the architectural grandeur of building styles, which included Spanish, Moorish, and French Renaissance; Renaissance; Greek and Classical Revival; Neoclassical; and Beaux Arts. Some but not all of the extant buildings, including cigar factories, are protected as national and Florida historical heritage sites.

Latin Coffeehouses: "Caffeine Nation" or a Level Playing Field

What the mutual aid societies and cigar factories had in terms of order and structure was exactly what coffeehouses, with their unstructured meetings and parley, lacked, which is why they were so appealing for their informal and sometimes inflammatory conversation.[23] Ray Oldenburg analyzes the general public good performed by cafés, coffee shops, and other such places, explaining the essential function that public meeting places have in established and aspiring democratic societies. Oldenburg describes some of the functions of what he calls the "third place" (the other two being home and work) as "ports of entry" for visitors and newcomers, as staging areas for social and political activities, multigenerational settings, and entertainment and mutual aid centers.[24] Tampa's Latin coffeehouses were and continue to be no different.

These sites became meeting places at which the curriculum of culture was the unwritten script of every day. When one takes into account that the curriculum of culture circulating at the factories and coffeehouses spilled over into homes, ethnic clubs, union halls, and theater, it becomes clear that cultural performance and performativity were constantly reiterated at all levels of Tampa immigrant society: "[Third] places are political fora of great importance."[25] Indeed, the subject of politics appears to have been and remains the most popular theme of coffeehouse conversation in Tampa. Perhaps most important, coffeehouses were "leveler" spaces, a mid-seventeenth-century English term referring to anything "which reduces men to an equality."[26]

Thus between 1886 and 1931 cigar workers met on a daily basis (perhaps twice a day) to discuss the contents of the cigar factory reader's morning or afternoon readings and other local, national, and global matters, a true example of performance and situated identity. More crucially, by the 1940s white, southern politicians adapted to and adopted this Latin custom and Latin fund-raising traditions and strategies for growing political support, having clearly identified them as spaces for potential influence, powerful evidence of how Latins in Tampa transformed their surrounding society.

"The Reader Lights the Candle": A "Radical" Workplace Education

Lectores, another crucial element of the Tampa Latins' curriculum of culture, were the men (seldom women) who read to workers in cigar factories while they worked.[27] It should be considered "radical" for two reasons: one, because the tradition is unique in an industrial context, and two, because in Tampa the content of the reading was not only mind expanding but also au courant with the local curriculum of culture. The custom traces back to early nineteenth-century Cuban jails, when *lectores* read to prisoners and, later, to 1864, when a reader was hired to read to cigar makers in Bejucal, Cuba. In Tampa, the lector became an essential part of labor culture.[28] Louis Pérez Jr. reiterates José Martí's idea that the "factories [were] like colleges, . . . schools where the hand that folds the tobacco leaf by day, lifts the text at night": "The *lectura* was itself a veritable system of education dealing with a variety of subjects, including politics, labor, literature, and international relations."[29]

The newspapers read to the workers by the lector tended to be in Spanish, locally produced or not, as in the case of *La gaceta*, from Ybor City (still existing after nearly one hundred years), *La traducción-prensa*, the *Diario de la marina*, and trade union labor-oriented papers like the *Boletín obrero*, *El internacional*, *Il obrero industriale*, and the *United States Tobacco Leaf Journal*. *Lectores* also read nonliterary materials to cigar makers, among them works by Karl Marx and Mikhail Bakunin. Some of the most widely read authors were Miguel de Cervantes, Honoré de Balzac, Fyodor Dostoyevsky, Cirilo Villaverde, Benito Pérez Galdós, Jules Verne, Charles Dickens, and Victor Hugo.

Broadly defined, performance and instruction were at the center of the lector tradition. Readers at cigar factories and the reciprocal engagement of the cigar workers with them created an undeniable performance dynamic. The relationship between the lector and his interlocutors/listeners was a performative strategy with which these immigrants negotiated and constructed their opinions and identities. The workers auditioned, hired, and tithed *lectores* a portion of their weekly salary to pay them, thus exercising agency in their own education and interpellation. Unfortunately, the lector tradition survived only about forty years. By 1931 cigar factory owners strategically decided to disallow the lector practice because they considered it a source of subversive, antimanagement propaganda and labor unrest. This loss could have been a veritable deathblow to immigrant identity, except that ethnic theater, especially the Tampa Cuban variety, essentially took over where the lector left off; 1931 was the same year when *lectores* were banned from the factories and locally written theater emerged.

From Factory to Footlights: When Cuban Workers Became Actors
Emilio del Río tells us in his autobiography *Yo fui uno de los fundadores de Ybor City* that the very day he arrived in Key West from Havana, in search of work in early 1886, he was approached by Proceso San Martín, president of the Instituto San Carlos, Key West's Cuban club (he was also director of its theatrical section).[30] San Martín queried del Río on the subject of theater in Cuba because he was looking for a small company to stage a popular drama, *Amor de madre* (1842) by Ventura de la Vega, at the San Carlos club theater. Del Río told the impresario that although the members of his family in Havana were not professional players, they had a lot of experience on the stage. San Martín, seeing potential in del Río and his family, took him to factory owner Vicente Martínez Ybor, who gave him a job and a pay advance so he could immediately bring his family over from Cuba to Key West. Within a few weeks he and two women debuted in the principal roles of the aforementioned

drama and became quite well known. He later performed in the same play in Tampa in 1887 after the great fire of March 29, 1886, that destroyed so much of Key West and helped trigger the relocation of a large part of the cigar industry to Tampa.[31]

In Tampa, also in 1886, Cuban cigar workers José Santos and Pedro del Río turned the former cigar leaf stripping building that Martínez Ybor had donated to his workers into Ybor City's first theatrical venue. The building was promptly named the Liceo Cubano and became home to patriotic, educational, and cultural activities. In early 1887 it opened with what would be Ybor City's first stage debut, a performance of the 1872 play *Amor de Madre*, by the Spanish playwright Ventura de la Vega. Given the lack of documentation, it is difficult to say, but it is very likely that this debut constituted the first theatrical performance of any kind, in Spanish or English, in all of Tampa.

Amateurs, professionals, and mixed groups alike, many of whose members were cigar makers or *lectores*, performed to extremely devoted audiences in the productions that ensued in Ybor City and West Tampa.[32] After the new Círculo building was built in 1907, with a nine-hundred-seat theater included (as well as cantina, pharmacy, library, dancing floor, gymnasium, and boxing arena), its *sección de declamación* immediately began contracting professional companies from Cuba, which brought with them several very popular *bufo* plays, and also worked on strengthening its own in-house company and repertoire.

The genre that fit this need best was *bufo*, an original Cuban genre born of a Spanish predecessor that incorporated a lot of native Cuban music that, among other things, reinforced its audience's connection with Cuba.[33] Typically, *bufo* plays can best be described as lighthearted, one- to three-act plays containing satirical language, double entendre, sexual innuendo, music, and dancing in a formulaic farce of high- and low-class society. Often they contain a stock character, the *negrito*, or black man, who is almost always played by a white man in blackface, although there are some notable exceptions to this.[34]

What made *bufo* so popular for Tampa audiences was its humor, musicality, and satirical nature. *Bufo* was extremely instrumental because it was a site where the immigrant community could process their experiences as transplanted but still very much connected Cubans. In addition, it was a site through which they proposed, reviewed, and promoted current and future possibilities. Following Augusto Boal's view of strategically purposeful theater, the instrumentality of Cuban-style *bufo* in this context often was to convert the members of its audiences from spectators to agentive actors, to inspire and promote reflection and discussion, and to "rehearse actions toward social change."[35] One could say, regarding the relationship of theater, performance, and performativity among Tampa's Cuban cigar workers, that they "[inhabited] a performance-based dramaturgical culture."[36] Any "division between performativity (the *doing*), and performance (the *done*) [had] vanished."[37] Performativity and performative language not only describe but also represent and produce social action. In this way, Tampa's Cuban theater was an "enactment of a composite experience that all participants (audience and players) recognized, and at the moment, responded to emotionally. . . . Multiple repeated performances [became] entrenched in performativity."[38] To contextualize this in the cigar workers' curriculum of culture, we must appreciate that memory is essential to performativity: "[Memory] is a mediator of performance and performativity as the repetition of collective memory becomes enacted in the doing."[39]

In the theatrical section of a 1904 issue of *Cuba y América: Revista ilustrada*, a Havana publication, Adrián del Valle, using the pseudonym Fructidor (a reference to the French Revolution), offers a rather benign view of popular theater in Cuba at the time based on his experience witnessing what he described as "light" theater:

> Esas obras ligeras [*sic*], que reproducen costumbres típicas, que copian, exagerándolos un poco, cieto caracteres populares; esas obras que, aún cuando se manifiestan dentro de llamado género chico, son obras de artes, porque hay en ellas . . . verdad, en dósis más ó menos grandes. . . . [Esas] obras . . . son preferibles á muchas obras de altos vuelos. ¿Qué sería del teatro si todos fueran dramas y tragedias?

> [Those light plays, which reproduce typical customs, which they copy and whose certain, popular characters they exaggerate a bit, even those appearing in *género chico* works [*zarzuelas*], are works of art, because they contain . . . truth, in more or less large doses. . . . [These] works . . . are preferable to many highbrow ones. What would be of theater if it were all dramas and tragedies?][40]

However, Nicolás Kanellos, in writing about the reception of *bufo* theater among the more conservative middle to upper classes, whose practices and values were often criticized in *bufo*, notes that on May 29, 1911, "Chalo," the critic from the *Diario de Tampa*, one of several, locally published, Spanish-language newspapers, "soundly censured Miyares's company [one of the visiting troupes] for their 'terrible *zarzuelicidio'*" (*zarzuela* murder).[41] While the critic explicitly mentioned director-actor Miyares's poor singing, there is no specific mention of audience response. However, it would not be unreasonable to assume that the critic considered the *zarzuelas*, some of them locally written, in bad taste because of their satirical nature and abundant use of street language and images. *Bufo* was similarly criticized forty years earlier in colonial Cuba, when it emerged as a popular tool for sharp criticism of the island's colonial condition. The productions were clearly "hitting a nerve." In fact, the working-class public's purported taste for "low brow" satire was attacked in the 1910s, in Tampa, in the same way it had been in Cuba, in the 1880s, potentially for the same reason. Yet a few years later, Miyares's troupe continued being invited from Cuba to play in Tampa; his company later performed a run of highly popular, parodic, and sharply critical *zarzuelas*, some locally written.

What the theater critic had perceived as lowbrow, popular humor was in fact a native Cuban theatrical form that had evolved from an earlier Spanish genre. *Bufo* came into vogue during the tense pre-independence period in Cuba and persists, in altered fashion, to the present day, both in Cuba and in Cuban immigrant communities (a variety of this form of theater can be found in present-day Miami). This originally Spanish-Cuban *bufo* genre eventually became inherently Cuban, then Tampa-Cuban. Tampa playwrights used it as an efficient tool with which to comment on social, economic, political, and cultural realities in Cuba and among Cubans and other immigrants in Tampa.[42] However, even in the first ten or fifteen years of the twentieth century, Cuban theater in Tampa had not yet entirely found its own voice, its own purpose; it still modeled itself on its island precursor thematically and in terms of characters. During this period the Círculo was still contracting Cuban professional touring companies, which, in any event, emphasizes the frequently seamless nature of Cuban culture on either side of the Florida Straits at that particular time.

A Two-Way Mirror on Cuba and the United States: Theater during the "Dance of the Millions"

The 1920s were the heyday of imported Cuban theater at the Círculo Cubano. Some of the best-known Cuban companies played there, as well as at other national and local venues. These highly regarded Cuban companies, which dominated marquees in Havana, contributed substantively to local efforts to bolster and promote Cuban identity, contributing to the local curriculum of culture by emphasizing themes embracing working-class ethics, workers' rights, job and economic instability, and US influence in Cuba. One of the plays, performed by the Baby-Colina group joined by both the Círculo's own adult and children's groups, was *Las vacas flacas* (*The Skinny Cows*), a parody of a prosperous period in Cuba during the late teens and 1920s known as *las vacas gordas*, "the fat cows" (equivalent to the United States' own Roaring Twenties), and the economic downturn that ensued. It seems that the play's (unknown) writer knew as early as 1923 that the period's "sugar-coated" prosperity would not last forever. According to Kanellos, in 1924 Cristino R. Inclán, a professional who sometimes played with the Círculo's *sección*, performed a monologue titled *Un tabaquero huelguista* (*The Striking Cigar Maker*), which gives ample evidence of the more serious, critical matters that were often addressed in popular theater.[43] Other plays from this period, performed by the "Bolito" Gutiérrez troupe, also clearly support the idea that Cuban theater at this time in Tampa addressed major social and political concerns among Tampa's cigar workers and Cubans, locally or abroad.

The mid- to late twenties saw a series of plays with local themes, among them *El tabaquero* (*The Cigar Maker*), *La honradez de un obrero* (*The Honesty of a Worker*), *Con todos y para todos* (*With All and for All*) by Ramón S. Varona, *The Cigar Leaf Stripper*, and *Cigar Making Machines or Death of the Industry*, the last one a reference to the incipient mechanical takeover of cheap cigar manufacturing by machines, which meant fewer jobs. However, two unpublished plays from the late 1920s that I recovered from the Special Collections Department at the University of South Florida, in Tampa, reveal the multiple viewpoints that existed among people of different social classes in Cuba and Tampa regarding their attitude toward their Cuban identity and US influence in Cuba. Specifically, one deals with a white, upper-middle-class Cuban who aspires to a seat in the Cuban senate and is a "wannabe *yanqui*"; the other with a similar male character who goes out of his way to prove to people in the United States that, under President Gerardo Machado, Cuba was progressing economically and was a great investment opportunity for American

Figure 1. Scanned frontispiece of "LOS ESPEJUELOS DE MACHADO," a one-act comedy by A.H. Ramos & Bolito (1927). Cuban Club records, Boxes 30-33. Special Collections Department, University of South Florida, Tampa, Florida.

speculators. Such topics, as well as the new migratory obstacles and government corruption, were inspired by and reflected in what was "reported" by newspapers, shared by *lectores*, discussed by cigar workers traveling to and from Cuba, and, of particular interest, depicted in popular theater.

Los espejuelos de Machado (*Machado's Spectacles*), a 1927 one-act play by Antonio H. Ramos and Roberto "Bolito" Gutiérrez, is a perfect example of a play that was written and performed transnationally. Its two authors were Cuban, its cast Cuban and Tampa Cuban. In this play, Mr. Fotoplay, a correspondent for US film magazine *Photoplay*, travels to Cuba at the request of a Cuban arriviste during the time of Prohibition (1920–33), a period that in great measure overlaps with Machado's first term. *Photoplay* was one of the first film fan magazines to focus on the lifestyle of the rich and famous among Hollywood's array of stars—an image that was promoted in Cuba and internationally. Yet the second half of the twenties was also a period of economic instability in Cuba, due to the sugar markets' ups and downs and expenditures resulting from Machado's construction of many public works, which made him famous.

Mr. Fotoplay's assignment is to photograph the wonders achieved by this president of a favorite tourist paradise for his US readers. However, the money generated by these grandiose projects was "distributed" very unevenly and better served the interests of Cuban investors and American interests, which set off a dramatic increase in protests by workers, trade unionists, and students who were swiftly and brutally repressed by Machado's forces. The Yankee photographer stumbles on all this quite by accident, as well as on Cuba's other reality, which his guide and other ordinary Cubans try to explain to him as he tours.[44]

Wealthy protagonist Don Jaime is responsible for inviting Mr. Fotoplay to gather visual evidence of the "new" Cuba, which reflects his own financial success, and that of his associates, more than any real improvement for everyday Cubans. When he tries to discuss with his wife, Doña Sinforosa, the wonders achieved by Machado, she, with newspaper in hand, retorts, "Déjate de guatequería y lee" (Stop your foolishness and read). We can assume that she is referring to articles about Machado's darker side: his dictatorial aspirations; violence against communists, workers, and students; reorganization of the army; and generally brutal tactics.[45]

When Mr. Fotoplay arrives, Don Jaime orders his black servant, Tintorero (Spanish for Dyer, a reference to his skin color), to serve as his guide around the city. The photographer, who is arrogant and insists on seeing only what he wants to see, follows him and discovers an unexpected reality. At this point the authors stage a play within a play, deploying a metatheatrical strategy so that Mr. Fotoplay, whose lens is preset to see only what interests the US public and pro-Machado Cubans, has a heteroglossic encounter with a "population" whose diverse opinions about their reality totally belie Don Jaime's.

All the interlocutors with whom Mr. Fotoplay interacts—both people and personified, inanimate things—offer a rhymed and musical criticism or compliment of their shortsighted president. Calles (Streets), for example, praises the splendor of the capital city's architectural wonders; the Gallego (Galician) lauds the president because his extremely poor family had arrived from Spain and was now doing well because of his successful business; la Prensa (the Press), we are told, publishes only the truth, without delay, documenting what is good or bad in the country; el Político (the Politician) does not want Tintorero to let Mr. Fotoplay say anything negative; Cuba Libre (Free Cuba), a drunken woman, explains that she drinks to forget her sorrows and is anxious for the freedom the island had when she fought for independence; Liborio is from Camagüey and owns a huge farm called "Cuba." He cultivates potatoes, cassava root, beans, and tobacco, and wants to grow something other than sugarcane so he can be independent of the sugar market. He wants to plant apple bananas, a native, small-scale crop. The character Apple Banana sings about his superiority, and Tobacco praises Liborio for having planted tobacco, Cuban tobacco being the best in the world. The Drunkard defends Bolshevism, shouting that Capital should die, and that he wants a social revolution; he says there is more hunger than justice, and the Constitution allows him to speak to the president and that he has a message for him. Uncle Sam congratulates Liborio for having sustained himself after the world sugar market's collapse; he reminds him that he is his friend, that he has proved that. Liborio expresses gratitude and acknowledges the United States' greatness but adds that he puts his faith in God and tells Uncle Sam that he doesn't need his help. Finally, Liborio shows Uncle Sam a copy of the new trade agreement Machado has signed with Spain (something the United States wanted to prevent). At the play's end, the curtain goes down, and the Cuban National Anthem is played. Throughout the entire play the heteroglossia Mr. Fotoplay encounters presents a seemingly endless array of direct and indirect reasons Cubans love or hate Cuba's current reality and its president. These voices offer a panoply of specific and personal perspectives regarding Cuba vis-à-vis the United States or Spain, political and economic independence, the trappings of monoculture, and

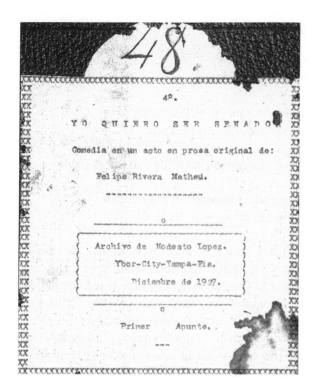

Figure 2. Scanned frontispiece of "YO QUIERO SER SENADOR," a one-act comedy by Felipe Rivera Matheu (1927). Cuban Club records, Boxes 30-33. Special Collections Department, University of South Florida, Tampa, Florida.

corruption, topics of extreme interest to Tampa audiences not only because of their strong connection to their Cuban identities and the island but also because of the economic dependence of the Tampa industry on Cuban tobacco, connection to cultural and labor institutions and practices there, and their ambivalent multipositionality as transnational residents—literal or figurative—of both places.[46]

Another transnational play written, presented, and witnessed by audiences on both sides of the Florida Straits was a 1927 work titled *Yo quiero ser senador* (*I Want to Be a Senator*), by Felipe Rivera Matheu. It features a very conceited member of the Cuban bourgeoisie who thinks he deserves a seat in the Cuban Senate. His pretense and affectation lead him to speak to his family in Peninsular Spanish. Yet he has also decided that English should replace Spanish in his household because it is the language of power and progress, and it could also guarantee him his coveted Senate seat. He is even willing to "sell" his daughter in marriage to an American banker. In one scene Don Serafín explains his designs, in a mixture of Spanish and bad English: "Gud nay . . . Under-stand? . . . Güel . . . Ol ray . . . Blanca se casará con Mister Roberts tan seguro como que hay God in the escay" (Good night . . . Understand? Well . . . Alright . . . Blanca will marry Mister Roberts as sure as there is a God in the sky). He then raves: "Jau greyt. Jau puri. Jau excelent. Jau biuriful. Jau . . . jau . . . jau . . ." (How great. How pretty. How excellent. How beautiful. How . . . how . . . how . . .).[47]

However, the daughter already has a suitor, an actor, and he decides to use his skills and Don Serafín's lust for English and power to beat him at his own game. He takes on the role of a rich American banker—in disastrous Spanish—but Don Serafín praises the suitor's language skills in his own terrible English, hoping to make points with him:

> SERAFÍN: Pero, dígame, mister, ¿cómo usted siendo americano habla tan
>   bien el castellano?
> RAÚL: Oh, mocho poquita. Solo dos mesas en Puerta Rica. [*sic*]
> SERAFÍN: Pues, lo habla usted como un nativo del país.
>
> [SERAFÍN: But, tell me, mister. How do you, an American, speak Castilian
>   so well?
> RAÚL: Oh. Very little. Only two tables [months] in Puerto Rico.
> SERAFÍN: Well, you speak it like a native.][48]

The marriage takes place immediately, and it is only afterward that the trick is revealed—in English. In addition, Don Serafín receives a letter from his party's Nominating Committee for Senatorial Candidates letting him know that he has not been selected as a candidate. He immediately realizes that his intense faith in English and in the benefits of imitating American customs has been in vain. As it has all backfired, he addresses his household to quickly retract his position on English: "Ahora quiero advertiros una cosa. Desde hoy, no quiero volver a oír aquí, en esta casa, ni una sola palabra en inglés" (Let me tell you all something. From now on I do not want to hear a single word of English spoken in my home).

In addition to its obvious hilarity and criticism, this play is very revealing in two significant ways. First, it was written by Cubans for island Cubans but was totally "readable" by Cubans in Tampa despite its focus on the social, political, and economic situation *in* Cuba. The Tampa Cuban and Latin public, broadly speaking, was totally in tune with and appreciative of the play's thorough exploration of an individual citizen's reactions to and opinions about political corruption; economic dependency; a failed, "real" independence; and the influence of American imperialism on the island, most notably, after 1900. After all, Tampa Cubans were living not in the "belly" but in the veritable bowels of "the beast," as Martí described the United States in an unfinished letter to Manuel Mercado on May 18, 1895, one day before his death in the battle for Cuban independence.[49] However, the other element of these plays that distinguishes them as transnational is the sociolinguistic and cultural situation of their plots and the binational recipient audiences. Their bilingual wordplay requires that their audiences be linguistically competent enough to recognize and understand their malapropisms and horrible pronunciations of Spanish and English, a potentially logical assumption given the incipiently bilingual/bicultural nature of the communities in Havana and Tampa. These plays are both agents and sites of exchange and create a "contact zone," as Mary Louise Pratt sees it, through language and circumstance.[50]

Conclusion: Ingredients for a Continued Command Performance

By the end of the tumultuous 1920s, the content of local plays clearly indicated that what had begun as essentially "foreign" theater had evolved into an immigrant theater now acutely attuned with how national and local events impacted the Tampa

Latin community. To mark the end of this decade, the Círculo's own company staged works written by a club member, Leopoldo González. One of them was the timely farce *La picada de la mosca o el pánico de los bancos* (*The Fly Bite, or The Run on Banks*), an obvious response to the stock market crash of 1929. This and other plays suggest the harsh economic and political realities both in Cuba and in Tampa, as well as the strategic assimilation, hybridization, and nostalgia of this now relatively mixed-ethnic Tampa Latin community as late as the Korean War.[51] Immigration to the enclave continued through the 1930s, 1940s, and 1950s for various reasons: the Spanish Civil War; World War II, which directly involved Spain and Italy; fascist, dictatorial, or corrupt governments in all three countries; and family-based immigration. In the late 1930s the Works Progress Administration established the only Spanish-language Federal Theatre Project in Tampa, thanks to two local entrepreneurs who convinced Washington, DC, to form a troupe there and not in perhaps more noteworthy cities with a Hispanic theatrical tradition.[52] The inward focus of a number of other plays dealt with the linguistic and cultural chaos of ethnic mixing; ambiguously uncomfortable feelings regarding racism—on the part of southern whites against Cubans, in general, and on the part of white Cubans against black Cubans and Americans—and ensuing hardships due to the cigar industry's decline and labor strife during and after the 1930s.[53] Tampa Latin theater offers a window onto what the curriculum of culture, as experienced through popular theater, tendered as a hermeneutic for analyzing and interpreting the complexities of the community's self-realization as well as its various difficulties—the negative impacts of American (political, economic, cultural, and linguistic) influence on both bourgeois and working-class Cubans; the ways that members of different classes saw and experienced the same phenomena; and how these experiences affected conceptualizations of national, binational, or transnational identity. By means of this theater, they "[recognized and reclaimed] their own struggles and experiences through the characters they were representing. . . . [By bringing] . . . fictional characters to life, [the actors] not only spoke of the characters, but of themselves of their own personal experiences."[54] It was a project that took on the task of creating community by finding ways to facilitate the sharing of family histories, life experiences, cultural traditions, and hopes and fears for the future.[55] The Tampa Latin curriculum of culture that was presented and experienced by actors and audience members alike circulated from the stage, to cigar factory readings, to coffeehouse discussion, to homes, and then back to the stage, to start the cycle over again. This repeated activity was both reiterative and citational. Following Judith Butler, these actions ("performances") were influenced by and responded to the Tampa Latin society's needs and demands, as well as by prior "texts" from cigar factory readings, union activities, mutual aid society activities, home conversations, or other plays. This activity was not "theatrical self-representation or free-play, nor [could] it simply be equated with performance."[56]

Regarding the impact of this curriculum of culture on the broader community beyond the Latin enclaves, Cuban cigar culture in Tampa thoroughly transformed living and working spaces in a segregated, Jim Crow city and fundamentally impacted its landscape, foodways, and identity. Through this veritable invasion of Cuban (and other Latin) people and mores into a white, southern-dominated space,

Cuban and Latin cultural and social values were passed on from one generation to the next within the community, and to non-Cubans, via reverse assimilation, as seen through transformed food traditions and new cultural practices, the shape and purpose of certain buildings, and the established and sustained political and economic relations with the countries from which the Latin immigrants came.

KENYA C. DWORKIN Y MÉNDEZ is professor of Hispanic studies at Carnegie Mellon University. She is working on two book projects, tentatively titled *Before Latino: How Cuban Theater in Tampa Shaped an American Immigrant Society* and *A Nation in Black and White: The Writing of the Cuban Nation, 1868–1934*.

Notes

1   Tampa Latins are the historical and contemporary descendants of Cubans, Spaniards, and Sicilians/Italians in Tampa. The name was applied to them by the city's mainstream, southern, white population and adopted by the "Latins" themselves, given that *Latin* was English for *latino*. The term's eventual use by the immigrant community reflected a more collective view of the group identity that began to emerge in the late 1930s as a result of prolonged cohabitation, common agendas, and external assimilatory pressures. *Latin* in Tampa includes not just Spanish speakers from Cuba and Spain but also Sicilians and Italians. I submit that members of the community were willing to adapt the English, identifying appellation because they saw it as a translation of *latino*, originally an adjective describing anyone who spoke a language derived from Latin. In the United States the Spanish word *latino* was later transformed into the English *Latino* to describe people of Spanish-speaking ancestry. The English term *Latin*, in the Tampa context, predates the twentieth-century US use of *Latino* for referring to Spanish speakers and their descendants in this country.

2   Bierstadt, *Aspects of Americanization*, 16.

3   For a general overview of the impact of immigration to the United States between 1880 and 1920, see Hirschman and Mogford, "Immigration and the American Industrial Revolution."

4   For a summary of the founding of Tampa and Ybor City, see Mormino and Pozzetta, *Immigrant World of Ybor City*; Long, "Making of Modern Tampa"; Muñiz, *Los Cubanos en Tampa*, 9–29; Galvez, *Tampa*; and del Río, *Yo fui uno de los fundadores*, 2–10. For a description of the founding of West Tampa, see Méndez, *Ciudad de Cigars*.

5   Greenbaum, *More than Black*; Greenbaum, "Afro-Cubans in Exile."

6   There were working-class Spaniards who had already migrated to Cuba from Spain as a result of Spain's rapid economic decline in the nineteenth century. See Cascón, "Desde la otra orilla." The Sicilians who migrated to Tampa were escaping poverty due to a total dependence on agriculture, poor soil, malaria, high rents, absentee landlords, exploitation, forced conscription, and epidemics after Italy's unification in the late nineteenth century. See Bencivenni, *Italian Immigrant Radical Culture*, 7; and Mormino and Pozzetta, *Immigrant World of Ybor City*.

7   Winsboro with Jordan, "Solidarity Means Inclusion," 279.

8   See Bourdieu, *Field of Cultural Production*.

9   See Bourdieu and Passeron, *Reproduction in Education*; and Bourdieu, *Field of Cultural Production*.

10   See Bandura, *Social Foundations of Thought and Action*.

11   Bodnar, *Transplanted*, 22.

12   Mirel, *Patriotic Pluralism*, 13.

13   See Lichterman, "Piecing Together Multicultural Community."

14   Wirtz, *Performing Afro-Cuba*, 274, referring to Bakhtin, *Dialogic Imagination*, 455.

15   See Bellah et al., *Habits of the Heart*.

16   The words in the section heading, taken from his final words that day, became the title eventually given to a speech delivered by José Martí to mostly Cuban cigar workers in Tampa, at the Liceo Cubano, on November 26, 1891. See Martí, "Con todos y para el bien de todos."

17   For a description of the mutual aid societies, see Long, "Immigrant Cooperative Medicine Program"; and Mormino and Pozzetta, *Immigrant World of Ybor City*, 175–209.

18   See Curl, *For All the People*.

19   See Greenbaum, *More than Black*, 12.

20   A small but important group of immigrants (many of them Jews) from Germany and other eastern Europe countries, for instance, Romania, built the German-American Club in 1901.

21   Numerous other ethnic clubs and lodges also had their own buildings (e.g., Los Caballeros Leales de América [The Loyal Knights of America]) in Ybor City. They were often less comprehensive in their offerings but drew on a very specific membership. Another example is the Centro Obrero (Labor Temple), a more union and politically oriented club. See Leto, *Fraternidad*.

22   The vast majority of the major clubs had their own theaters, which sometimes also served as movie houses. Although almost all the film fare was American, the live performances (comedies, dramas, musical revues, *zarzuela*, and opera) were Cuban, Spanish, or Italian. Additionally, some clubs offered a gymnasium; a cantina for cards, chess, and dominoes; a billiards room; a boxing arena; and a small bowling alley.

23   In the early twentieth century explicit political activity was prohibited at the clubs, due in part, at least, to Tomás Estrada Palma, Cuba's first (American citizen) president, who asked the patriotic clubs to stand down during the early, postindependence period in Cuba. On December 21, 1898, in a circular he inserted in the Cuban émigré newspaper *Patria*, he asked the clubs all to dissolve, their purpose having been fulfilled. Since many of the associations created in these clubs later translated into mutual aid societies and other fraternal organizations, the new institutions' bylaws adopted the nonpolitical stance called for by Estrada Palma. The non-Cuban organizations in Tampa followed suit. See Muñiz, *Los Cubanos en Tampa*.

24   Ray Oldenburg provides an exhaustive list of social scientists, psychologists, urban planners, and others who have written on the subject of the "great, good place." For authors, essays, or book titles, or full bibliographic citations, see Oldenburg, *Great Good Place*, xvii–xxv.

25   Oldenburg, *Great Good Place*, xxiv.

26   Oldenburg, *Great Good Place*, 23. Oldenberg accurately describes the leveling effect the third place has, particularly on members of the upper class, stating that "[those] who on the outside command deference and attention by the sheer weight of their position enjoined themselves in the third place enjoined, embraced, accepted, and enjoyed where conventional status counts for little. They are accepted just for themselves and on terms not subject to the vicissitudes of political or economic life."

27   The section heading refers to Mormino and Pozzetta, "Reader Lights the Candle."

28   See Tinajero, *El Lector*.

29   Pérez, "Reminiscences of a Lector," 445. See also Pozzetta and Mormino, "The Reader and the Worker."

30   See del Río, *Yo fui uno de los fundadores*.

31   For more information about the establishment of Cuban and other theater in Tampa, see Kanellos, *History of Hispanic Theatre*; Dworkin y Méndez, "Cuban Theater, American Stage"; Dworkin y Méndez, "From Factory to Footlights"; Dworkin y Méndez, "Tradition of Hispanic Theater"; and Dworkin y Méndez, "La patria que nace de lejos."

32   In addition, in keeping with the influence of the local curriculum of culture and its manifestation in mutual aid society practices, the proceeds from performances of plays and other entertainment were often used to benefit sick or injured workers and widows and to support humanitarian recovery efforts in Cuba or Spain (e.g., after a hurricane or during the Spanish Civil War). This tradition continued well into the 1950s, and there are even some examples from the 1960s.

33   For a detailed account of the artistic and political origin and development of the Cuban *bufo* genre, see Huidobro, *Persona*, 69–79; Tolón, *Teatro lírico popular de Cuba*, 19–31; and Cortina, *Cuban American Theater*, 7–17.

34   Dworkin y Méndez, "La patria que nace de lejos." A full discussion of *bufo* and blackface theater in Cuba; its iteration and evolution in Tampa, in which the *negrito* character is a key distinction between the Cuban form and the new, evolving Tampa form; and the issue of white Cuban racism and discrimination toward black Cubans (and black Americans) will appear in a forthcoming manuscript.

35   Prendergast and Saxton, *Applied Theatre*, 69.

36   Denzin, *Performance Ethnography*, x.

37   Dwight Conquergood, quoted in Sommerfeldt, Caine, and Molzahn, "Considering Performativity."

38   Conquergood, quoted in Sommerfeldt, Caine, and Molzahn, "Considering Performativity."

39   Mieke Bal, quoted in Sommerfeldt, Caine, and Molzahn, "Considering Performativity."

40   Del Valle, "Notas teatrales," 122. This and all other translations from Spanish to English, or adaptations of Spanish, English, and Spanglish, are mine.

41   Kanellos, *History of Hispanic Theatre*, 162.

42   Kanellos, *History of Hispanic Theatre*, 163. The children's theater became another bastion of

Tampa Latin culture and a site at which this younger generation experienced the curriculum of culture. By 1922 three renowned figures had taken 1920s Círculo Cubano theater into an important, new decade of professional-level local theater. Cuban actress Carmen du Molins began to work with the Círculo's *sección de declamación*, along with two other local actors, Víctor Fernández and Arturo Morán, both professionals in their own right. Kanellos credits Fernández with creating a children's theatrical section at the Círculo Cubano.

43   Kanellos, *History of Hispanic Theatre*, 122.

44   For an excellent analysis of Cuba's development and social, cultural, and economic relapse after 1902 and during Machado's role, see Macías Martín, "La diplomacia española ante el 'Machadato.'"

45   See Benjamin, "Machadato and Cuban Nationalism," for a very good study of the kinds of Cuban nationalism that emerged during the first thirty years of the Cuban Republic and, specifically, of the rise and fall of Machado, the social and political impact of his presidency, and his treatment of opposition groups.

46   Ramos and Gutiérrez, "Los espejuelos de Machado."

47   Matheu, "Yo quiero ser senador."

48   Matheu, "Yo quiero ser senador."

49   Henke and Nicholson, *Transnational Exchange*, 1, quoted in Foster and Altamiranda, *From Romanticism to Modernism*, 248.

50   See Pratt, *Imperial Eyes*.

51   *Un black out en Ybor City*, a 1943 farce written by the Tampa Cuban cigar makers and playwrights Salvador Toledo and Jaime Fernández, staged for Círculo Cubano audiences the need for ethnic groups to join forces, fight fascism, and support the Allied effort in Europe. *El general Pelusa o El arma secreta*, a 1950 farce by Toledo, revealed anxieties about the Korean conflict, particularly about the possibility of another, great and prolonged war; "yellow peril" manifestations of anti-Asian racism; and allusions to the atomic bombs of 1945. See Salvador Toledo, July 1950, 1979, Playscripts, box 33, University of South Florida Libraries Special Collections, *Cuban Club Records, 1852–1989* (also in my personal possession). I recovered both texts, and others, in 1996 in West Tampa, photocopied them, and gave them to the University of South Florida Libraries.

52   Dworkin y Méndez, "When a 'New Deal' Became a Raw Deal."

53   *Tabaqueros a coger el cheke* [sic], a dateless farce probably written during the Depression by Toledo and Fernández, explored interethnic marriage and generational change using hilarious wordplay to represent the linguistic confusion that ensued when a Cuban and Sicilian married and had a Tampa Latin daughter. *La familia Tinguillo en Clearwater*, a 1947 farce by Toledo that was rewritten and again presented in 1952, referenced white southern racism toward white Cubans that prevented them from visiting certain beaches, and changing perceptions among the white Cuban population regarding in-group and out-group, antiblack racism. While the play did not outrightly condemn it or propose ways to improve the situation, it conveys a remarkable shift in thinking to an audience for whom its ideological context was all too real. Playscripts, box 33, University of South Florida Libraries Special Collections, *Cuban Club Records, 1852–1989* (also in my personal possession). I recovered both texts, and others, photocopied them, and gave them to the University of South Florida Libraries.

54   García, "Creating Community," 20.

55   Gavin Bolton, *New Perspectives on Classroom Drama*, quoted in García, "Creating Community," 20.

56   Judith Butler, quoted in Sommerfeldt, Caine, and Molzahn, "Considering Performativity."

Works Cited

Bakhtin, M. M. *The Dialogic Imagination: Four Essays*, edited by Michael Holquist, translated by Caryl Emerson and Michael Holquist. Austin: University of Texas Press, 1981.

Bandura, Albert. *Social Foundations of Thought and Action: A Social Cognitive Theory*. Englewood Cliffs, NJ: Prentice-Hall, 1986.

Bellah, Robert N., Richard Madsen, William M. Sullivan, Ann Swidler, and Steven M. Tipton. *Habits of the Heart: Individualism and Commitment in American Life*. 2nd ed. Berkeley: University of California Press, 1996.

Bencivenni, Marcella. *Italian Immigrant Radical Culture: The Idealism of the Sovversivi in the United States, 1890–1940*. New York: New York University Press, 2014.

Benjamin, Jules R. "The Machadato and Cuban Nationalism, 1928–1932." *Hispanic American Historical Review* 55, no. 1 (1975): 66–91.

Bierstadt, Edward Hale. *Aspects of Americanization*. Cincinnati, OH: Kidd, 1922.

Bodnar, John. *The Transplanted: A History of Immigrants in Urban America*. Bloomington: Indiana University Press, 1987.

Bourdieu, Pierre. *The Field of Cultural Production: Essays on Art and Literature*, edited by Randal

Johnson. New York: Columbia University Press, 1993.

Bourdieu, Pierre, and Jean-Claude Passeron. *Reproduction in Education, Society, and Culture*, translated by Richard Nice. Thousand Oaks, CA: Sage, 1977.

Cascón, Patricia Prieto. "Desde la otra orilla: La experiencia migratoria de los españoles en Estados Unidos, 1880–1930." August 25, 2016. publicacionesdidacticas.com/hemeroteca /articulo/074018/articulo-pdf.

Cortina, Rodolfo. *Cuban American Theater*. Houston: Arte Público, 1991.

Curl, John. *For All the People: Uncovering the Hidden History of Cooperation, Cooperative Movements, and Communalism in America*. Oakland, CA: PM, 2012.

del Río, Emilio. *Yo fui uno de los fundadores de Ybor City*. Tampa, FL: N.p., 1950.

del Valle, Adrián. "Notas teatrales." *Cuba y América: Revista ilustrada* 18, no. 10 (1904–5): 122.

Denzin, Norman K. *Performance Ethnography: Critical Pedagogy and the Politics of Culture*. Thousand Oaks, CA: Sage, 2003.

Dworkin y Méndez, Kenya C. "Cuban Theater, American Stage: Before Exile." In *The State of Latino Theater in the United States: Hybridity, Transculturation, and Identity*, 103–29. New York: Routledge, 2002.

Dworkin y Méndez, Kenya C. "From Factory to Footlights: Original Spanish-Language Cigar Workers' Theatre in Ybor City and West Tampa, Florida." In vol. 3 of *Recovering the U.S. Hispanic Literary Heritage*, edited by María Herrera-Sobek and Virginia Sánchez Korrol, 332–50. Houston: Arte Público, 2000.

Dworkin y Méndez, Kenya C. "La patria que nace de lejos: Cuba y lo cubano en la vanguardia de Martí." *Cuban Studies* 36 (2006): 1–22.

Dworkin y Méndez, Kenya C. "The Tradition of Hispanic Theater and the WPA Federal Theatre Project in Tampa–Ybor City, Florida." In vol. 2 of *Recovering the U.S. Hispanic Literary Heritage*, edited by Erlinda Gonzales-Berry and Chuck Tatum, 279–94. Houston: Arte Público, 1996.

Dworkin y Méndez, Kenya C. "When a 'New Deal' Became a Raw Deal: Depression-Era, 'Latin' Federal Theatre." *Transmodernity: Journal of Peripheral Cultural Production of the Luso-Hispanic World* 1, no. 1 (2011): 10–28.

Foster, David William, and Daniel Altamiranda. *From Romanticism to Modernism in Latin America*. Vol. 3. New York: Garland/Taylor and Francis, 1997.

Galvez, Wenceslao. *Tampa: Impresiones de emigrado*. Havana: Establecimiento Tipográfico de Cuba, 1897.

García, Lorenzo. "Creating Community in a Theatre Production." *Journal of Multicultural Perspectives* 1, no. 2 (1999): 20–24.

Greenbaum, Susan. "Afro-Cubans in Exile: Tampa, Florida, 1886–1984." *Cuban Studies/Estudios Cubanos* 15, no. 1: 59–73.

Greenbaum, Susan. *More than Black: Afro-Cubans in Tampa*. Gainesville: University Press of Florida, 2002.

Henke, Robert, and Eric Nicholson. *Transnational Exchange in Early Modern Theater*. Burlington, VT: Ashgate, 2008.

Hirschman, Charles, and Elizabeth Mogford. "Immigration and the American Industrial Revolution from 1880 to 1920." *Social Science Research* 38, no. 4 (2009): 897–920.

Huidobro, Matías Montes. *Persona, vida y máscara en el teatro cubano*. Miami: Ediciones Universal, 1973.

Kanellos, Nicolás. *A History of Hispanic Theatre in the United States: Origins to 1940*. Austin: University of Texas Press, 1990.

Leto, Emanuel. *Fraternidad: The Mutual Aid Societies of Ybor City*. Tampa, FL: Ybor City Museum Society, 2001.

Lichterman, Paul. "Piecing Together Multicultural Community: Cultural Differences in Community Building among Grass-Roots Environmentalists." *Social Problems* 42, no. 4 (1995): 513–34.

Long, Durward. "An Immigrant Cooperative Medicine Program in the South, 1887–1963." *Journal of Southern History* 31, no. 4 (1965): 417–34.

Long, Durward. "The Making of Modern Tampa: A City of the New South, 1885–1911." *Florida Historical Quarterly* 49, no. 4 (1971): 333–45.

Macías Martín, Francisco Javier. "La diplomacia española ante el 'Machadato' y la crisis cubana de 1933." Thesis, Instituto de Estudios Hispánicos de Canarias, 1998. ftp://tesis.bbtk.ull .es/ccssyhum/cs50.pdf (accessed July 15, 2017).

Martí, José. "Con todos y para el bien de todos." Speech delivered at the Liceo Cubano, Tampa, FL, November 26, 1891. www.damisela.com /literatura/pais/cuba/autores/marti/discursos /1891_11_26.htm (accessed July 21, 2017).

Matheu, Felipe Rivera. "Yo quiero ser senador." Unpublished playscript. University of South Florida Libraries, Special Collections, *Cuban Club Records, 1852–1989*.

Méndez, Armando. *Ciudad de Cigars: West Tampa*. Cocoa, FL: Florida Historical Society, 1994.

Mirel, Jeffrey. *Patriotic Pluralism: Americanization Education and European Immigrants*. Cambridge, MA: Harvard University Press, 2010.

Mormino, Gary R., and George E. Pozzetta. *The Immigrant World of Ybor City: Italians and*

Their Latin Neighbors in Tampa, 1885–1985.
Urbana: University of Illinois Press, 1987.

Mormino, Gary R., and George E. Pozzetta. "The
Reader Lights the Candle: Cuban and Florida
Cigar Workers' Oral Tradition." *Labor Heritage*
5, no. 1 (1993): 4–26.

Muñiz, José Rivero. *Los Cubanos en Tampa.* Havana:
N.p., 1954.

Oldenburg, Ray. *The Great Good Place: Cafés, Coffee
Shops, Community Centers, Beauty Parlors,
General Stores, Bars, Hangouts, and How They
Get You through the Day.* St. Paul, MN: Paragon
House, 1989.

Pérez, Louis A., Jr. "Reminiscences of a Lector:
Cuban Cigar Workers in Tampa." *Florida
Historical Quarterly* 53, no. 4 (1975): 443–49.

Pozzetta, George E., and Gary R. Mormino. "The
Reader and the Worker: 'Los Lectores' and the
Culture of Cigarmaking in Cuba and Florida."
International Labor and Working-Class History,
no. 54 (1998): 1–18.

Pratt, Mary Louise. *Imperial Eyes: Travel Writing and
Transculturation.* London: Routledge, 1993.

Prendergast, Monica, and Juliana Saxton. *Applied
Theatre: International Case Studies and
Challenges for Practice.* Bristol: Intellect, 2009.

Ramos, A. H., and Roberto "Bolito" Gutiérrez.
"Los espejuelos de Machado." Unpublished
playscript. University of South Florida
Libraries, Special Collections, *Cuban Club
Records, 1852–1989.*

Sommerfeldt, Susan, Vera Caine, and Anita
Molzahn. "Considering Performativity
as Methodology and Phenomena." *Forum
Qualitative Sozialforschung/Forum: Qualitative
Social Research* 15, no. 2 (2014). www
.qualitative-research.net/index.php/fqs
/article/view/2108/3670.

Tinajero, Araceli. *El Lector: A History of the Cigar
Factory Reader.* Austin: University of Texas
Press, 2010.

Tolón, Edward Teurbe. *Teatro lírico popular de Cuba.*
Miami: Universidad de Miami, 1973.

Winsboro, Irvin D. S., with Alexander Jordan.
"Solidarity Means Inclusion: Race, Class, and
Ethnicity within Tampa's Transnational Cigar
Workers' Union." *Labor History* 55, no. 3
(2014): 279.

Wirtz, Kristina. *Performing Afro-Cuba: Image, Voice,
Spectacle in the Making of Race and History.*
Chicago: University of Chicago Press, 2014.

Latino, the Word

JOSHUA JAVIER GUZMÁN

Abstract   This brief meditation on *Latino* the word underscores a politics of loss at play in the emergence of the new term *Latinx*. The term *Latinx* reveals how a performance of negation, identified in the very telling word *no* in Lati*no*/Chica*no*, takes seriously the ex-factor marking the collective phenomenon known as *latinidad*. If the shifts from *o* to *o/a* to *@* and now *x* are about political inclusion, it is not through liberal incorporation but through the inscription of linguistic and symbolic cuts, which hemorrhage something remarkably unnamable.
Keywords   Latinx, Latin@, Latina/o, communism, borderlands, negation, Norma Alarcón, Jean-Luc Nancy

I n his notes to a 2009 conference in London titled "On the Idea of Communism,"
Jean-Luc Nancy begins by exclaiming "Communism, the word. Not the word before the notion, but the word as notion and as historical agent."[1] In his brief annotations, Nancy traces the "strange story" of the word *communism*, insisting that "no history, no etymology either can produce anything like [the] sense [of communism]." Here Nancy meditates on the metaphysical comportments of the word in order to deliver, once again, the word—*communism*—back to its inscription as notion, "as presence, as feeling, as sense (more than meaning)." He continues by sketching an argument for property, not as material possession but as in what is proper to the ontological ground of the commons, which he gives the name *Mitsein*, understood as "being-with." Property speaks to the *co* in communism, that is, the shared exchange of something that escapes equivalency such as love, friendship, and art. "Communism" then becomes about questions of presence and sense to the extent that they both mark—together—the activation and subsequent limitation of politics. Communism is being-with (as opposed to being) *in the world*. *Communism*, the word, does things in the world. For the philosopher, communism ought to be understood as the ineffable sense of being-in-common, a phenomenon initiated by the very naming of a seemingly impossible though ongoing political project.

At the same time, this also seems to be the underlying assertion in Nancy's reading of the word *mestizaje* in his 1994 essay "Cut Throat Sun"—an argument that will eventually come under scrutiny.[2] Norma Alarcón takes Nancy to task on

ENGLISH LANGUAGE NOTES

56:2, October 2018 DOI 10.1215/00138282-6960834
© 2018 Regents of the University of Colorado

this argument in an underrecognized debate about Chicano identity and its production of community through what Nancy calls the "cut" and Alarcón theorizes as
"identity-in-difference."[3] Though both thinkers share a suspicion of the autonomous subject of knowledge, for Nancy mestizo identity mostly lies in its cutting
and repetitive inscription in meaning, those "borderlands of meaning," to echo
Gloria Anzaldúa. Meanwhile, Alarcón's groundbreaking concept of "identity-in-
difference" is a paradox through and through. Identity-in-difference involves a naysaying of sorts, a remapping of recognition away from the subject of knowledge into
the interstial spaces of meaning. In a sense, Alarcón performs her refusal of Nancy's
supposed "knowing" what *mestizaje* can mean, even if this meaning is obstructed by
a cut, a border, or a gap. Though I will not linger on the differences between Alarcón
and Nancy here, I do want to underline how both thinkers offer us a different way of
working through the problem of naming the thing that escapes knowability and
meaning, a problematic performed by the very term *Latinx*.

　　Latinx has recently emerged in the early parts of the twenty-first century to
demarcate those afflicted under the sign of *latinidad*. First showings of the term
appeared in the queer blogospheres, traveling among younger queer communities
of color with the promise of gender fluidity. Before *Latinx* there was *Latin@* with its
use of @ to signal inclusion of those outside the gender binary propagated by the
Spanish use of *o/a*.[4] Also gaining prominence on a fledgling internet, *Latin@*
became more difficult to use with time. Perhaps this was because of the term's
inclusion of that clunky at-sign, even if its largeness (and unpronounceability) was
supposed to showcase the term's openness and inconclusivity. Hovering around
both *Latinx* and *Latin@* is the now standard use of *Latina/o* as a way to make more
explicit not only the two gender variants but also the very "cut" in "Latin" identity
(lest we forget that *Latin* was also a term used, however anachronistically, to identify
the Latinx population while not relying on gender pronouncement even if it did
occlude indigenous genealogies within the term).[5] The slash in the word *Latina/o*
might have given solace to those who believed that something must have existed
between *o* and *a*. Yet there is a recalling of the "/" in the *x* through a doubling and
a crossing. In this double-crossing we see a double negation circumscribing an
absence, which expands outside meaning into a sense of something more, something like an opaque presence. Despite these nominal variants, the problem remains:
how to name a group of people residing in the United States who have been historically displaced not only from Latin America but from the symbolic realm as well.
The experience of historical and psychic displacement cannot be more incongruous. Both perform a refusal of determination, yet their respective, material effects
differ in the way we come to measure their constitutive losses. In which case, *Latinx*
gives a name to the measurement of a loss in language as well as material losses
in resources, money, care, housing, land, community, country, political representation, representation, sovereignty, justice, and so on. If *x* marks the spot, it marks
here the political refusal to mean anything whatsoever. Instead, the nagging insistence of the *x* to collapse the universal into the particular is met with histories of
dispossession to only yield a resounding politics of negativity—there is no liberal
incorporation here and no good feelings about finally being captured, represented.

What was always written into the word *Latino* (as well as *Chicano*, or *Cubano*) is the very word given to refusal—*no*.

In light of Alarcón's and Nancy's theorizations, the radical potential of *latinidad* comes not from its names but from the naysaying it repetitively performs in language and in history. Those who are optimistic about the word *Latinx* as the new, more inclusive linguistic software update that more accurately represents all the different people who *are* Latinxes will inevitably be disappointed by the failure of language to ever be used *properly* by those who claim to *know* what Latinxes *are*. This is to say that *Latinx*, the word, means nothing if it is not understood first as a notion colored by a melancholic attachment to a name that once captured us all yet never really existed. In short, *Latinx* reminds us of the inadequacy of language, reflected back to us in the subjects it produces under the sign of *latinidad*.

JOSHUA JAVIER GUZMÁN is assistant professor in the Department of Gender Studies at UCLA. He is coeditor of a special issue of *Women and Performance: A Journal of Feminist Theory* titled "Lingering in Latinidad: Aesthetics, Theory, and Performance in Latina/o Studies" and is working on a book-length project tentatively titled *Suspended Satisfactions: Queer Latino Performance and the Politics of Style*.

Notes

1. Nancy, "Communism, the Word."
2. Nancy, "Cut Throat Sun."
3. Alarcón, "Conjugating Subjects," 127–28.
4. Rodríguez, *Queer Latinidad*, 138.
5. Rodríguez, "Latino, Latina, Latin@."

Works Cited

Alarcón, Norma. "Conjugating Subjects: The Heteroglossia of Essence and Resistance." In *An Other Tongue: Nation and Ethnicity in the Linguistic Borderlands*, edited by Alfred Arteaga, 125–38. Durham, NC: Duke University Press, 1994.

Nancy, Jean-Luc. "Cut Throat Sun." In *An Other Tongue: Nation and Ethnicity in the Linguistic Borderlands*, edited by Alfred Arteaga, 113–23. Durham, NC: Duke University Press, 1994.

Nancy, Jean-Luc. "Communism, the Word." Paper presented at the conference "On the Idea of Communism," Birckbeck College, University of London, March 13–15, 2009. commoningtimes.org/texts/nancy -communism-the-word.pdf.

Rodríguez, Juana María. "Latino, Latina, Latin@." In *Keywords for American Cultural Studies*, edited by Bruce Burgett and Glenn Hendler, 146. New York: New York University Press, 2007.

Rodríguez, Juana María. *Queer Latinidad: Identity Practices, Discursive Spaces*. New York: New York University Press, 2003.

Keep up to date on new scholarship

Issue alerts are a great way to stay current on all the cutting-edge scholarship from your favorite Duke University Press journals. This free service delivers tables of contents directly to your inbox, informing you of the latest groundbreaking work as soon as it is published.

To sign up for issue alerts:

1. Visit **dukeu.press/register** and register for an account. You do not need to provide a customer number.

2. After registering, visit **dukeu.press/alerts**.

3. Go to "Latest Issue Alerts" and click on "Add Alerts."

4. Select as many publications as you would like from the pop-up window and click "Add Alerts."

read.dukeupress.edu/journals

Printed and bound by CPI Group (UK) Ltd, Croydon, CR0 4YY

13/04/2025

14656480-0005